SLAVES IN PARADISE

JESÚS GARCÍA

SLAVES IN PARADISE

~

A Priest Stands Up for Exploited Sugarcane Workers

Translated by Richard Goodyear

Foreword by
Seán Patrick Cardinal O'Malley, O.F.M. Cap.

IGNATIUS PRESS   SAN FRANCISCO

CONTENTS

FOREWORD TO
THE ENGLISH EDITION

Father Christopher Hartley and I first met many years ago when he was working in New York City, and what impressed me most about him was his missionary zeal and his priestly spirit. I was acquainted with a little bit of his history, namely his desire to be helpful to Mother Teresa in her ministry, his generosity in serving the Hispanic population in the United States, and his desire to become a missionary to those on the peripheries, those who are often forgotten and neglected.

This desire to become a missionary led him to accept the Lord's invitation to bring God's love and salvation to the Haitian and Dominican people in the Dominican Republic. His experience in the Dominican Republic with the exploitation of Haitian workers had a very profound effect on Father Hartley, and his witness to the world helped to raise consciousness about the suffering and the injustices they endured on the sugarcane plantations of San José de los Llanos. Like so many migrants in this century, the Haitians who left their country in search of paradise were actually fleeing extreme poverty, and they found themselves living in a new land, in search of a better life, as cutters of sugarcane. The pages that follow are a witness to Father Hartley's experiences as a missionary working among these poorest of the poor.

Unfortunately his prophetic voice did not elicit the supportive response that we would have hoped for within the Church in Santo Domingo, and so Father Hartley had to leave his beloved ministry there. But following the gospel injunction, he shook the dust from his sandals and went to another mission to continue to announce the joy and the liberation of Christ. He is now in a very remote part of Ethiopia, ministering to God's people and witnessing to the presence of the gospel in a heavily Muslim population.

Many Americans have already been exposed to *The Price of Sugar*, the very powerful documentary about Father Hartley's experiences with the Haitian workers in the sugar industry. But this written documentation is an important contribution, because it exposes more of the sad realities that these workers face each day. Theirs is indeed a desperate situation. In today's world people are becoming more and more aware of the horrors of human trafficking and the exploitation of workers. This book demonstrates what is currently occurring in the Dominican Republic among the Haitian workers. Many of these so-called Haitians are really Dominicans, having been born in the Dominican Republic, but they are often treated like people without a nation and are made to feel unwelcome, even while their labor is contributing mightily to the economic growth of the country.

Father Hartley's mission of love is fueled by his strong prayer life and his intimacy with God. You will discover in the following pages a man who always makes time for prayer, often spending hours before the Lord. His devotion to the Blessed Sacrament and to the worthy celebration of the Liturgy was at the core of his evangelization and helped to shape his heart after the image of the Good Shepherd, who lays down his life for his sheep.

We hope that this book will help to raise consciousness and to shed a light on this dark episode in the recent history of our hemisphere. Many of the tensions that exist between the two nations of Hispaniola are the outcome of a tragic history, which has resulted in an unfriendly and racist attitude that perpetuates hostility and division between these two peoples who share the same island. We hope that the Church leadership in both the Dominican Republic and Haiti will be able to work together to bring about healing and reconciliation based on justice and respect.

I pray that this book will inspire us all to a deeper faith in God and love for the poor. The two go hand in hand, as Father Hartley's mentor and teacher used to say: "We cannot say that we love Jesus only in the Eucharist—naturally, we want to put that love into action, serving the poor. We cannot separate the Eucharist and the poor." May these words of Saint Teresa of Calcutta, her heroic example, and her saintly intercession continue to inspire us to become missionaries of charity throughout the world.

+ Seán Cardinal O'Malley, O.F.M. Cap.
Archbishop of Boston
January 17, 2017

FOREWORD TO
THE SPANISH EDITION

This book is a true gift to the reader, as it has also been a true gift and blessing to me: a galvanizing and heartening proclamation of the wonders wrought by God's mercy for the benefit of the Church and mankind.

Unquestionably, the principal figure in this story is not Father Christopher Hartley so much as it is God. In effect, this account is akin to the Acts of the Apostles: the protagonist is God, who has vouchsafed for the benefit of all mankind his mercy, his immense love, and the grace he has poured out and spread all over the world through the apostles, which we see in what God has done through this priest, this missionary, in the sugarcane plantations of the Dominican Republic.

Anyone who reads this book will not find a superhero here in Christopher, my good and dear friend and brother. He will find no more than a man of God—a faithful and reliable subject and servant of the Lord—who with deep sincerity seeks nothing more than to fulfill the Lord's will: to affirm that the neediest of men, poor and suffering, share in his infinite loving-kindness, his eternal mercy, his extreme closeness, that they may share in his salvation, which is of the whole person and resides only in that union with the Lord. Every page of this book attests to God's love for and his salvation of the Dominicans and the Haitians in the *bateyes*[1] of the sugarcane plantations of San José de los Llanos (Saint Joseph of the Plains).

This book bears witness to a mission among the poorest of the poor. We have here a fulfillment of one of Isaiah's prophecies, as when in Nazareth Jesus said of himself, as an evangelist of the poor: "The Spirit of the Lord is upon me, because he has anointed me to preach

---

[1] As Father Christopher writes in his first letter, a *batey* (pronounced "bah-TAY"; plural *bateyes*, pronounced "bah-TAY-ess") is a village or hamlet inhabited mostly by Haitian immigrant workers. The *campos*, on the other hand, are villages or towns of about two hundred to seven hundred mostly Dominican inhabitants.—TRANS.

good news to the poor. He has sent me to proclaim release to the captives and recovering of sight to the blind, to set at liberty those who are oppressed" (Lk 4:18).

We are in the province of the 2012 Synod of Bishops on the new evangelization. Father Christopher Hartley Sartorius was sent to San José de los Llanos, and during his years there (1997–2006) he did nothing but evangelize everyone—at opportune and inopportune times, at every moment. He evangelized in plenty and in want, but in the name of God and with God's strength, which emanates from the Eucharist, from prayer, and from listening to and welcoming the Word, in communion with the Church. This is a book that exudes hope, that engenders happiness and a zest for life, that awakens a fervent desire to do likewise: to evangelize. The witness borne here by this beloved and admired missionary conveys happiness and light, as he conveyed that same happiness, and hope, to those brothers in San José de los Llanos living in such suffering.

The journalist who introduces and provides the setting for this story, told through letters written from the mission, acts as a chronicler and a witness—as a guide who does not force his observations into a predetermined mold but rather presents us with the whole reality he experienced, alerting us to an unfolding story of salvation. He does somewhat the same thing as Luke, who in Acts recounts that great first mission of the apostles, who carried out the mandate of the Lord with the fortitude of the Holy Spirit.

Speaking of evangelization, of the new evangelization, which may more often be the subject of theorizing than a vocation to be acted upon, this book tells us in substantive, vivid, and inspiring terms what the new evangelization is and how to conduct it. Certainly, one of the things that impresses me the most is the missionary's ardor; "new in its ardor", John Paul II said of the new evangelization. Christopher found that ardor in prayer, in "a close sharing between friends" as Saint Teresa said, meaning "taking time frequently to be alone with him who we know loves us".[2] How many hours and hours of prayer there are in this story! And, inseparable from prayer, the Eucharist.

---

[2] Teresa of Avila, *The Collected Works of St. Teresa of Avila* (hereafter *Collected Works*), trans. Kieran Kavanaugh, O.C.D., and Otilio Rodríguez, O.C.D., vol. 1 (Washington, D.C.: ICS Publications, 1976).

There is no new evangelization without the Eucharist. From it springs all the humanly unimaginable strength of active love, of charity that does not uncaringly turn a blind eye to so much misery, poverty, pain, and injustice.

The book is a page of Christology, of the proclamation of Christ, who identified himself with the ill, with those who weep and suffer. The proclamation of chapter 25 of the Gospel according to Matthew, a true kerygma, the living substance of the gospel, is realized in this story and in the letters that we read here.

Any reader of this book will feel himself called to evangelize and to say before God: "Here am I; send me whither thou wouldst; thy will be done, as revealed in thy Son." He will also feel called to conversion, to follow Jesus Christ, to open the door to him without fear as he follows the missionary work of Father Hartley, inspired by the Holy Spirit and in communion with the Church, in which Jesus Christ lives, where he is present, and through which he acts.

I need not go on. I need merely ask that this book be read with an open heart, with total receptivity, in happiness and joy for the great works and the mercy that God manifests to us. I give thanks to God. I also thank Christopher Hartley, because he has been a faithful servant of the Lord in his mission, which is always accompanied by the cross, for the Lord does not reveal all of his strength without the cross, the manifestation of the love of God, who is Love.

+ Antonio Cardinal Cañizares Llovera
Rome, September 2012

I

DRINKING COFFEE WITH COCOLA

Beginning when the Spaniards arrived, Dominican children were taught, in the oral tradition that was passed on by parents to their children and by grandparents to their grandchildren, whether in Spanish or in Creole[1] or in some less widespread dialect, how the Virgin of Mercy herself played a role in the Spaniards' wresting of Hispaniola from the hold of its Taíno Indian inhabitants. According to what the elders told those children, clothed in *mestizo* skin in an uncommonly wide variety of tones and shades, the Virgin of Mercy appeared between the Spanish forces and the indigenous inhabitants and, spreading her cloak over both sides, repelled the arrows being shot by the Indians so that they rebounded against them, resulting in a massacre, the beginning of the end of the Taíno Indians on the island, the end of their world.

This story was told, and accepted as true, for centuries. For years, images depicting it were painted on no small number of Christian churches, until someone realized that such an appalling story could not be told to the descendants of the Taíno and Carib Indians who populated the island. The story was simply regarded as authentic history. Very few people doubted it, and no one disputed it in public—until a schoolgirl in San Pedro de Macorís, in the south of the Dominican Republic, to the astonishment of her fellow students and the horror of her teacher, stood up and challenged the abominable legend, as from then on she would put in his place anybody who recounted it: "Señorita, doesn't this mean that the Virgin of Mercy isn't as good as people say she is?"

---

[1] The Creole language is spoken on various Caribbean islands by people of mixed race.

Any other child in the Dominican Republic would have kept quiet. No one had ever before raised his voice against the Virgin and against history. But for little Noemí, who is now Doctor Méndez, the law is a vocation, and she has raised her voice against injustice and abuse since her childhood, especially in cases where the victims are most vulnerable, as the Indians were at the time of the Discovery. Noemí's forthright audacity earned her a week of punishment, in the form of not being allowed to play during recess, but it was worth it. She went home savoring the respect that is the reward for telling the truth, standing up for it, and taking it as her flag. When she was a lively young girl it was written in her heart that, once she had grown up, she would be an advocate for those who stand up for themselves and fight.

That moment in school said so much about this little Dominican girl, and it was not an easy road that led from there to her law degree, which she proudly holds and firmly puts to practical use to this day, in cases that are more impossible and contentious than revising the story of the Virgin in front of the entire school.

Noemí is the seventh child of Manuel Méndez, Don Manolo, a Dominican peasant who worked all his life in the sugarcane fields. As his wife, Cocola, Noemí's mother, tells us, "Manolo knew a lot about sugar."

This grandmother's eyes are as immaculate as refined sugar, her skin is the color of brown sugar, and her gaze combines the sweetness of sugar and the bitterness of fresh-filtered coffee—which in her house, by the way, is as intense as a quarrel but goes down your throat harmlessly, as though it were caressing it. And so, over the six cups of coffee that are sitting here and there around the table in front of us, the conversation at Cocola's house flows the way the smell of coffee suffuses the room, and time goes by unnoticed without our being aware that something marvelous has enveloped us. The sugar, as though it were the notary of time taking minutes of the meeting, sits in the middle of the table, for in the Dominican Republic, and especially in Los Llanos and San Pedro de Macorís, which is where we are, the life and death of its people revolve around the sugarcane and its precious crystallized molasses.

Around Cocola's sugar, spilled on the table, we learn interesting things, important things—things that, when you hear them, are interesting the way a documentary film would be if you saw it from inside the screen. Listening to this woman talk nonstop is a documentary without music but with aroma, and with flavor, and with silences that say much more than an overcharged sound track.

Sitting there with her, we learned in the time it took to drink two coffees the process of turning sugarcane in the field into sugar on the table, how a guava tree is planted, what it would be like to feel an earthquake shaking your chair or a hurricane lashing your house, bringing it down as easily as a puff of wind would flatten a house of cards. We also learned a very significant part of the story that will be the subject of these pages, in which we propose to follow the trail of some letters written from a batey, from the canefields, from the mission of a Spanish priest who recorded the feelings, ideas, thoughts, and experiences that sprang from his heart as every morning unfolded, and at every sunset, for eight unforgettable years in the Dominican Republic.

Our missionary's thoughts are at times as sweet as molasses, but at others as bitter as the thickest coffee. His letters describe a missionary's discovery, in his daily routine, of the human miseries endured by the very poorest of men, and of the most heroic virtues. And this half-Spanish, half-English priest gives us a window not only on the faults and virtues in his surroundings and the mission in which he worked, but also on his own faults and virtues, and on how in the midst of the chaos of poverty and despair there's a presence that's stronger than evil and sadness, that raises man from his humiliation and distress to the greatest heights of human dignity: goodness and hope. Through reading the letters in this book, we will come to know the work of this missionary priest, from the world around him to his innermost self, and from there back again to the entire world, passing through the filter that is the presence of God in the human heart. This exercise will at some points distill, from the mixture of observation and intuition, a text that is intense because of its social content, yet warm and intimate because of its vitality; a text that is sometimes sublime, not because of the talent of the author but because of the spiritual power radiated by the letters and by the acts they recount.

These letters I am describing, which put us on the trail of the missionary who signed them, came into my hands shortly after they were written, when the missionary no longer had a mission, when he was no longer in the Dominican Republic. As I read them, I developed a keen appreciation for what they revealed—the God who could be seen in events that, very often, were beyond the control of the missionary priest. The stories that he tells in his letters are overwhelming. The letters have the freshness of the man who wrote them in the heat of the moment, describing unsparingly and fully, and with his heart on his sleeve, the reality of life in the mission.

The letters were written from inside the bateyes of the Dominican Republic. As Cocola drinks her coffee and gazes into the distance on our first stop along the path traced by those letters, she tells us that the bateyes are small peasant villages that grow up in the middle of the canefields. They are where the workers of the canefields live, workers who come from elsewhere and do not have their own homes. Originally, before 1848, the bateyes were built a mile or more from the plantation. Given the nature of sugarcane, which was until very recently the main source of foreign currency in the Dominican Republic, the bateyes were in effect isolated from each other, leaving room between the thick growth of sugarcane for no more than tracks that converged on the *ingenio*, the refinery where the cane is processed to yield sugar in a form that can be sent by freighter to the United States or some other country in the Americas.

In general, the population of the bateyes is made up of migrants who have been coming, for more than two centuries, to work the cane. There was a time when they came from the islands of the British Caribbean or Puerto Rico, and in the nineteenth century some were even seasonal workers from depressed regions of Europe, such as Belgium and northern France. From time to time there have also been a few Chinese, many Cubans, and also Jamaicans. They have always come through neighboring Haiti, the country that shares the island of Hispaniola with the Dominican Republic.

There are also Dominicans who live in the bateyes, but they are relatively few. They usually buy or rent houses in what they call *campos*, small rural hamlets with a minimum of infrastructure, although they have more and better-connected services than the bateyes.

It was in one of these bateyes surrounded by sugarcane that Noemí's jet-black eyes first saw the light of day. Her humble origins are intermixed with the Haitian migrants who came to the Dominican Republic, fleeing an extreme poverty that condemned them to exile in search of a better life among the canefields. While she absently stirs her coffee, Cocola tells us that she married Manolo when she was little older than a girl, barely fifteen years old. Ten years later she was already the mother of eight children, Noemí among them.

The canefields offer little more than back-breaking work, so Manolo and Cocola decided to move their family to the city of San Pedro de Macorís, where they could a provide a better future for their children, who ran here and there with the Haitian children in their batey. They were a happy family who had almost nothing, and Cocola remembers how well they lived together in the batey, loving each other and sharing with their Haitian neighbors the little they had, which was barely enough for themselves.

Even so, they decided to leave. They knew very well that the future of a boy in a batey went no further than working in the canefields. At most he might become a cart driver or, with a little luck and some skill, an accountant. A girl's future was more foreseeable: to have her first child in her teens and dedicate herself body and soul to a home in which there would never be anything left over for tomorrow.

So they left, and the change was for the better. Today, among this family of children born into the misery of the bateyes, there are lawyers, doctors, architects, and engineers. All of them have degrees, so they have broken the family tradition of occupations that came down from their ancestors—slaves who worked for some Spanish or French master in the everlasting canefields of the Dominican Republic or salaried workers like Don Manolo, who did not live in the institution of slavery but in living conditions that were almost inhuman, spending their lives working somebody else's lands. This is how the children of Manolo and Cocola conquered their lives and their futures, and those of their children and grandchildren—by leaving behind them the batey where they were born, hoping never to return except to bury their dead.

Little Noemí nevertheless missed the batey, and on weekends and during the summer she would go whenever she could, by oxcart, to the little shack where her father still lived as a worker in the canefields. Noemí belonged to the batey. The batey was her home. Her life breath needed this air, a mixture of Haitian melancholy and Dominican sweetness, so that she could go on living during the week. The batey and the Haitians shaped her vocation as a lawyer, the first glimmer of which had cost her a week of punishment, with no recess, for questioning the goodness of the Virgin of Mercy in the story told above.

Cocola then remembers an anecdote about Noemí that says so much about her sparkling personality. Before they moved, the little child accompanied her mother as she went from batey to batey, from hut to hut, distributing the clothes that Cáritas[2] sent them. Cocola was always a fervent Christian and took the opportunity presented by this distribution of clothes, or other things, to evangelize and tell the Haitians the story of one Jesus of Nazareth, a worker like them in Roman Palestine, who traveled through the world proclaiming, with his life and example, the liberation of slaves, the consolation of the oppressed, and the presence of God in the poorest places on earth. She told them that, being God, he had become man, and a poor man like them. A worker like them. If he had been made flesh in the Dominican Republic instead of in Judea, she said, he would not have been a carpenter but a cutter of cane.

The anecdote Cocola remembers was about one of those afternoons of distribution and catechism that memory cannot place with precision. There were so many such afternoons. We do not know what the little girl, no more than nine years old and with a vocation for the law, might have said when a Haitian neighbor to whom she was delivering clothes told her in front of her mother: "Child, you'll grow up to be a lawyer to defend the Haitians who live in the bateyes." Rarely has a sentence been more prophetic in the history of the Dominican Republic: once she had attained her admission to the bar, Noemí Méndez found herself plunged into an exceptionally thrilling story, worthy of being told on the screen, in a decisive legal battle that extends beyond race, color, nationality, and caste. She found herself in a struggle for freedom and human dignity about which I first learned from the letters in this book.

The story told here has been sought and brought to light through conversations and cooperation with the sugarcane workers and the other residents of the bateyes, and with their elders who have been away from home for more than eighty years and have clouded eyes from

---

[2] Cáritas Internationalis is a humanitarian organization of the Catholic Church that consists of 162 national organizations dedicated to social aid, development, and service. It was founded in 1897 in Freiburg, Germany.

having stared so long at the ground and missing fingers from having cut cane and more cane. We have traveled the sugar plantations of San José de los Llanos and San Pedro de Macorís, talking, asking, and sitting down to listen to stories. All the stories revolve around the same thing: sugar. It is at the center of the table and the center of the conversation. This sugar—as those who plant it and work in it say—is not sweet, as it is in Spain, and not white either. Here in the bateyes of the Dominican Republic, the sugar is red like the blood of the sugarcane cutters and bitter like the tomorrow of one who has nothing.

2

HISPANIOLA

The island of Hispaniola was inhabited by Taíno and Carib Indians when, on December 5, 1492, Christopher Columbus landed on its north shore in the second stage of his first voyage, building the fort named La Navidad—Christmas—with the wreckage of the *Santa María*, which had run aground on the beach.

The Taínos gave the Spaniards a warm welcome and helped them build the fort. Columbus continued his voyage once the fort was built, leaving behind a small detachment that is considered the first European settlement in the West Indies. Those men had come from arid Castile, unyielding Extremadura, or the rainy Basque country. We can imagine how, after seeing this territory, they lay down that first night thinking they were in a paradise where it was never cold and where food fell from the trees without being cultivated. Spellbound by those beaches of never-ending sun and warm water, which seems less like salt water than fresh because of its softness to the touch, many of those men decided never to return to Spain.

The exceptional conditions of the island made the life of the indigenous inhabitants very easy. The temperature was consistent throughout the year, ranging from sixty to eighty degrees, a tree would yield enough fruit for a week if you threw a single stone at it, and the sea offered plenty of fish to anybody who reached out for it. So the Taínos had a much weaker constitution than the Europeans. In fact, when Columbus came back to Hispaniola on his second voyage, Navidad had been destroyed by fighting among the Spanish colonists themselves and between them and the Indians, who gradually came to see how the former used them to do the most difficult work. And the Indians, being less used to hard work on account of their milder environmental conditions, and being more susceptible to the infections that were passed on to them by the Spaniards, saw their population dwindling.

In the face of the hostilities he was up against, the Admiral decided to establish another settlement to the east in what is today the Dominican Republic, called La Isabela in honor of the Catholic Queen of Spain. The paradise of enviable weather and crystalline seas hid a danger, though, of which the Spaniards were almost unaware, and two hurricanes destroyed Isabela in just two years, reducing it to a mere footnote in the history books. Columbus therefore ordered his brother Bartolomé to seek a site in the southern part of the island and to establish what is today the capital of the Dominican Republic, Santo Domingo. Santo Domingo is not spared the fury of hurricanes, but the hurricane seasons of the years that followed simply treated Hispaniola more leniently than they had before. Instead of enduring a hurricane every year, the inhabitants of Santo Domingo were subjected to one every four or five years.

The local population had already been substantially reduced by 1501. The hard labor and disease to which the Indians were subjected, as already noted, together with the flight of some to other islands and the mixture of races with those who remained, spelled the end of a race that had occupied these islands since God had put them there. In the first two decades of the sixteenth century, the Spaniards introduced two elements in Hispaniola that have shaped the history of both Haiti and the Dominican Republic, and that shape them even today— the slaves imported from Africa and the sugarcane brought from the Canary Islands.

The first African slaves arrived in Hispaniola between 1503 and 1509; the date varies among sources. The sugarcane came soon after, in 1511, and the first sugar mill on record was already operating by 1516. The mere existence of a sugar mill implies a large number of manual laborers who are productive, strong, and also cheap. The cultivation of sugar is, now as it was then, viable only as a low-cost operation. Sugarcane requires immense tracts of land to yield a profit to the owner, because the price of sugar is very low and a great deal of cane yields just a handful of *cabos*. In addition, cane attains a height of ten feet and has a very strong stalk, which makes the canefields dense to the point of impassability. And transporting it, because of the length of the stalk, is no simple matter. The arrival of slaves from Africa, therefore, increased considerably, in step with the planting of cane, the construction of sugar mills and the production of sugar.

By the grace of God, from the confusion that originated not in the discovery of a new world but rather in the coming together of three different cultures—European, indigenous, and African—some Spaniards conceived the idea that neither the blacks of Africa nor the Indians of America were animals, but rather that they had souls and therefore human dignity. One of those Spaniards was Friar Bartolomé de Las Casas. He had come from Seville to the Americas as a young man in 1506, following in the footsteps of his father, who had accompanied Columbus on his second voyage. Las Casas worked as a miner in the gold mines of Hispaniola—which have since been mined out— and took an active part in the Spanish conquest and settlement of the island. When he went back to Seville, he studied to be a priest and entered the Order of Preachers. After his studies in Rome, he decided to return to the Indies, renounced some holdings that he had there, and began to explain to the Europeans that these people were God's children as much as Spaniards were—which embroiled him in quite a few conflicts and earned him quite a few punishments—and to tell the Indians that God was alive in the person of Jesus Christ.

The sixteenth century, as it unfolded in Hispaniola, was marked by violence, evil, and drama. Sugar became the most important sector of the economy, and the canefields acquired central significance for the landholders and the governing class. Many African slaves fled to the mountains on the Haitian border. At the same time, the waters of the Caribbean became infested with English, French, and Dutch pirates who terrorized the Spanish navy by boarding and looting its ships and who began to enlist Africans and mestizos from the mountains and the territory that is Haiti today.

It was the French who, in the late-seventeenth and early-eighteenth centuries, decided to invade and conquer the western part of the island. Or, rather, they decided to occupy it, as a good part of it was abandoned by the Spanish because it was not as rich in mining potential and arable land as the eastern part, which is today the Dominican Republic. The French kept the poorest part of the island, which, in addition, was populated by fugitives and exiles who came with nothing to a land that offered nothing. These are the roots of today's Haiti, the poorest country in the Americas, and the roots of the racial problems that have afflicted, and continue to afflict, the Haitian and Dominican populations of Hispaniola.

Haiti gained independence from France in 1804, after a bloody slave revolution against the landowners that lasted more than ten years. The Haitian population was black, and by the time they attained independence they had come to identify white skin with the invader, the oppressor, the tyrant, the slaveholder. With that perception ingrained in them, the Haitians expropriated the lands of the white landholders— or, depending on the point of view, obtained restitution from them; restricted the use of the Spanish language (it was impossible to restrict the use of French); and outlawed many of the traditional European customs. Whites were forbidden to own land, and all relations with the Roman Catholic Church were cut off.

The island was thus divided between two national and racial realities. In the west, Haiti had a black population, the French and Creole languages, and a syncretic religion with African roots that led to the expansive spread of voodoo. In the east was the Dominican Republic, with the Spanish language, the Christian religion, and a "white" population, although racial mixing actually runs so deep that you cannot tell by a person's skin color whether he is a Haitian or a Dominican. But this national marker has produced a situation in which, for them, a man who was born in the Dominican Republic with skin as black as night is a white, while a Haitian the color of café au lait is a black— and, in each case, in the most derogatory sense of the word.

Since we do not propose to write a historical treatise, we will jump to the twentieth century, at the end of which the first of the letters that brought us to the Dominican Republic was written.

The twentieth century was the century of dictatorships, and Hispaniola would not want for totalitarian regimes at either end of the island. So, after an invasion by the United States and a series of revolutions, Rafael Leónidas Trujillo Molina (1891–1961) was elected president. Of Spanish, Haitian, and Dominican descent, he established absolute political control in the Dominican Republic with severe repression of human rights.[1] He governed the country for thirty-one years, from 1930 until his assassination in 1961. Along the way he left no small

[1] Jonathan Hartlyn, "The Trujillo Regime in the Dominican Republic", in *Sultanistic Regimes*, eds. H. E. Chehabi and Juan J. Linz (Baltimore and London: Johns Hopkins University Press, 1998), 85–112.

trail of blood, generally the blood of Haitians, such as the thousands of workers killed in the "massacre of *perejil*", when he ordered his troops to kill, en masse, the population of Haitian origin who lived in the campos and bateyes of the agricultural areas, especially in those that bordered Haiti.

The sources differ as to the number of victims. It is said that there were between twenty and thirty thousand. What all the sources agree on is the name by which this atrocious ethnic-cleansing operation is known, because the Dominican soldiers and police, unable to distinguish between Haitians and Dominicans by the color of their skin— no matter how much some of them insist they can—required their potential victims to pronounce the Spanish word for parsley: *perejil*. Since Haitians speak Creole or French, in which the *r* is pronounced softly, it was relatively simple to guess, though not with certainty, who was Haitian and who was Dominican. Many Dominicans were also killed, not for the color of their skin or their nationality, but for having a speech defect that prevented them from properly pronouncing the *r* in *perejil*.

Trujillo had accused Haitians of being squatters who were seizing land and rustling cattle, but at the same time he hid from the Dominican population, for as long as he could, the fact that he had murdered thousands of innocent, defenseless poor people. What Trujillo could not do was restore the color of the river Dabajón, known today as the Massacre River. For weeks it was tinged a deep red from the blood of the bodies that were thrown into the river so that they would be carried off by the current and their memory erased.

If the Dominican Republic had its tyrant in the person of Trujillo, Haiti had its own in that of Papa Doc (François Duvalier, 1907–1971), a doctor and politician born in Haiti's capital, Port-au-Prince, of African and indigenous descent. He was the president and dictator of Haiti from 1957 to 1971. Interestingly, during the few years in which his dictatorship overlapped with Trujillo's, the two signed a nonaggression pact, which shows how much they feared one another. While he was in office, Papa Doc used murder and exile to sideline his political rivals, and some sources attribute about thirty thousand deaths to him. It goes without saying that his political ideology brimmed with extreme hatred toward Dominicans and that the fact he was black helped him to be elected president.

After his death in 1971 he was succeeded by his son Jean-Claude, known as Baby Doc, who was overthrown and went into exile in France in 1986. After he fled to that country, his father's tomb was publicly vandalized.

In 1997, when the first of our letters was written, the Dominican Republic was under a democratic government led by Leonel Fernández (born in Santo Domingo in 1953), a Dominican lawyer and politician educated in the United States, who had to struggle from the moment he took office, in 1996, with a poor economy that for centuries had been based on the declining sugar industry. Most of the country's population were unaware that, at their core, the canefields harbored a reality left over from the days of landowners, masters, fear, poverty, and human misery that recalled or smacked of the days of slavery. They were no longer brought from Africa. They came—many of them tricked into coming—from neighboring Haiti. And they came to cut the cane.

3

NOEMÍ MÉNDEZ AND CEDAIL

Noemí Méndez earned her high school diploma and her law degree when she was very young. She was barely twenty-one years old when she graduated. This circumstance is attributable to the simple fact that no one asked how old she was on her first day in primary school, an omission that remained uncorrected through the day she obtained her high school diploma at the age of seventeen, and then on through the day she finished her graduate education. At that point she was so young, and she looked so young, that she doubted anyone would hire her as a lawyer. And so it proved.

A law office did hire her, but not as an attorney. Her first job was as a lawyer's secretary, and was unpaid. Yes, she was paid nothing. Her boss maintained that what she would learn as a secretary in the office would be compensation enough. What the attorney did not know was that Noemí began to educate herself, because in her free time she kept on visiting the bateyes where she was born and raised, gaining a new perspective on the unspeakable poverty and unpredictability of life in those villages. She was no longer the Noemí born in the batey of Las Pajas who went there to spend the weekend. She was no longer the little girl who, clinging to her mother's skirts, distributed clothing and food while she observed and absorbed how life unfolds in those houses made of wood and cane. Noemí was now a lawyer. She was almost as slight and still as outspoken as before, but she had the perspective of one who has studied, who has learned that some conditions in the batey are not as they should be, that life is not as rosy as she used to paint it from the innocent vantage point of a child.

As though it were a diversion for her, she began to help the cane workers with their minor problems—little everyday things that had nothing to do with working conditions or human rights. But, without realizing it, during those first years of her practice as a volunteer lawyer, Noemí devoted herself above all to translating what she learned about the batey into the language of the law. Little by little she began to see an endless train of typographical errors in the script that governed how the men and the women in the batey lived. Those imperfections began to come to life one morning at the end of 1997.

In the meantime, Noemí made progress in her life and in her profession, and she was hired by the Dominican Center of Legal Advice and Research (CEDAIL in its Spanish acronym). CEDAIL was founded by the Conference of the Dominican Episcopate in 1979 to provide education, support, advice, and assistance in human rights to the impoverished and marginalized parts of the population—migrant workers, peasants, vagrants, abused women, and so on—to contribute to the establishment of structures that will bring about a new order of justice and equality in the exercise of fundamental rights.

The sugar industry was beginning to go into decline at the time, though that was not obvious, and notwithstanding CEDAIL's attempts to help the neediest people in the campos of the Dominican Republic, there were many men and women in the most isolated bateyes whom no one ever reached, until the end of 1997.

The Dominican sugar industry is divisible into two types of sugar mills, according to their ownership, and each of those two groups is divisible again into two, according to their respective types of batey. In the second half of the twentieth century, the sugar mills were owned either privately or publicly, in the latter case through the State Sugar Council (CEA in its Spanish acronym), an entity founded by the government that succeeded the Trujillo dictatorship to manage the production of sugar by the twelve sugar mills that then belonged to the state. The living conditions of the workers in the bateyes differed depending on whether they were publicly or privately owned: in the bateyes of the CEA sugar mills, the law of the state was applied, whereas in the privately owned bateyes, whatever happened behind closed doors was given free rein without comment by anyone. But it was true that the workers' way of life was as harsh in one case as it was in the other.

Every sugar mill had its central batey, where the mill workers lived next to the mill, and its rural bateyes surrounded by the fortress-like canefields. In those rural bateyes, which we will be addressing in these pages, life was hardest for the workers.

In the 1990s the price of sugar on the international market suffered a considerable decline, making it barely profitable without extremely cheap manual labor, and the state-owned sugar mills lost their viability. Many of them closed or were privatized, creating an extremely difficult social environment for their workers. The lawyers and staff of CEDAIL, of which Noemí began to be a part, were up against poverty, a lack of legal protection from the state and the industry, unemployment, and living conditions that were below what a worker deserved. It was administrative work, in contact with the workers and carried on with an emphasis on charity similar to that of the Church, that served, and continues to serve, to help many people live their lives with a little less pain within the sea of bitterness that is the lot of the Haitian migrant worker in the Dominican canefields.

During our visit to the Dominican Republic in January 2011, in which we followed the trail blazed by these letters, some of the inhabitants of the poorest, most unspeakable bateyes we visited told us that, when Noemí began to work for CEDAIL, the living conditions of those workers were so bad that they needed not a little help but a revolution. The conditions of those men and women, as they thereby attested, were so dire that, at the end of the twentieth century, thousands of them lived in barracks or huts no larger than a hundred square feet, without water or electricity, without sanitation. They cut cane from four in the morning until five in the afternoon for less than two euros per ton, eating only one meal per day. They were unable to leave the bateyes for they had no labor contracts, no work visas, and no passports. Our witnesses told us that the situation was a legacy of the time of slavery's abolition, which no one had ever bothered to put into full effect, either out of ignorance of the cane worker's plight or by turning a blind eye to it.

Elderly men and women told us that in their ninety-five years of life they had known nothing but the batey and the sugarcane. Turning things around, they said, would take more than a little aid, more than charity. What was needed was a revolution that, like a hurricane, would demolish the obsolete and outdated concept of the batey that has lived on into the twenty-first century, and with it the prevailing ideology—almost that of a slaveholder—about the sugarcane workers.

What was needed was something that would do away with a status quo that no one questioned or found surprising, in which whole generations of Haitians, and also of Dominicans, have lived and died without anybody moving even a single fiber of a single stalk of sugarcane for them, for their dignity, for their labor, for their humanity.

The oldest among them told us this, and so too did some of the younger ones who raise their heads to look at the sky and to ask the good Lord when he will turn his attention to them to change that situation of bitter, blood-red sugar. And many said that God has heard them, that he has answered by sending a hurricane dressed as a missionary. Father Christopher Hartley Sartorius arrived in San José de los Llanos in the autumn of 1997, in the middle of hurricane season. Depending on whom you ask, he was a hurricane for the worse, and also for the better. The key question we asked when the local elders told us this was, "Can a hurricane do some good?" The answer given by those in the batey who knew him was devastating: "To reverse a desperate situation you have to destroy first so you can start over from zero, from the foundations. When you're tackling a project like that, a hurricane certainly does help you get the process started."

4

FATHER CHRISTOPHER

As she did every morning of her life for more than seventy years, Mother Teresa of Calcutta woke up early to offer up her personal prayers. This small, wrinkled Albanian nun, missionary, and founder of the Missionaries of Charity devoted at least three hours every day to sitting and praying in front of her tabernacle. Her tremendous labors on behalf of the poorest of the poor always ran through her profound faith that the little metal cabinet in her chapel contained the same Christ who inspired, strengthened, supported, and awaited her. Even during all those dark years when she did not feel his presence there, she simply believed it.

On the morning of September 5, 1997, Calcutta teemed as it always did with people in every nook and cranny eking out a living as best they could. Mother Teresa performed her routine tasks as though there was nothing to it. She prayed, answered some letters, and worked as usual, despite having felt pain in her chest and back since the early hours. It was past ten o'clock when one of her sisters entered her room and found her in bed tossing and turning in pain. Her hands were cold, her pulse was racing, and in a thin voice she asked for air, saying, "I can't breathe." At that very moment, when they were about to place the oxygen mask on her face, there was a power outage in Calcutta that prevented Mother Teresa from getting the air she needed.

The light that illuminated Mother Teresa during her time on earth was not extinguished by her death. As just one example out of many, that same day one of her favorite sons was arriving in the fields of the Lord in the Dominican Republic. As a priest with a missionary's vocation inspired by her, he would spread the flame ignited by Mother Teresa among the poorest of the poor in the bateyes of the sugar plantations.

While darkness was taking possession of Calcutta, the sun shone fiercely and the wind blew gently in San Pedro de Macorís, in the south of the Dominican Republic, where immense fields of sugarcane spread as far as the eye could see to the east, the north, and the west. A couple of hours before, the plane from New York had landed in Santo Domingo with a passenger on board who did not have a return ticket. He was Father Christopher Hartley Sartorius. He arrived in the Dominican Republic with the eagerness of a missionary on his first mission. Not for nothing was he the spiritual son of Mother Teresa of Calcutta, the most emblematic and popular missionary of the Roman Catholic Church in the twentieth century, who that same day was on her way to heaven.

Father Christopher did not yet know, while he was aloft in that airplane, that Mother Teresa had died in Calcutta of a heart attack. At that hour of the afternoon, no one in San José de los Llanos knew. They knew neither that Mother Teresa had died nor that Father Christopher was one of her favorite sons. They neither knew nor cared. They were happy because a new priest was coming to them.

Looking forward as he still was to telling Mother Teresa about his first contact with his mission, Father Christopher was recalling how she had always been a part of his vocation story. It all had begun many years before, on December 25, 1976, in Madrid, under a Christmas tree in the house of a well-to-do, aristocratic Hispano-British family.

Christopher's father gave his son of seventeen, as a Christmas present, a book titled *Mother Teresa: Her People and Her Work*. The images in this book touched young Christopher, at that time an impetuous and ungovernable adolescent, deep in his heart. Those photographs so impressed him that he secretly said to himself that those people, those poor and miserable men, would from that moment be the reason for his existence and his vocation. He decided to lead a life radically removed from the wealth, opulence, and comfort in which he had been born and raised. Two years before, when he was barely fifteen years old, Christopher had already decided to be a priest. But that book was one more step toward his destiny, turning his priestly calling into a missionary vocation.

The first Hartley Sartorius of his generation has never been able to put into precise words the moment that he received his vocation. He can only contextualize that moment, saying that he was fifteen years old and wanted for nothing in his life. His father was a successful businessman who had devoted his career to a family marmalade business in Great Britain. When Christopher was a child, the family sold the business at a good price to devote themselves to other things. His mother, Pilar Sartorius y Álvarez de las Asturias, is from an aristocratic Spanish family. Christopher's maternal grandfather was the third Count of San Luis.

What then made young Christopher an unhappy and troubled youth? He had an unruly and complex character, and business was not, in any way at all, for him. Nor was the aristocracy, and still less a career in diplomacy. His father remembered, in a documentary produced in the United States in 2007, that Christopher was a "rebellious, difficult" boy.

His brother and sister have described him as a very "competitive" person, who both in school and at home gave his parents, teachers, siblings, companions, and friends constant headaches. This was a boy who always wanted to win, to be the best, and who did not like school at all or, rather, who hated it.

The young Christopher was bitter, bad-humored, sad, and distressed, and he felt misunderstood. He cared about nothing, was motivated by nothing, and vented his discontent in fights and quarrels with anybody who happened to be around. He was far from being a model boy. And suddenly, for no reason at all, lying in his bed on a March afternoon, he felt he was loved to the utmost, and he decided to be a priest, going off to the seminary in Toledo at the age of just fifteen, to the astonishment of everybody, the misgivings of many, and the relief of a few at the disappearance of this earthquake disguised as a teenager.

He was seventeen when his father gave him the book about Mother Teresa, and at eighteen he had the chance to meet her in person at the London home of the Missionaries of Charity. Christopher spent his summer vacations there to get to know them. He saw in Mother Teresa a woman of extraordinary strength. Unmoved by sentimentalism, she could be extremely tough on occasion. She was a woman who loved Christ and whose only goal was saintliness. Beholding her courage and compassion in the presence of injustice and poverty, the young seminarian decided to take her as his guide and model, his point of reference, his exemplar.

As he struggled to advance at the seminary during the years that followed—he continued to find it difficult to earn passing grades—

Christopher spent his summers in one or another home of the Missionaries of Charity. One year he even took advantage of a promotion by Pan Am to go around the world in eighty days, visiting the homes of Teresa of Calcutta's daughters in many countries.

In the summer of 1980 Christopher stayed in Spain. In Leganés, near Madrid, permission had been granted to the Missionaries to establish a home there. Christopher, along with some classmates at the seminary in Toledo, went to get it up and running. When Mother Teresa came to Spain, Christopher became her shadow because he was bilingual, acting as her interpreter and guide wherever she went.

In the summer of 1981 Christopher again visited Calcutta. He was about to begin his final year at the seminary, but he returned gravely ill. He brought with him malaria, typhus, intestinal bacteria, and scabies. At the beginning of October, he was sent home from the seminary with a dangerously high fever, and the doctors did not know how to treat such a collection of rare diseases.

That December, the young men in his class were up for ordination as deacons. But Christopher had fallen a half semester behind and did not return in time to be ordained with his classmates. His recovery from the illnesses was very slow and full of complications. He was weak and very thin. So when his classmates were ordained as deacons, one of the acolytes in the ceremony was as scrawny as a stick and as pale as a sheet, and he did not stop crying throughout the ceremony. When he arrived at the seminary, he was the only member of his class who was still in street dress.

In the spring of 1982 those who had been ordained deacons the previous December were scheduled to be ordained priests in Toledo. Don Marcelo,[1] then the archbishop of Toledo, talked with our young missionary and asked him what he should do with him. Christopher must have had the same idea that the prelate had in mind for him: to be ordained a deacon on the day his classmates were ordained priests, and ordained a priest on the day the members of the following class were ordained deacons. When Don Marcelo heard his own thoughts in what Christopher told him, he asked him: "Would you like to be ordained by John Paul II?"

---

[1] Don Marcelo González Martín (1918–2004), cardinal archbishop of Toledo from 1975 to 1995.

On May 13, 1981, with two shots, Ali Agca made it impossible for John Paul II to visit Spain in the following October, as had been planned. The Polish pope's visit to Spain was postponed until fall 1982, when he would ordain 141 Spanish seminarians. Christopher was not eligible to be one of them, but behold the works of God: the seminarian who cried like a child over not being ordained a deacon with his classmates in 1981 leaped for joy when his bishop told him that by a special dispensation he would be ordained on November 8, 1982, in Valencia, by Pope John Paul II. His illness of the year before turned out to be a piece of luck.

Barely three weeks after being ordained, the twenty-three-year-old Father Christopher, one of the youngest priests in the Toledo Diocese, took possession of his parish of Robledo del Mazo. Serving this rural community was not easy for the cosmopolitan city priest, who was a Londoner by birth, a citizen of the whole world by vocation, and a restless soul. To put it briefly, this first assignment did not go well for the fledgling priest. He has often acknowledged, however, that he learned a lot in those two years as a village priest. He still has fond memories of the people of the Sierra Toledo, and the unmet needs, the shortages, and the loneliness of the simple parish helped him to mature and to understand, on the ground, the day-to-day life of the very many anonymous priests whose services are indispensable in Spain.

In the end, the experience helped him to grow in his vocation as a missionary priest, for in his heart, which was like a volcano on the verge of eruption, he felt that his calling was elsewhere. With inspiration, and with the help of Bishop Marcelo, he left Robledo del Mazo in 1984 for New York, to work in the Bronx with the Missionaries of Charity Fathers. He was there for eight years, serving particularly the Puerto Rican and Dominican populations. He so devoted himself to his mission that he became an integral part of the archdiocese of the legendary Cardinal John O'Connor,[2] who saw him as a gifted young man and sent him to study in Rome.

In the Eternal City Christopher earned a doctorate in dogmatic theology, became familiar with the ins and outs of the Vatican, lived day-to-day life very close to the pope, and at the same time learned

---

[2] John Joseph O'Connor (1929–2000), archbishop of New York from 1984 (cardinal from 1985) to 2000.

Italian. Everything pointed toward his ordination, before long, as a bishop somewhere in the world. He had more than enough credentials, and he did not lack for charisma or initiative. Some said, as a way of highlighting his respect for all that is holy, that when it came to celebrating the liturgy, living as a priest, and preaching the gospel, he was more old-fashioned than the Council of Trent. And so by 1995 he had returned with his doctorate to New York, to be a parish priest. But it was not just any parish. The post that awaited him was nothing less than the venerable Cathedral of Saint Patrick. No small thing.

For two years Father Christopher enjoyed the pomp and the prestige of being the parish priest of the best-known Catholic church in New York. The cream of American Catholicism, the highest class in the city, gathered at Saint Patrick's every Sunday, and Father Christopher was very much at home in that environment, like a fish in water. He had been born as one of them, and he was one of them. And though in the past he had by vocation rejected all vestiges of blue blood, the good life was affecting him in the same way that skin is tanned by being exposed to the sun. He never stopped serving the Missionaries of Charity whenever he could, however, and he always spent his vacations at a mission. And so, invited by a seminary classmate, Father Antonio Diufaín, he was introduced to the Dominican Republic. On every one of Father Christopher's visits there during those two years, Father Antonio invited him without fail to join him in the parish next to his, which had been without a priest for a decade.

The reality is that Father Christopher had developed a taste for his role in New York. Life was good there, and comfortable. Yet the problems of his parish did not move him as much as his gnawing inner recollection that he had once, some time ago, secretly promised God that he would dedicate his life and vocation to the poorest of the poor, to those whom Teresa of Calcutta treated like the living Christ in his suffering among us, deep in the world's most horrible depths. New York had obscured his desire to be a missionary and to dedicate himself to the poorest, the neediest, but the embers of that desire remained; and they were rekindled in the priest's prayers and solitude, especially when he sought silence for his conversations with God in the convent of the Sisters of Bethlehem. It was his periods of solitary prayer that kept him firm in his secret commitment to go on a mission one day.

To ease his conscience, Father Christopher decided to resolve the problem of that commitment by putting his immediate future in the hands of Archbishop O'Connor, and he did it as someone might ask his father to send him to war—as an absurd act of madness. He assumed that, having sent him to study in Rome, the bishop would never even let it cross his mind to send such a priest to a remote hole in the Dominican Republic.

"I had other plans for you," the archbishop admitted, "but maybe God's plans are different. Go there, and at the end of a year you'll have to decide whether to come back or stay there as a missionary."

Father Christopher left the archbishop's house in a state of shock. He had put his idea of being a missionary in the hands of his bishop more to ease his conscience than out of conviction—so that he could say, when asked, that it was the Church that would not let him forsake all that he had and devote himself to the poor. He saw, however, that in less than a half hour his bishop had swept aside the reluctance that, all by himself, he had developed in his years of ruminating about his future, his position, and his career. To obey, the only thing Christopher could do that morning was to buy an airplane ticket to the Dominican Republic. A one-way ticket, not round-trip.

5

LETTERS FROM THE MISSION

Father Antonio Diufaín had been in the Dominican Republic for several years. Though he was older than Christopher, he was his junior as an ordained priest. But he was unquestionably Father Christopher's best teacher and support in the mission to which he invited him.

Antonio had fairly recently begun to work with a Dominican lawyer who, in her free time, gave classes to women, taught catechism, and did it with the ease of one who knew the fields and bateyes in which she had been born. In addition, Noemí Méndez had the benefit of her experience with CEDAIL to familiarize herself with the current problems of the campo and the batey. At the end of 1997, Father Antonio Diufaín introduced Noemí to Father Christopher.

As she later admitted, she did not take to him: "He was rude, coarse, and suspicious. He kept me waiting in the street, out in the hot sun, for more than a half hour and then gave me the third degree to find out who I was, where I came from, and why I was there. He did not realize it was his friend Antonio who had sent me to him, to help him with some courses in the parish, and that I was not the least bit interested in being there with him."

All we have for now from this missionary priest, who was so unpleasant and coarse in his very first dealings with Noemí, is a handful of letters written from the mission that give us a glimpse into the missionary's life. All the same, Noemí admits that she misses him now: "Meeting Father Christopher changed me—as a person, as a lawyer, and as a Christian. Rarely have I seen such conviction in a follower of Christ." After hearing her describe this change in her judgment of Father Christopher, one wonders what goes through the missionary's mind and heart. What moves a man like this priest Hartley—

by extension, any missionary—to give up everything to go and live among the poor? Why would a person "who has it made" complicate his life that way? How does a person think, feel, and live when, despite his faults, he is capable of giving himself wholly to making life better for others?

The purpose of this book is rooted in these questions and in preserving these letters in their original form, as faithful reflections of a missionary's experience. I want to pause here briefly before approaching the first of the letters. This book is neither a beatification proceeding nor a criminal trial—not of Father Christopher or of the people with whom he shared his missionary experience in the Dominican Republic; not of those who helped him or of those whom he helped; not of those whom he confronted or of those who confronted him. Anybody looking for a superhero in these pages would do better to buy a Batman comic book. A superhero is nowhere to be found here. The point of this book is nothing more than to understand, through his heart, through his vision, through his judgment, the social reality with which a missionary is faced, and how and why—with his virtues and defects, with his fears, his doubts, his decisions, good and bad—he addresses that reality. In fact, this book is no more than a Christian witness of someone who, following his vocation, has found himself face-to-face with the real life of a large number of poor men to whom nobody has ever given anything—as what follows will show.

～

Go into All the World and Preach the Gospel to the Whole Creation

Having made our purpose clear, we now turn to the first letter by our missionary, written a few weeks after his arrival in the Dominican Republic. We will see in it the eagerness and the initiative of one who has arrived at his pastoral assignment called by God and sent by his Church, to help the poor and to evangelize in a place where not a single sacrament has been celebrated for years. The first thing that noticeably marks him as a missionary is his absolute confidence in prayer—especially, in this case, in the prayer of contemplative nuns. And although it is true that he solicits financial support, the father gives a lesson on the spiritual meaning of the act of giving. One who does so can have learned it only from being with the poor and praying with them, elevating the absolute good of prayer, and of renunciation, above the donation itself.

Finally, we need to say that this first letter, in the optimism that it exudes amid so much drama, resembles what a child would write to his parents on his first day at summer camp. The writer gives off such energy that it seems nothing and nobody will be able to get the better of him. And we will see the same throughout the other letters, not because of his own strength and energy but rather because of the strength and the energy he receives from God. Little by little the disciple diminishes himself and leaves space for the Master. He is in this first letter an unseasoned missionary, even in his ignorance of the realities that attend his vocation, and above all of those that will exceed what he bargained for, however well-intentioned his motivations may have been. We must bear in mind that, although Father Christopher had already lent a helping hand to many missions, he had never had one of his own.

Along with his eagerness, the letter radiates his astonishment. Poverty seems to be everywhere around him, but the letter reflects the fact that, in his mind and heart, he is already imagining a multitude of projects to be carried out alongside the unremitting celebration of the sacraments. This priest does not seem to be motivated by the simple act of giving assistance and consolation, of sinking wells where there are none or building houses with roofs for beggars. This first letter makes it indisputably clear that, always and everywhere, he is motivated by his evangelistic and apostolic zeal, although in the process he sees that he has to think and to act like a walking nongovernmental organization, resolving problems and coping with emergencies at every turn. Although the material necessities described by the father were extreme, the spiritual ones were no less so. A population of more than twenty-five thousand was awaiting Father Christopher in San José de los Llanos. Many of them had never seen a priest in their lives, many others did not even know if they were baptized, and many more knew that they were not.

The father also explains the reason for writing these letters and sending them to his close friends and family, and although in this first letter he cites the bateyes, he is unfamiliar with the wretched living conditions of the Haitians in the heart of his parish, in San José de los Llanos.

~

"Go into all the world and preach the gospel
to the whole creation." —Mark 16:15

Dear friends of the mission:

I've finally arrived at the mission to which the Lord has sent me! Most of you know that I'm in the parish of San José de los Llanos, in the province of San Pedro de Macorís (Dominican Republic). We're in the eastern part of the country, in the middle of an endless sea of sugarcane that surrounds us on all sides, on an immense plain. It's the most extensive plain in all the Caribbean Islands.

The city of San Pedro is on the southeast coast of the island. The area to which I've been assigned extends from the coast to almost the middle of the country. I live in the city limits of Los Llanos, and it's my responsibility to attend, in addition, to thirty-eight campos (villages or towns with about two hundred to seven hundred Dominicans) and bateyes (villages made up of Haitians, most of them here illegally, who live in and for the cane).

It's impossible to calculate the population. Ask as I might, nobody knows what it is, and there are hardly any censuses. The only thing I do know is that there are people here—people everywhere. Especially many, many children, who are the great treasure and wealth of this marvelous country. I haven't yet had time to visit all the campos, I go to two or three new ones per week. There aren't even three feet of asphalt on these roads, just mud, mire, muck, and water. The roads are actually nothing more than the tracks of ox carts and tractors that drag the cane to the *ingenios*—the mills that process the sugarcane. No cars travel these roads. Only four-wheel-drive vehicles can avoid getting bogged down in the mire, and when they do bog down they have to wait for a tractor or a team of oxen to pull them out. Perhaps the most urgent need I have at this point is to get such a vehicle, because the one I have now is on the verge of giving out.

Of the thirty-eight campos, only fourteen have anything resembling a little chapel or "arbor"—no more than a shelter made of sticks and thatched with palm fronds and banana leaves. In the rest, Mass is celebrated in the open air. I take with me what I need for the Mass in a briefcase that the Carmelite Mothers of San Francisco (California) gave me.

The heat is unbearable right now. I don't remember ever having sweated so much in my life—perhaps when I went to India during the monsoon season. To write a letter, I have to put a towel or some cardboard under my forearm, so the sweat doesn't destroy the paper. I won't even describe what it's like to sweat when you're celebrating Mass, just imagine it. The weather doesn't change much during the year; it may be a little cooler during the winter, although as you can imagine it isn't cool enough to require a coat!

Among the many surprises that were waiting for me when I arrived, the one that surprised me the most, by far, was definitely the poverty. The poverty is horrible, and only somebody who has lived it can truly know its depth. These people are poor because they simply have nothing, absolutely nothing. That's what it is to be poor, you see, to have nothing.

I go into these people's huts, which are thatched with palm fronds and made out of royal palm wood. There's nothing inside. Everything's rudimentary; they have no electricity, no running water, barely a place to sit. They don't have the most minimal cooking utensils or toilets, or the means of taking a bath. They use rudimentary latrines that they themselves dig in the ground and are a steady source of infection. You often see children as young as four walking along, wearing filthy underpants and carrying a rusty old can, bringing water to their little house.

A few days ago I went to celebrate Mass and acquaint myself with one more of my many small villages. It's called Los Castro. The hut in which I celebrated the Eucharist was filthy, the worst I've seen so far. When I was done I asked if there were any sick in the village, and they showed me the house of two old women who lived in a hovel under terrible conditions, with no hygiene and nothing to eat. They gave me a dilapidated wooden box to sit on while I heard their confessions.

When we finished, I asked again if there were any sick in the village, and I realized that they whispered to each other something like, "Shall we tell him, or not?" They finally took me to a hut of no more than a hundred square feet, with no windows. A man literally lifted one of the walls off the ground so I could go in, while the people who had just participated in the Mass commented: "He's going to go in, he's going to go into So-and-so's house." When I got inside I saw an old, skeletal man. Wearing nothing more than a pair of dirty underpants, he was lying on a cot made of rope. Everything stank of urine and excrement. The villagers, meanwhile, were milling about at the entrance, to see what the father was doing.

The man became anxious when he saw me and was capable only of repeating, almost unintelligibly: "I have a Bible, I have a Bible . . ." as though to tell me that he was Catholic. In fact, he did have one. When I left I asked if he had any relatives, and they told me that he did in the next village, so I went there. When I found a member of his family, I asked permission to take him to Mother Teresa's home for the elderly, in the capital. So tomorrow I'm going to fetch him with one of the lay missionaries who's working as a nurse in the next village, where my friend Antonio Diufaín is.

All the water we have here is contaminated. We have to boil and filter it. You can buy five gallons of "purified" water (God knows what they mean by "purified") for fourteen pesos (a dollar) . . . if you can pay that. Almost everyone here suffers from stomach problems caused by amoebas and no end of other creatures that live in the water. Talk about poverty! A few days ago, at a dispensary in the village, a little seven-month-old girl died because there was a region-wide power outage, and they couldn't start the "*planta*" (an electric generator with a diesel engine) because they didn't have the money to buy fuel. For want of electricity they couldn't give her oxygen, to combat a little asthma attack. When they asked her mother what she might have given her that would have sent her into such a critical condition, she said that, in her little campo, it was customary when children weren't breathing well to give them their own urine, boiled and mixed with a little sugar. No comment.

Just now, for anybody who wants to participate in the work of the mission, we have four priorities or specific projects.

First: We urgently need an all-terrain vehicle to take us from one place to another. The one I'm currently using is almost ready for the junkyard, and when I'm driving it mile after mile, between two endless walls—real walls—of cane, I think to myself: "If this heap stopped moving, nobody would find me for a month." To give you a laugh, the roads are so long and untraveled, especially at night, that it has occurred to me to get some flares in case I get bogged down so that the villagers will know that they have to come rescue me and will know where I am.

Second: The parish house has been abandoned for several years, and it needs to be restored (it has to be painted and equipped with a connection for electricity, the brick wall that encloses it has to be rebuilt, and a little stove and other basic furniture have to be bought). This is important and urgent because some college students have contacted me and are willing to give a piece of their life to work in this mission. Imagine how important this is for me, to have some partners who want to offer their Christian commitment, their youth, their talents, and their academic specialties. We need many arms and hearts here! We would be able to accommodate them in this little house, but I need it ready by December, which is when I expect the first of them to arrive.

Third: The parish has begun a dining hall for a hundred of the poorest children in the village. Unfortunately, the budget is totally inadequate for what we need in order to attend to these small children. For that reason, we can't now give them any water other than the purified water I referred to above. I would like to try to give a stipend to a young woman from here so that, in addition to feeding the children, we could give them some education and buy them some school supplies and materials for catechesis. It's wonderful to see the children every morning, although when I see them I'm always left thinking: What will become of them tomorrow?

Fourth: This may be our most ambitious project for now. It involves building, little by little, a chapel in each village. This would provide a place to celebrate Mass, catechize children, house mobile dispensaries when we get them, and shelter the people of the village during hurricane season, which sows destruction and devastation everywhere. Consider, in this connection, that even in the filthiest little hamlet there are an evangelical church and an Adventist or Pentecostal church.

I'll be describing in future letters a great deal more about the needs and possible projects and programs with which you can help financially. Of course, if you truly want to support the mission, what we need most is your prayer and sacrifice because what's most essential to us here, thanks be to God, can't be bought even with all the gold in the world. More than anything, we need priests. Many more priests. Pray with all your soul that there will be others whose hearts burn with the missionary spirit and who will throw themselves into the work to the exclusion of everything else. We're fifteen priests in this new diocese, including our poor bishop, who has to work as just one more of us.

I would like in this first "Letter from the Mission" to thank many, many people who've helped me and generously continue to do so: first and foremost, my parents, my brother and sister, and my brother-in-law and sister-in-law, who are already deeply involved in this mission, without whom we wouldn't have been able to get even this far. Among those who deserve special mention in my gratitude are the cloistered communities who in silence and solitude accompany me through their life dedicated to Christ, their Spouse, and who bring to all of us missionaries the grace and strength we need to persevere. The Carmelite Mothers of San Francisco (California) have given me a precious tabernacle that I have in my oratory, for which I always remember them in my poor prayers. They've also given me a precious monstrance for the adoration of the Most Holy Sacrament, which we're now using in the parish. And they've given me many liturgical vestments, a briefcase for the celebration of Mass out among the fields, altar cloths, enough books on spirituality for a doctorate . . . well, everything! Likewise, the Carmelite Mothers of Buffalo (New York) have given me purifiers, corporals, a tabernacle, and so on. I also thank the Carmelites of Talavera de la Reina, who've given me so many, many things throughout these years. Many of the vestments I use every day were made by their own hands—you can imagine with how much love. They've just sent me a great number of chalices, which will lend dignity to each of these little chapels.

I thank very much the Sisters of Bethlehem for their help and prayers. They've given me some beautiful icons that I have in my oratory; one that I especially love is of Saint Joseph, who, as you know, is the eponym and spiritual head of our parish. It's difficult for me to do justice to the debt of gratitude that I owe to these sisters, for in their monasteries I've always found a place for silence, retreat, solitude, and prayer. I urge you to visit and help them!

I thank the Oblate Sisters of Jesus the Priest for all the help they've given me in their witness and their life given as a sacrifice of love for priests. One of my most wonderful memories of this summer, in preparation for the mission, was my visit to their community in Javier (Navarre). I had an immense desire to go there and commend myself to Saint Francis Xavier, the great missionary and patron of missions.

The Oblate community prays in the choir built over the very village church in which Xavier was baptized, and in which the very image of the Virgin before which he prayed the Salve Regina as a child is still venerated.

Incidentally, I had just had a wisdom tooth pulled, and I was able to go to Javier thanks to my cousin Paul, who took me there.

Believe it or not, in my last conversation with Mother Teresa, at the end of June in New York, when I told her that I was going as a missionary to the Dominican Republic, she was overjoyed and told me not to fail to write to her in Calcutta to ask for the establishment of a foundation of her sisters, the Missionaries of Charity, to whom, as you know, I'm so devoted. Well, while the foundation's being established, the sisters of that congregation who are already working in Santo Domingo, the capital, have offered to come one day a week to help me in the campos.

Perhaps the person to whom I most owe thanks is my friend Father Antonio Diufaín, my classmate and friend since the seminary in Toledo. He was the first to arrive here. We're twelve miles—forty-five minutes—from each other. His "yes" to God has made mine possible. If he hadn't urged me to come, in all probability I would never have reached this land, these blessed people. His needs and mine are very similar, and we all manage things together, sharing all the aid that reaches us. Truly, there are wonderful people in this world who silently go about their work and give of their best from the heart. May God be their reward!

Should anyone ask the reason for these letters and those that are to come, let me say that their fundamental purpose is to share with you the wonders that the Lord wants to work among these people. For that reason I don't want at all to give anybody the impression that it's a matter of simply giving money. What I truly want is for people to change their hearts, to read these lines as an invitation from Christ to change their lives. For there's poverty everywhere, right under our noses for anyone who wants to see it, in our own houses and families; but this poverty, the poverty here, is so shocking, shouts so loudly, that it's impossible to ignore it as we do other cases of poverty—I, first and foremost.

I would like to be of what help I can to you, through this epistolary dialogue, so that you may think every day of these people. Don't give from what you don't need; don't give because I'm the one who's asking and you know me. Give not from your excess, but rather give as an act of sacrifice, deprive yourself of something. You could spend the money on something that isn't bad in itself, that isn't even ostentatious, but choose instead for the love of Christ, who's living here as one of the poor, to give it to them. This can be very useful to those of you who have small children or adolescents. Don't give them everything they may wish for. Remind them that there are others who have nothing and that in addition there are people who, out of love for Christ, go to live among those who have nothing, the way Christ did, as Saint Paul said: "Though he was rich, yet for your sake he became poor, so that by his poverty you might become rich" (2 Cor 8:9). I don't just ask you to give. I ask you to give of yourselves. With the cross, with sacrifice, though it be a small thing, but do it with all your love.

This summer I also had the opportunity to go to Lisieux to commend myself to Saint Thérèse of the Child Jesus, who, as you know, is the other patron saint of missions. She said: "To love is to give all, and to give oneself."

To all of you who have already helped with your prayers and financially, I thank you with all my heart, but above all, as a priest, I want you yourselves to experience the grace of the mission. Don't forget these wonderful people in your day-to-day life. They're our brothers; they've been redeemed by the same Blood of Christ. They're the extension and living presence of Jesus Christ in our midst, who said to us all: "I was hungry and you gave me food . . ." "Lord, when?" "As you did it to one of the least of these my brethren, you did it to me" (Mt 25:35–40).

Here in the Dominican Republic they deeply venerate Our Lady the Virgin of Altagracia, and I commend you all to her. Pray for me as I do always for you before the tabernacle of the mission.

> With my most loving blessing,
> Father Christopher

P.S. The mail doesn't get delivered here, so we've opened a mailbox in the capital, to which Antonio or I go almost every week.

Christmas in the Canefields

The clock has not yet struck five in the morning, and you can already hear the soft sound of feet shuffling along the roads between the canefields, from one batey to another, in San José de los Llanos. An enormous throng of men are walking, machetes in hand, following their overseer, the little boss who, on horseback and holding a rifle, directs them to the face of the cane, the part of the field that is to be cut that day. Many of these men have no papers. Not from the past, not for the present, not in the future. To the state, they are nobody, not even ghosts. To the sugar company, they are no more than cutters of cane. Can they mean anything to anyone?

They make it through the early morning chewing on sugarcane, having had no breakfast. That is how they make it to the dawn, and through the whole morning, and a good part of the afternoon, with very little rest and nothing to eat, cutting cane like machines, to the point of losing the feeling in their hands. That is their life. That is how it has always been, every day, every morning. Every afternoon, until they come back, ground down by work, with somewhat less than twenty cents of today's euro per ton of cut cane.[1]

The harvest of 1997 has begun, but the date does not matter. Nothing has changed in the last two hundred years in these bateyes populated by Haitians. Nothing since they arrived here, or since their parents arrived, or their grandparents, or so many of their ancestors. This is not fiction. It is what Francisco tells us, sitting in the doorway of his house (for lack of a better word for this thatched-roof cement hut of no more than a hundred square feet in which he lives). Here he keeps all his possessions: a half dozen machetes, a pair of waterproof

---

[1] The workers were paid forty Dominican pesos per ton of cut sugarcane, so this figure virtually equates to the euro of today (2012).

boots and some gloves, two rags with sleeves that he calls shirts, a rusty pot, and three half-spent candles. There is also an old suitcase that serves as a closet but would never serve as a suitcase.

We are in Bayaguanita, a batey that is cut off for almost six months of the year, during the rainy season. Francisco, who is seventy, arrived in the Dominican Republic as a boy of eleven, fleeing the hunger that devastated his family in Haiti. He dreamt, he tells us, of earning money to send home. But he never sent anything home, and he could not even return home himself. Now there is neither family nor house left for him in Haiti.

Francisco sleeps on a hard old bed with rusty springs. There is no bathroom, not even a sink. Water is brought to the batey in cisterns from time to time. The oxen that work for the Company have better living conditions in 1997 than the workers, who in some bateyes use the oxen's leftover water to drink and wash. Francisco tells us all this in a mixture of Creole and Spanish. And he goes on, "When I had to stop working they gave me a final payment of twenty-one pesos. As if I could live on that for the rest of my life. What you see is all I have. It's all I have left."

Francisco clutches a metal crucifix, of a hand's length, which he shows us with a smile. "Nobody's going to take this away from me. It gives me strength and hope."

His bitter expression, carved over his years of misery and toil under the tropical sun of the canefields, turns into a smile when he hears Father Christopher's name. His face lights up.

"Everything changed when Father Christopher arrived, in 1997. Ever since, through the parish, we the workers have united. He united us around an idea, which was to seek a contract from the Company, providing for a pension for retirement, among other things."

"It certainly was earned," chipped in Noemí Méndez, our guide in the bateyes. "It's required by law."

Those three months from September to December 1997 gave Father Christopher a chance to start familiarizing himself with his surroundings. He writes his second letter for Christmas, and it already reflects a little of the importance that the poor cane workers attribute to him. At that point, Father Christopher had not yet made it to Bayaguanita and did not know Francisco. But in just three months the father has realized that in his mission there is more than just material and spiritual need. There is something in the air, an undercurrent that marks the character of the people, that makes them evasive, silent, introverted.

The father has already learned a considerable amount about the place he is in. He has learned about the cane, about sugar, about the industry, about the people, about the difference between Dominicans and Haitians. He did it by trudging through the little campos and the occasional batey closest to the roads, to which he went simply to evangelize. His words begin to be harsh, and he even suggests the idea that there is human trafficking when people say that the workers "are brought here".

Also in this letter he tells us for the first time, without mentioning its name, about the existence of a powerful family, the owners of all those lands and of the agricultural cultivation of the canefields. It is evident that the missionary has informed himself little by little about the hard conditions in which the people live, and that, little by little, no longer a mere observer, he has become one of them. One more of the poor whose pain and unconsoled grief he makes his own. It can seem like the passing anger of a specific moment, but this priest considers himself to be the pastor of the sheep in his parish, and he begins to make their suffering his own.

Also evident is the father's eagerness for a project that, over time, did not turn out so well: the arrival of the volunteer missionaries for short stints of one or two months. As we make our way through the text, we will see how that experiment became impracticable, either because of the very conflictive circumstances of the mission or because of the sometimes utopian character of these summer vacations that generated such a high level of interest at the time among young people of Catholic background. In what he says about this project of welcoming missionaries we see the father's rebellious nature, as he reacts against the comfortable circumstances in his background, challenging the comfort in which the entire world has seemingly installed itself. It is as though the father so enjoys the life choice he has made that, in some part of his persona, he cannot understand any other choice, although it is true that he again offers a great lesson on the meaning of giving of oneself, of abnegation, not for the purpose of *feeling* good about oneself but for the good that it actually does.

In this letter we see that this priest is active, that he has immediately set about celebrating Mass, and a great many baptisms, in places where they have not been celebrated for years, and that he has begun a kind of catechizing as best he can, amid so much ignorance of the gospel. He is still the same eager missionary who arrived three months before, but who has, after simply contemplating the cane and what happens in the canefields, already begun to adapt and respond to the situation. He recounts this in his second letter, on the eve of Christmas.

~

"Maranatha: *Our Lord, come!*"

Dear friends of the mission:

This year God will be born in the silence of the canefields. Yes, friends. Here, too, in these Caribbean lands, the poor cry out for the coming of the Son of God. Here, too, we're preparing for the birth of Christ. Steeped in the awe-inspiring silence of these endless plains of cane, my people, my poor people, from the simplicity of their indigence, look up to the sky every night in anticipation of Jesus' birth.

Do you know? The nights here are unsurpassably beautiful. I didn't know until I arrived in the Dominican Republic that God had set so many sparkling stars in the sky. This Christmas God will be born here, swaddled in the canefields' silence and the stars in the sky. But it's so strange for me to think that Christmas is coming in the midst of such heat! For me, who thought it couldn't be Christmas unless the weather was cold! For me, when I've just spent thirteen freezing winters in New York, it's so strange to see Christmas trees and at the same time be constantly sweating . . .

If you saw the beauty of the cane at this season . . . it's very high, almost fifteen feet tall. Friends, the cane has bloomed! At this time of year, when you look toward the horizon, all the canefields are covered with thousands and thousands of beautiful white feather dusters. The land is bursting with fruit, bursting with life. The harvest will begin soon, the cutting. This season brings a period of frenetic activity in this remote, uncompromising corner of the world, with the to-and-fro of carts, oxen, tractors, and peasants carrying machetes. And as I wind through those roads, I think I've become a little more contemplative just by contemplating . . . the cane! The desert monks say, speaking of their cloistered life: "Listen to your cell and your cell will teach you everything." One day when I was making my way along a track of muck and mire, paraphrasing them, it occurred to me: "Listen to the cane, and the cane will teach you everything." If the cell is truly the meeting place of God and the monk, these fields are certainly the cell, they're the monastery, they're the meeting place of the missionary and God. I ask God for the grace to have the clear eyes I need to see, to learn to look more deeply and penetratingly every day at the mystery of his love and his presence in everyone and everything around me.

The lessons of a canefield

Looking at the cane, so tall, so quiet, swaying from side to side with the wind, I've learned above all that the cane speaks. Yes, it speaks. Of the life and death of the poor men bent over with pain, bent over with silence, bent over with exhaustion, bent over with blood and death. I sometimes wonder: How many human lives has this merciless cane devoured? These fields are watered with the blood, tears, and sweat of countless lives of Dominicans and Haitian migrants, who've come here—been brought, even—looking for paradise on earth, only to find themselves with nothing more than a loincloth and a machete in the hell that is the cane.

How many generations of young lives have been wasted for a wage of misery and exploitation! And to think that all the cane in this part of the country—hundreds and hundreds of miles of cane—belongs to just one family! How many lives have been wasted, dear God, to enrich, to make scandalously rich, a single family . . .

Incidentally, did you know that even though the Dominican Republic is one of the leading producers of sugarcane in the world, the sugar consumed here is almost all imported? I'm a priest, not an economist. Can you explain to me why, when I'm drinking my morning coffee and looking out the windows of my house at so much cane, the sugar that I've stirred into my coffee has to come from outside the country? To think that most of my people don't earn enough to be able to buy sugar . . . Oh, mystery of mysteries! Forgive me if I upset you with these questions. The famous Brazilian bishop Hélder Câmara[2] used to say, very correctly: "When I give food to the poor they call me a saint, when I ask why they're hungry they call me a communist."

To all of you I say, simply, thank you. It's utterly impossible for me even just to list the names of the many, many people who are helping

---

[2] Hélder Pessoa Câmara (1909–1999), bishop of the Diocese of Olinda and Recife from 1964 to 1985.

me move forward with the projects that we have in the mission. I feel overwhelmed and almost embarrassed by the very great generosity of all of you. I think, for example, of a young Polish couple, parishioners of mine in New York. They're custodians of a building, and whenever a tenant leaves, they gather everything that has been left behind in the apartment and on Saturdays spend the whole day selling it in the street, with the help of their two small children, as they would at a flea market. Bursting with happiness, they called me not long ago to tell me they were sending $264. What can I say when I see such love, such generosity? I can only give thanks to the Lord for the goodness of so many simple people who will never see their names on the front page of a newspaper, but whose names, beyond any doubt whatsoever, are already written in God's heart.

Thanks to everybody's extraordinary generosity, we've already received enough funds to buy the all-terrain vehicle that we needed. It will be of incalculable help to the mission. The vehicle has been ordered. They assure me that it's already on board a ship that's coming directly from Japan! We're now in the throes of the endless red tape involved in taking delivery and getting a license for it, tax-free.

We've received a good part of the money we need to fix up the house I told you about in my previous letter, which we'll use to house the young lay missionaries. The house is nearly finished already; we've completed the high brick wall around it and are now working on the interior, the windows, the kitchen, the bathroom, and the water tank that we're putting on the roof as a reserve and precaution against the daily water and electricity outages.

After I wrote my latest letter, they told me that the parish had a space in the middle of town that had in the past been useful in programs aimed at improving the lot of women (to teach sewing, pastry making, cooking, baking . . .). The place was collapsing, and some construction materials had been donated for it. Because of the urgency, I threw myself into the work, and with two construction projects going simultaneously I'm becoming quite the master builder . . . This latter space will be ideal for when this large group of missionary youths arrives this summer, because either the boys or the girls will be able to sleep there, where we're installing showers, a big kitchen, a laundry, and so on . . . Even a septic tank!

Another great boost that we've received since my last letter came from Santo Domingo itself. It involves the children's dining hall that I've mentioned to you. About a hundred of the poorest children in San José come every day. We were spending about $430 a month on food, cleaning supplies, and so forth . . . until one fine day the owner of a big supermarket in town introduced herself to me, and since last month she has been donating all the food. Also thanks to her, we've gotten three companies to donate pasta, flour, and cookies for the children. It's extraordinary to see how God helps us. What a good Father God is!

Missions and missionaries

I've now received calls and letters from quite a few young people who are ready and willing to come for one or two months during the summer, and others who are even considering giving a year of their lives to the mission. This generosity on the part of so many young people is admirable. Pray for them and encourage them. For many young people who don't know what to do with their lives or who are discerning a vocation, I'm convinced that it's in giving themselves to others, for the love of Christ, that they'll find the answer and the strength to make of their entire existence a true "yes", complete and permanent, to the free love of God, who has called them to life, who has created them through love and for love. Ensconced in our middle-class mediocrity, it's impossible to do anything worthwhile with the life we've been given to offer up until, leaving behind nothing but ashes, it's silently consumed by love.

We sometimes have to step out of our daily routine to change direction and make radical decisions, whatever path God may have for each of us. You will all agree that there are lives that are worth living and lives that haven't been worth anything—unlived, badly lived, irrelevant lives, although sometimes they meet with "success" and the world applauds them. There are lives that leave a mark and lives that pass through the world just to pass, "passing" by everything and everyone . . . There are paths that, if they're followed, lead to heaven, and paths that lead nowhere. Let us ask ourselves: Where will the footprints I'm making today lead others?

Adventures and misadventures of an apprentice missionary

A few days ago, on Saturday, on my way to celebrate Mass in one of my most abandoned, faraway villages, I lost my way in the middle of the cane. I had had to go first to a batey of Haitians to let them know when the next Mass would be, and when I left there—what with the fact that the roads through the cane have neither stoplights nor names, and they all look the same anyway—I headed out into the unknown. As I went along, the mud got muddier and muddier and the muck got muckier and muckier, until I reached a curve where I sank in up to the middle of the hubcaps. Even with the traction of four-wheel drive, I couldn't go forward and I couldn't go back. I got out of the car with my two excellent, intrepid altar boys, put on my knee-high waterproof boots, the famous Wellingtons, and the boys and I began to hack away at the cane with our machetes, because on other occasions I had been able to free myself from the mire by putting armloads of cane under the tires.

But not this time. By the grace of God, my friend Father Antonio Diufaín and I are connected by radio, in case of an emergency. I called him and asked for help. He was also traveling at that moment, heading in his vehicle for one of the most distant villages to celebrate Mass. He told me that if I didn't succeed in freeing myself, he'd come to save me after his Mass. We were about two hours apart by terrible roads. He was a much more seasoned veteran of such struggles than I was, and he suggested to me on the radio that, if nothing else worked, I should make a fire so that the people of one of the villages on the plain would come to the rescue.

In the end, it was my altar boys who decided to walk down the road to see if they could find a tractor. They found one. I never thought I'd be so happy to hear the grumble of a tractor. I can't tell you the relief I felt when I began to hear the sound of a motor approaching and then, suddenly, saw an immense tractor with a Haitian at the wheel, and my two altar boy experts up next to him, with a triumphant air and a look of, "And what would you have done without us?"

So I made it to the village of Los Nepomucenos. Instead of arriving at three in the afternoon I appeared at five thirty, up to my ears in mud. I was dead tired, so dirty that you couldn't tell the color of my clothes. In the thatched hut that serves as a chapel there were still some twenty people waiting for me. They didn't know anything, and only three of them had been baptized. They didn't know how to respond during the Mass. They didn't remember how many years it had been since a priest had been there for baptisms, catechesis, first Communion, and so on . . . There's so much left to do!

Although I can't yet say, as the great Francis Xavier did when he wrote to his mentor, Ignatius of Loyola, in Rome: "My arm is worn out with baptizing", you can nevertheless be sure that the greatest happiness that the Lord has granted me in the brief time I've been here is the number of baptisms, of children and adults, that I've celebrated. I'm up to more than 260 at this point.

But don't think that I baptize, in any old way, just anybody who comes along. The process is this: first a team of evangelists is organized, and I send and accompany them to a given village. They go from house to house spreading the gospel, and they gather together those who want to participate in an appointed place, at an appointed time. The team of evangelists—who are always people from Los Llanos— is later divided into three groups: one that attends to the children, another for the young people, and a third for the adults, depending on the number of people who attend the assembly. Then the evangelists take a simple census of the people—how many of them are baptized, how many need one or another of the sacraments—and give me all that information. The group or assembly that has been formed is going to be kept together as a continuing group and will always meet at the same place and time, so that even if the Holy Mass can't be celebrated often, the group will continue to meet with a catechist as a permanent group of prayer and instruction.

Finally, a short baptismal course is offered to parents and godparents, at the end of which they're given a card that says they're now qualified to have their children baptized. The group of evangelists and catechists helps me at the end of the course with all the paperwork, such as verifying the birth certificates and other information necessary to enter the baptisms in the parish records.

Retreats

Antonio's life, and mine here in the mission, aren't all activity, of course. We've worked out a plan for us to go on retreats a couple of days a month. There are very beautiful places here in the Dominican Republic. For our October retreat we went to Carmelo de Baní, in the southern part of the island. A wonderful place for silence, prayer, and meditation. The Carmelite Mothers received us with immense affection. We undertook to help them with confessions of their community, as the scarcity of clergy makes it hard for them to find confessors who'll come to them regularly. For our Advent retreat we're going to go to Jarabacoa. There's a community of Trappist monks there founded by the Trappists of Cóbreces (Santander, Spain).

The Missionaries of Charity

One of the great pieces of news since my last letter is the priceless help I'm getting from Mother Teresa's Missionaries of Charity, as though she herself, from heaven, had sent them to me. They come to Los Llanos very early every Wednesday. From here we go together to the bateyes. In the evangelizing plan I've made, Wednesdays are dedicated exclusively to the Haitian bateyes. Of the eight bateyes for which I'm responsible, we regularly visit three. Two sisters join us: one, Sister Magda, is the mother superior. She's from Catalonia, a doctor by profession, and she has worked in Haiti for almost eight years. She therefore speaks Creole perfectly and also knows the culture, customs, music, and so on. The other is Sister Josette Marie. She's Haitian, so you can imagine the help she is to me.

We devote the mornings to visiting families, house by house, making a little census of the number of people and their spiritual and material needs. In addition, the sisters go to the little school and give classes in religion and the catechism. We come back here at midday for lunch. In the afternoon we return to the same batey that we visited in the morning and celebrate Mass. Although almost no one can receive Communion, they're nevertheless delighted to come, to sing, to pray. They bring their own Creole songbooks. The sisters have gotten me a photocopied missal in Creole and are giving me lessons so that I can learn how to conduct Mass in their own language. I'm going slowly still; I'm not yet a star!

Between the two biggest bateyes that we visit we have about a hundred children to baptize in early January. It will be a day of great joy for them and for the whole Church. It has been years since anybody was baptized there. The preparation process for the children and their parents is similar to the one described above.

The Missionaries of Charity have taken another dying man from my campos to their home for the elderly. I'll never forget the day I met him. It was the first time I had been to that village, Los Nepomucenos. Shortly after our arrival, the sky darkened as though night were falling. It was three in the afternoon. Suddenly, in the middle of our processional hymn, and with all of us squeezed into our reinforced asbestos-thatched chapel, rain began to pour in such deafening torrents that, small though the church was, the deluge drowned me out no matter how loud I shouted. The children screamed in fear, and the congregation huddled together against the wind, while the water came in at us from all sides. From behind the altar I saw through the door that the rain, instead of falling vertically, was strangely flying from left to right. It was literally raining horizontally, in what was my first experience of the hair-raising force of a tornado.

It got so dark that I could see absolutely nothing. There was no electricity, which is why we always go to the campos during the day. The only thing I could think of to do was to go out into the rain, wearing my chasuble, get into the car, turn on the headlights, and shine them through the doorway of the chapel so that I could see the missal and thus finish the Mass.

That was when I saw this elderly man for the first time, lying in a corner of the chapel, wrapped in rags, a repellent sight. He was missing some fingers. He was emaciated with the chronic hunger that he had endured his entire life. When I asked the others, I found out that he had no family, that he dragged himself from one campo to the next, begging a bite of food and a place to spend the night. He was a complete human ruin. Finally, one day last week, the Missionaries of Charity called me to say that there was a free bed in their home, and I took him there. There he will live and die, surrounded by love, attended to like a son of God by sisters who have taken seriously Jesus' words in the Gospel: "You did it to me."

Gautier

I wanted to sink my teeth (I mean, evangelically!) into Gautier, a village on my long list. As you approach these parts from Santo Domingo, it's the first village of many that appear on the road. Let's say that it's the entrance to my parish. From there to Los Llanos is a little more than fifteen miles. What first comes into view as you go along the road and are about to enter Gautier is a huge billboard announcing the Pentecostal church. And that is so, friends, because for now (and do I mean for now!) this village is lost to the Catholic Church. Yet the largest congregation isn't the Pentecostals but rather the Episcopalians. What makes it worse is that their liturgy and rites are in many ways so similar to ours that a great many people, in their ignorance, think it's either Catholic or similar or not different enough to matter . . .

I'm told that about ten years ago, a Colombian priest, who was lame and up in years and the last priest to have lived in Los Llanos before my arrival, tried to celebrate Mass in Gautier but was practically thrown out of the village. They made fun of him and played merengue music through very powerful loudspeakers during the Mass so nothing could be heard . . . The poor man had to give up.

I confess that, after I learned all this, every time I went by the entrance to the village, my blood boiled and I racked my brains to see what I could dream up to do about it. Since it's a big village and has a school with more than six hundred students, it occurred to me one day to talk to the director of the school. Providentially, he lived here, in Los Llanos. We hit it off, and he invited me to celebrate Mass one morning at the school, for all the students, with the excuse that they had just inaugurated a new school building.

I went there last week with my briefcase at the ready. It was one of the most wonderful experiences I can remember. There were almost three hundred students, and none of them had ever seen a Mass! They were spellbound, amazed, as they watched what I was doing. Since they didn't know how to respond, I told them what they had to repeat. But that wasn't the best thing, which came when I was about to begin the Mass and five ladies introduced themselves to me. As though they were telling me a secret, they said to me: "We're Catholics, the only ones left in the village, and we go, on foot or by whatever transport we can get, to Los Tanquecitos"—a nearby village in the diocese—"so that we can attend Mass." So we've organized the first Mass with them and an enormous number of people whom I've invited from other campos and Los Llanos, to help them start their church.

The Episcopalians have an enormous church in Gautier, and almost all the other sects have smaller ones. The Catholics have no place of worship other than the hearts of these five women—which make no small cathedral! I've already appointed a group of my best evangelists (the marines among my catechists, or the all-terrain vehicles) so that a new campaign of evangelization and catechesis will be launched at that Mass. I ask you to commend it to the Holy Virgin. I will report to you in future letters how this develops. For now, I'll celebrate Mass in the former school building.

I'd like to conclude this Christmas letter by once more giving thanks to all of you who've helped me so much throughout these first months of my life in the mission. Remember that Christmas is when the Son of God was born of a Virgin Mother, that he comes to redeem our sins and give us new life, eternal life, and that this life and this coming are accessible to men always and everywhere only through the Church.

With my most loving and grateful blessing for all, and promising you my prayers before the tabernacle of the mission,

Father Christopher

~

I smile because he changes the lives of all of us.

Francisco's eyes well up when he recalls the old days and explains to us the impact of the missionary in his life while he shows us a smile that fills the dismal hut with hope.

"Now I want to see him again before I die," the old man adds. "When they told me he had left, I shed a tear. Sometimes, I sit and look out at the fields and hope that his all-terrain vehicle will appear, and another tear falls. I don't know if he'll ever come back, but I love him like a father, like a brother. I would love to see him return. But in case he doesn't, I ask God to bless him and protect him in his mission, helping the poor, wherever he is. He brought us to Jesus, and there are more poor people to bring to Jesus. I don't know how to read or write. I'm poor and illiterate, but what I do know is that the Lord came with Father Christopher to be among us. I belong to the Lord. I live here with God."

We ask Francisco about the father's temperament, and he laughs again. "He sure had quite a personality, but that made him good, too. There's a man here who got sick one day. His name is Eugenio Valdés. We called the Company to ask for a doctor, but nobody came for him. I had dysentery, and I made a visit to the doctor, in Los Llanos, and told Father Christopher that Eugenio was very sick. The father asked me if they hadn't come to see him because of the shape the roads were in, and I told him the roads were open. How was I going to get out of here if they weren't? His face changed color. He didn't say anything, but he got very serious, and that same night he showed up at Eugenio's house to take him to the doctor. They kept him for two weeks for I don't know what. What I do know is that if the priest hadn't shown up with his four-by-four, Eugenio would have died, and yet there he is, alive and working. That's how the father was. He had quite a temper, which sometimes was a bad thing, but also it was sometimes a good thing."

It Is Always Good Friday in the Canefields

Every now and then some Scalabrinian nuns,[1] missionaries who for many years before 1997 did what they could to help, would look in on San José de los Llanos. They attended to the basic needs of the people in the little campos and in the town of Los Llanos itself, visiting sporadically. They had earned many people's affection, and they were not lacking in courage or apostolic zeal in their dealings with anybody, whether they were Dominicans or Haitians. The sugar companies' overseers and foremen denied them access, though, to the bateyes in Los Llanos.

When Father Hartley arrived, because he knew very little about the bateyes and the problems of the Haitians, one of these nuns, with the best of intentions, informed him that the nuns had been warded off when they tried to gain access to the bateyes. Good heavens! Christopher's father said that Christopher was rebellious as a boy and that the only time he was not was in 1997, when he obeyed his bishop and the Church. But when he had his mind set on evangelizing he would not make an exception for an overseer, a watchman, or anybody else. If there were people in those bateyes, he would go to seek them out, which is what he was there to do as a missionary and the parish priest of Los Llanos.

So, warned by a nun—at this point, not about the danger involved in evangelizing in the bateyes but about the prohibition against setting foot in them—he decided one fine day to drive into a sugarcane plantation, not knowing what he would find. He had asked the bishop of San Pedro de Macorís for his thoughts beforehand, and the bishop gave no opinion because he was unaware of the situation. So the bishop let

---

[1] The Scalabrinian missionaries are a religious congregation founded in 1887 by Blessed Giovanni Battista Scalabrini. They are active in more than thirty countries around the world.

the Spanish priest do as he thought best, advising him not to poke his nose into a hornet's nest but unaware that, quite simply, the hornet's nest had come into being in his diocese years before the diocese existed. It was just a matter of time before somebody would see it and realize what was going on. Those were living men and women in there. They were not a figment of someone's imagination, or an apparition. They were a reality among whom the Church—despite her apostolic tradition, her liturgy, her charity, and her social doctrine—had, for whatever reason, not made her presence felt.

It did not take the father long to decide whether he should go into the bateyes. The spark was struck by a young Haitian man whom he did not know, who one day blurted out to his face, apropos of nothing in particular, "Are you ever going to come celebrate Mass for us?"

This was an arrow to the father's heart. He was afraid to go in to evangelize, but it was his duty. Yes, Father Hartley was a rebel, but he was not foolhardy. In fact, alarmed by the warning, he decided not to enter the canefields alone and asked his friend and comrade in the trenches, Antonio Diufaín, to go with him. That way, if anything happened, they would both suffer the same fate, which would be whatever God willed.

God's will was that both priests should see in the bateyes, with their own eyes, what no one had told them about in the outside world. Some people were afraid to. Many just did not know. Yes, both Father Antonio and Father Christopher knew before they went into the batey that the life of a cane cutter was harsh, but what awaited them in the bateyes of Los Llanos was beyond harsh: it was inhuman.

Father Christopher has recounted what he saw with his own eyes that day and in the following days: how men were living below the level of animals. He saw the absence of the most basic sanitary facilities in the bateyes. Some of these villages did not even have latrines, and the men and women who lived there did what they had to do out in the fields, behind a bush.

In those first visits, the missionary saw sick men and women who were getting no medical attention. He saw filthy, starving children who had only one meal per day, many of them with no possibility of going to school, condemned from birth to being illiterate and having no future other than to work all their lives in the canefields. He saw children—yes, children, ten or eleven years old—working like adults, cutting and hauling sugarcane.

Father Christopher saw, and he has described it this way, little villages of square houses, lined up in parallel lines along a muddy, unpaved street and surrounded by canefields that looked like walls. He saw men working in the fields, the women and children in the batey, waiting for the father of the family to bring home something to eat. A bag of rice, a handful of corn, or perhaps, that day, nothing.

In these first visits, the father saw many very young mothers and guessed—from their ages and what he saw of their homes—that there was prostitution with the consent of the families, and incest. Sometimes, in those huts of less than a hundred square feet, parents, sons, daughters, grandchildren, and nieces all lived together, all of them slovenly but doing the best they could in conditions fit more for pigs than for men.

What they saw touched both priests to the heart. They had not known it, but there were conditions in their parishes that went beyond poverty, because the people they saw were not just poor. They were workers being paid a pittance and who, in the opinion of both priests, were being exploited, to say the least.

This risky excursion took place before the second letter, but it was not until the third that Father Christopher wrote freely about it, revealing in unvarnished language some of the things he saw that were not only unfit for human beings but also illegal in the Dominican Republic, as Doctor Méndez recalls.

For the Haitians in the bateyes that the father began to frequent, the appearance of a foreign priest had an effect not far from what it would have been if a Martian had landed. Many of them had never participated in a Mass. Many of them had never spoken with a foreigner. None of them knew that they were living under something called the rule of law. As Noemí Méndez explains, "First we had to teach these people that the law applicable in the bateyes was that of the state, not that of the Company. That the police and the judges outranked the overseers and foremen. They had no concept of the individual or of rights."

So the Haitian workers' biggest problem was not their condition: it was their ignorance about that condition. As Father Christopher and Doctor Méndez have explained countless times, these men and women were Haitians, and their life was simply, to them, how life was. They were unaware of any rights beyond the right to live in the batey and to cut cane for a pittance. That was where they had been born, many of them, and that was where they were going to die.

The father learns during this period that the fields where these mostly Haitian cane cutters work belong to a company in the sugar industry. The bateyes are a part of the industry. In fact, they were built by the Company decades ago, in accordance with the customs and norms of the past, in a pattern that, no matter how you looked at it, obviously had become obsolete by the beginning of the twenty-first century.

The Company paid the workers some forty pesos per ton of cut cane, but in many cases it paid them not in cash but in vouchers. Those vouchers were valid only at the batey's grocery store, which was also owned by the Company. When the vouchers were exchanged for food, the workers were charged a commission of up to 20 percent. So, for the cane cutter who was paid a hundred pesos, his purchasing power was reduced to eighty when he bought whatever there was in the Company's grocery store, the only place to buy things in the whole batey.

Father Christopher Hartley's righteous indignation is aroused by the plight of the cane cutters, although at first he does not know how to respond other than to vent his anger in his letters. Father Antonio is also angry, but each of them has his own distinct personality; and although they often were kindred spirits in many ways, they sometimes acted differently. Not better or worse, just differently.

Under the problematic circumstances in which they find themselves, it is difficult to come up with the right response. A case of dire need like poverty becomes in Father Christopher's eyes a situation of humanitarian conflict, social injustice. As he himself has explained hundreds of times, it was not simply a matter of the poverty of people born in a place that lacked everything, but rather of the injustice done to men who deserved a fair wage, having earned it by the sweat of their brow, but who were not compensated accordingly.

The father understood as time went by that, in order to bring his preaching to life, he had an obligation to raise his voice so the voiceless could be heard, so they would be known. All of this fostered Father Christopher's desire to go beyond celebrating Mass and baptizing, to raise his parishioners' consciousness of their worthiness as children of God, which in turn raised their consciousness of the human rights they had by virtue of the simple fact that they were human beings.

He celebrated his first Mass in a batey in December 1997, in the batey of Cánepa, next to the road. But it was not until Lent of 1998 that the very complex reality being lived out in his parish began to be known beyond the Dominican Republic. In his third letter, explaining the things he learns as he learns them, Father Christopher decries some of the unjust conditions in which these men live.

The author of this letter also insists on catechizing about the good done by giving, not only to him who receives but also to him who gives. He shows his readers the pain of Lent, the preparation that derives from his experience in the wretched bateyes where he writes, but always illuminated by the hope of the Resurrection. This is a missionary who, though he is an exceptional witness to a daily Good Friday, does not lose sight of Easter Sunday.

~

Dear friends of the mission:

We will all be deep into a new Lent by the time you hold this letter in your hands. "A time of grace and salvation" that God offers his people so that we may return to him with all our heart. Lent is a new spring, the rebirth of an eternal life that rises anew out of the ashes of our limitless desire to be reborn to a life in Christ.

It's Lent here, too, in the Dominican Republic, in the mission of Los Llanos, though these plains of sugarcane that extend to the horizon don't so much seem to be bursting with spring as they resemble an immense, collective via crucis.

These vast expanses of sugarcane are now dotted with small but muscular Haitian men, sons of God, brothers of Jesus Christ, your brothers and mine, of dark skin and with the face of Good Friday. In a loincloth and with a machete, they cut incredible tracts of land one after another. To see Christ's Passion reenacted in such a horrific passion play, in the lives and faces of these people, is a meditation that can't fail to strike us over and over again in our deepest conscience. A Haitian earns about forty Dominican pesos per ton of cane loaded into a cart—that is, after it has been cut and its long leaves have been peeled off, leaving just the cane. Cane costs about four hundred pesetas,[2] or two American dollars and eighty-five cents, per ton. Draw your own conclusions.

Living waters

I have days when it seems to me that I've done nothing but baptize since I arrived at the mission six months ago. My count is now approaching four hundred children and adults who, by the grace of the sacrament, are Catholics, sons of the most wonderful Father, who has loved them to the point of enduring the madness and infamy of his Son's death on a cross.

I had the first two baptisms of Haitian children in January. I assure

---

[2] The equivalent of two euros and forty cents in today's euro, in 2012.

you that they were a sight to see. The first was in the batey of Cánepa, where we baptized twenty-three children in a palm-thatched arbor. You can imagine how well the children had been catechized in preparation for the sacrament from the fact that the next day, a seven-year-old girl named Estela—whom I've nicknamed "Es-Tela Marinera"[3] for the blessed girl's mischievous personality—said to her mother: "Mamá, I'm the Church because I'm baptized."

You should have seen the happiness in the batey that Epiphany afternoon! I marveled at the tenderness of the parents, the care that the mothers had invested in seeing to their children being dressed in their Sunday best for the occasion. One of the mysteries that I haven't been able to solve is how they can find such clean clothes in the huts they live in, which are so very frightful. But, above all, I marveled at the loving-kindness of God, who could, once again, come down and humble himself so. What lessons I'm learning for life and the priestly ministry! Tell me if you can understand it: how can it be that I, a priest, a sinner like anybody else, in a filthy batey, with a plastic bowl in which a poor woman had washed a heap of tattered clothes not long ago, and with the cap of my canteen serving as a saucer, have been able to witness that wonder of wonders, the birth of twenty-three children into a life in heaven?

The second baptism of Haitian children was in the batey of Contador. With several thousand inhabitants, it's the biggest batey I have. We baptized seventy-three children at the same time! A spectacle worth seeing. I don't know where so many people came from. If it hadn't been for the help of four strong, seasoned sisters of the Missionaries of Charity, I would have committed hara-kiri. I consider the day's biggest success to be that I didn't drown a single child!

You should have seen the near riot that broke out in front of the bowl of water! All those mothers were worked up over whether their child would be the first, on top of which some of them had six or seven children being baptized on the same day. All in all, I assure you that it was the most beautiful thing that has been seen in this miserable batey in a long time. So much gratitude to God! So much love for the Mother Church!

---

[3] This is a play on the expression *es tela marinera*, colloquial Spanish for "she's some piece of work."—TRANS.

I went back to Contador recently, and the first thing the mothers asked me was, "Father, when will you come back here to baptize again?" To which I answered, "But we baptized seventy-three last month!" They replied, "Father, there were three times as many children who weren't baptized, and in these six weeks another thirty-four have been born."

More on Gautier

Many of you have asked me about the mission in Gautier, the village in which there were only five Catholic faithful left. Well, for God's glory and that of his Holy Church, Gautier is a new village and is standing out as one of the most fervent and enthusiastic. The night of abandonment and orphanhood was long, but since Christmas a new light has been born there. As I told you, we sent them a group of evangelists from Los Llanos who, for two months, have been faithfully gathering the members of the community together every Friday. As in the Acts of the Apostles, some of them brought others; and, in addition, there are more children everywhere than you can shake a stick at. I celebrate Mass there on the first Sunday of every month, and you should see how, because the attendance has grown so much and we needed more space, we've already changed the location of Mass three times. Mass is always celebrated outside: in the yard of a house, in the middle of a muddy road . . . The people bring benches, chairs, or whatever else will serve as a seat, and I bring my briefcase. You should see the joy of these people! This month we easily surpassed a hundred people. Last week we began catechizing the children, for whom I had to bring more than fifty books, and the numbers keep on growing.

A few days ago, the community leaders surprised me to the point of tears. They came to me with a sheet of paper, pulled out of a spiral notebook, bearing a great number of signatures that they had collected, asking me to send a letter requesting a plot of land on which to build a little church. Their enthusiasm is overwhelming and a pleasure to behold. Will we one day be able to say that we realized the dream of a village that yearned for no more than a humble roof under which to worship the living God as Catholics? God knows where the funds will come from . . . Continue praying for Gautier, I implore you. There you have another project to collaborate in.

Visitors who are a gift from heaven

Among the most wonderful things that have happened to me lately, the visit of my parents and my brother Billy and his wife, Elena, is without doubt the one for which I most thank God. They will tell you in their own words something about what they experienced here, including taking a bath every morning with the hose coming in through the bathroom window, and the baptisms in the batey of Cánepa! The truth is that without the unconditional support of my family and their very generous help, I never would have been able to get this far.

Young people this summer

Some young people have now contacted me about coming to work with us this summer. I'd like in that connection to give a brief outline of the plan.

The mission we're preparing will be conducted during July and August. We want to have two sessions, one for each month, although if some want to stay for two months, they may do so. But it won't be possible to come for less than a month. I'm truly sorry about that on account of the people who don't have more than a couple of weeks of summer vacation, but if we don't set that requirement, we'll spend our days going back and forth to the airport, and a lot of time will be wasted while the participants acclimate themselves, adapt to the work, and learn what they'll be doing here—and then have to leave. Also, getting along with each other will become quite complicated if there's that much turnover.

So who will be eligible to come? My answer is: anybody who has two hands with which to serve, a heart with which to love, and the Catholic faith. This isn't social work. We're not the United Nations, or Doctors without Borders, or the Red Cross. We're the Catholic Church, and we want to share our faith with those who are without it, because they don't know Christ, and with those whose faith is weak. How will we carry out this work? That's where there are many possibilities, but all of them will be based on this approach: We're Catholics, and we want to evangelize.

There may be various ways to evangelize: some will catechize, others may teach reading and writing, others may join together in organizing

camps for the poorest children, in which all sorts of classes may be offered, games, hygiene . . . and others may work in the Haitian bateyes,
where we may help in documenting the undocumented, in legally reg-
istering the children. A group may organize a medical facility along
the lines of a mobile dispensary. Some can help in building churches
in various villages. The list of possibilities is as long as the many needs
of the people.

It's very important to maintain a team spirit—not to come free-
lance, as tourists or in search of philanthropic adventure. This will be
a collaboration in a Catholic mission that has its structure, its style, its
life of prayer, its sacraments, and so on. We'll all have to participate
in communal life. No way can we have people who don't want to go
to Mass every day, or who want to sleep instead of getting up early
for morning prayers, or who aren't prepared to work with whatever
colleagues, and in whatever work, they're assigned to.

We need men and women who come motivated by love of Jesus
Christ to work in his name, who come prepared to embrace the crucified Christ, who is in the face and the pain of every brother or sister
who is suffering. If I don't take care about this, if I accept anybody
who has "goodwill" and a little spirit of adventure, I'll be cheating
those who expect to get from me and my co-workers the truth of the
gospel, as it's lived by the Church and as the Church teaches it should
be lived.

Donors and donations

I offer my most heartfelt thanks to those who've sent us their donations, in cash or in kind. Thanks to the help of so many, we've been
able to respond to some of the first needs that we've set ourselves
the task of meeting in the mission. With what you've sent us so far,
we've bought the all-terrain vehicle, with which we can reach places
that before were inaccessible, and we've been able to complete the
renovation of the existing parish house, in which we hope to house
the missionaries who come this summer.

I've received very generous donations that have truly moved me.
I would like to highlight especially those of the cloistered nuns and
donations by very poor people who've given from what they need to
live on. Finally, I publicly thank the anonymous donors who've made

their contributions directly into our account. I don't know who you are, but God does. He will be your recompense.

NGOs

Some people have been in touch with me to encourage solicitation of support from the funds of non-governmental organizations, generously offering to help me with all the related paperwork and bureaucracy. Well, after much prayer and thought, I've decided not to accept donations from institutions, especially not from those that collaborate in, finance, or support activity that is morally disapproved by the Church.

I will not accept funds even from the institutions of the Church, much less solicit funds from any NGO, regardless of its ideology and purpose. Most NGOs, as you know, are financed by taxes paid to the government that must be devoted to "humanitarian" work, a term that today describes almost everything. Promoting abortion and contraceptives is typical of the ideology of some of them.

When you're going through a difficult time, there is a terrible temptation to take money without much concern for where it comes from. I don't want to yield to that easy money, and I want to guard against that temptation. I don't want money at any price; I want anybody working with us to do it out of their love for God and for the poor. I want the donor to have a specific name and face. To help you understand this, which may be difficult and make little sense to some readers of this letter, I want to quote an extremely enlightening text about it by Pope John Paul II in a recent Encyclical Letter titled *Redemptoris missio*, on the missionary work of the Church. Speaking of the help that can be accepted and the help that can't, he says this:

> The material and financial needs of the missions are many: not only to set up the Church with minimal structures (chapels, schools for catechists and seminarians, housing), but also to support works of charity, education and human promotion—a vast field of action, especially in poor countries. The missionary Church gives what she receives, and distributes to the poor the material goods that her materially richer sons and daughters generously put at her disposal. Here I wish to thank all those who make sacrifices and contribute to the work of the missions. Their sacrifices and sharing are indispensable for building up the Church and for showing love.

In the matter of material help, it is important to consider the spirit in which donations are made. For this we should reassess our own way of living: the missions ask not only for a contribution but for a sharing in the work of preaching and charity toward the poor. All that we have received from God—life itself as well as material goods—doesn't belong to us but is given to us for our use. Generosity in giving must always be enlightened and inspired by faith: then we will truly be more blessed in giving than in receiving. (81)

I believe I'm called to live from divine providence, from people's charity, and from the generosity of my brothers in the Church. I want to live more and more fully and thoroughly from God's fatherliness, as one of his sons. Only those who haven't delighted in that fatherliness are entitled to call this "improvident" or "risky". For those who do know God, this is the safest way, the only safe way, to live. I therefore believe that I'm in a better position to testify that all of the relationships in a priest's life should spring from the pure charity that comes from above, and that all his activity should derive from that pure charity.

This may—materially—hinder many plans and projects that could be implemented if we were to solicit assistance, and I were to act, in a more ordered and systematic way. But I haven't come here to do that; the Spirit of the Lord hasn't brought me here to make, to construct, to organize. Jesus Christ and the Church have enjoined me to witness to the love of God, to be the bearer of a gift that's infinitely greater than I am, because it's God himself. If manifesting that love should seem to require some sort of economic assistance, then I'll be obligated to solicit it and, if God wills, he himself will move the heart of anybody who wants to help me. If no one helps me, then God did not will it—and so be it.

What is it to give?

I'm convinced that, in bringing me here, God has entrusted to me the mission of moving people not only to give but also to understand the profound meaning of Christian giving. Many give as a pagan of goodwill would give. Many who more or less have plenty of material resources believe that what's theirs is theirs, and they give of what they have because something—for example, an image of a scene of hunger, poverty, or sickness—arouses their sensibility, a purely natural feeling of pain, and often they give of what they don't need, without depriving themselves of anything and at no great cost.

He who gives in this way hardly grasps that the person who's suffering is his brother, is someone who in his essence is united with him —"that they may all be one . . . , so that the world may believe" (Jn 17:21)—redeemed by the same blessed blood of Christ. When the God Yahweh asked Cain, "Where is Abel your brother?", Cain answered, with no small surprise, "Am I my brother's keeper?" (Gen 4:9).

The problem is that these Dominicans, these Haitians, are your brothers—as are the Chinese, the Eskimos, and the Tutsis, of course —loved by the same Father to whom they pray every day in much the same way you do: "Give us each day our daily bread." They are redeemed by the same blood of Christ, entrusted to the Blessed Virgin as their Mother, as you are and I am.

What you have isn't yours; you're its trustee, not its owner. An owner isn't called to account for what's his, but you and I will be called to account by God for what we've done with what he has given us: "I was hungry and you gave me food" (Mt 25:35). Saint John the Evangelist goes further, speaking of charity: "But if any one has the world's goods and sees his brother in need, yet closes his heart against him, how does God's love abide in him?" (1 Jn 3:17).

Alms as an act of justice

Giving to the poor also has meaning as an act of expiation for our sins. It's a token of repentance and conversion. Giving what we have is a sign and testament that Christ has entered our house, our life.

Christian alms should spring from repentance, fasting, austerity, and the burning desire to change our sinful life. It's not about giving from what I have left over, but rather about depriving myself of something when I give, in sacrifice, for the love of God and of those who are without. Alms are a penance for our sins, for our wastefulness, for all that's superfluous in our lives. I can't give to another what I've spent on myself. Alms aren't a kind of tax that I pay to society so I can go on living as I have been, but rather the public manifestation of my recognition that I've done harm to others and want to change.

Therefore, if after I've given I go on living as I have been up to now, it means that nothing's changed. If one who gives has changed nothing in his heart or way of life when he gives, what he gives hasn't benefited him. What's more, giving may have done him great harm, because he feels more and more justified in carrying on in his way of life and, on top of that, in believing himself to be good. For that reason, if we don't want to change, it's much better and more honest, with God and with others, not to give. It means I'm not yet ready to give. Or I haven't yet received, or opened myself to receiving, the grace to transform myself and turn away from my sins.

Remember Zacchaeus, the miserly little man whom Christ called down from the tree. The signs of his happiness and conversion appear in the repentance with which he says to Christ, "Behold, Lord, the half of my goods I give to the poor; and if I have defrauded any one of anything, I restore it fourfold." And Jesus answers him, "Today salvation has come to this house, since he also is a son of Abraham. For the Son of man came to seek and to save the lost" (Lk 19:8–10). If the joy and peace of Jesus have truly entered your house, your life, you manifest that joy by sharing what you have with the needy. It's true that many have been very generous with me in these months of the mission, but it's also very true that many haven't been—and that many have given but in truth could have given much more.

Let us all think about whether we've been as generous as we could have been. Why haven't we been more generous? In most cases it isn't because we had nothing more to give, but rather for lack of love, because we're attached, very attached, to material things. Because we love money. And, therefore, Christ can't say of our heart that "joy has come into this house" as he says of Zacchaeus' house. We give, yes, but couldn't we give much more? Think it over.

You see, Zacchaeus was small in stature, but he was above all small of heart and of generosity. He wants to see Jesus but can't. He climbs a tree, which he uses as his pedestal, and Jesus says to him as he passes, "Zacchaeus, make haste and come down; for I must stay at your house today" (Lk 19:5). Isn't it odd that Jesus tells this man that, in order to see him, he must come down? The same thing happens to us: All of us want to see Jesus, but strangely, although we hardly ever want to recognize it, we don't see him. Why? Because we're small. Not small in stature, small in heart. Christ has passed by so many times in our lives and said to us, "Come down." From where? From the place to which you've climbed! That tree is the pedestal that all of us create to hide our inner smallness: our arrogance, our pride, our vanity, our attachment to material things, our eagerness to seem important, to be noticed. These, and the dribs and drabs of the lives of all of us, mean everything to us. How wonderful it would be, and what an extraordinary blessing of this Lent, if everybody were to ask himself: And I, what do I need to climb down from? We might think it would cost us too much, but that's not so. What's more, if we don't climb down we risk Christ's never entering our heart, and there's no greater misery than that. If Christ enters "my house", my heart, then my heart will grow and fill up with love, and I'll be able to delight in my happiness, the joy that the world can't give me because it comes from the gospel that the world doesn't know.

The sin of the Church

The sin of the Church in this respect is easy to see. For centuries, again and again, priests and missionaries, and anybody else who wanted to undertake any socially beneficial work, busied themselves with kowtowing to the rich in pursuit of the material means they needed. Sadly, too often, we've inflated the egos of the rich for our own benefit. At bottom we've deceived them: we haven't known how to appeal to the most beautiful part of the heart that all men have, rich or poor, which is love and generosity, so we've appealed to the basest part, which is vanity and pride. In addition, we've thereby swindled them, because we've deprived them of the chance to transform themselves. We've let them stay where they were. We've cared about our good works for the needy, without caring about the heart of the giver or why he gave. I don't want to fall into that. As a priest, I can't allow myself to do that. I'm a priest to everybody, not just to the materially poor. I have just one simple vocation: to declare and make present to every man the saving love of God that is manifested in Christ.

God's greatest gift to this mission

As I told you in my first letter, what we need most in the mission of Los Llanos can't be bought with all the gold in the world, but God wants to give it to us. What we need most, I told you, are priests. Keep this intention in your prayers.

Purina

Purina isn't a puppy food, but rather a human ruin whom the Missionaries of Charity and I found during a visit to one of the bateyes. She was lying on a filthy cot, in a windowless room of not even forty-five square feet, in the heat that is the order of the day here. She didn't speak. She became violent if somebody approached her. She was incapacitated and lying in the fetal position.

We went to see her whenever we could go to that batey. She kept getting worse and worse, looking more and more like a skeleton. Her mother looked after her as best she could but was convinced that someone *"había hecho un trabajo"* on her. That's their expression for witchcraft. Purina has two daughters, one of whom lives in the batey; the other one was adopted by a fine family in Los Llanos.

Finally, the sisters took Purina to their home for the elderly in Santo Domingo. You should see how this young woman has been transformed, with the ton of love they've given her and a little bit of food. There's no question about the fact that when you see such things, you realize that it's so easy to love, help, relieve the pain of humanity . . . Truly the sisters do extraordinary work. I don't know what I would do without them. They're experts in charity, and I'm no more than a beginner who has a lot to learn from them.

Holy Week

The truth isn't that we're approaching Holy Week here, but rather that these roads, these parts, resemble a perpetual Good Friday. Christ makes the climb to Golgotha in the person of every poor and abandoned brother, of everybody who feels poor and exploited by an absurd world that he doesn't understand. Imagine, my people's dream is very simple. They say here that the first words that a child learns are "New York" or, as they say, *"Nueba Yol"*. It's a shame that these poor people imagine paradise in this fashion.

And what will we do in Holy Week? I invite you truly to live it. Holy Week isn't "Holy Week vacation". It's the most beautiful week of the year, the one that distills all of God's love for man. Unlike us, God has given not of his excess but rather all that he had to sustain him: his beloved Son. Behold how much God has loved us! "For us and our salvation" he has given up his only-begotten Son on the cross.

Saint Teresa of Jesus used to tell her novices, when they asked her to teach them how to pray: "I am not asking you to do anything more than to look at him."[4] That's what the Church asks of us all: that we look at him, contemplate him, crucified, with a gaze from the heart. "They shall look on him whom they have pierced" (Jn 19:37). The nails, the lance, the crown of thorns, the gall, the wood of the cross, the marks of an ignominious death, the death of an innocent, of the only innocent. Christ who dies for you, loving you and forgiving you.

My friends, you can't go from the beach to the rites of Holy Week, or from après-ski to whatever church is handy, and purport to have lived the Easter of Christ. Who are we kidding? Isn't this ridiculing and mocking the flagellated, crucified Christ? There, over there, is the naked Christ on Good Friday, and here am I soaking up the sun, only to run out in the afternoon to go to church?

The Church is complicit in her cowardly silence, in not having said anything, in keeping quiet except to say that one thing is compatible with the other. I don't want to be an accomplice to this scandal. We hold our head in our hands, saying like the Pharisees how bad people are, when we ourselves show not the slightest sign of credibility. How is anybody going to believe us if we're the first unbelievers, living in this absurd contradiction?

If the cane became a candle

The via crucis I was telling you about at the beginning of this letter isn't a road without an end. It leads from Golgotha to the glory of the Resurrection. Although it's true that the Passion of Christ is relived every day in these canefields from the break of day on, it's much truer evangelistically that the victory of Easter manifests itself in these fields every day, and you—with your prayers, your sacrifices, and your economic support—are making it possible.

How many stories of redemption could be told by these rows and

---

[4] Teresa of Avila, *The Way of Perfection: A Study Edition*, trans. Kieran Kavanaugh, O.C.D., and Otilio Rodríguez, O.C.D., (Washington, D.C.: ICS Publications, 2000).

rows of cane! Yes, friends. The Church is present here in this forgotten, isolated part of the earth, to convert this calvary of cane into a
candle of glory. Yes, brothers. Here charity, the limitless desire that
beats in the heart of every missionary, to the point of willingness to
give his life if necessary, makes it possible for the cane of Good Friday
to become the tall paschal candle of the Sunday of Resurrection.

How many signs of the victory of the risen Christ I have the privilege of seeing, every day, in the midst of the appalling horror of the
poverty and misery of these people! The laughter of so many children,
inexhaustible in the imaginary games they play with nonexistent toys.
The rejoicing in the campos and bateyes every time another child
is born. The number of wonderful families who, though they live in
poverty and have a good many children of their own, also have what it
takes to adopt other children whose young parents have died. I think of
the joy of so many hundreds of people, of all kinds, to whom it seems
like the most normal thing in the world to walk five or six miles, with
children on their backs and shoes in their hands—their only pair of
shoes—to go to Mass. How can Christ not have risen, how could the
Lord not have been resurrected, when there are so many gestures of
heroic love that move even the hardest hearts! Together, if we all join
our efforts, we can make possible the miracle of redemption, wrought
anew one more time among men and women who no longer hope for
anything from anyone but who hope for everything from the Mother
Church.

Pray for me, that I may shout myself hoarse with joy. As the angels
said to Mary Magdalene when she cried inconsolably over the disappearance of Jesus' body from the tomb (Jn 20:11–13): "He has risen,
he is not here" (Mk 16:6). When the cane becomes a candle, the world
will know that Christ is not dead: he is risen, amen, alleluia! With my
most loving blessing to all of you for everything you have done to
help me, and a very special remembrance before the tabernacle of the
mission,

                                             Father Christopher

The Breath of Love over the Canefields

At the beginning of the seventeenth century, the north and east coasts of Hispaniola were nests of smugglers, pirates, and adventurers strategically placed to conduct trade between the islands of the New World and the continent, outside the control of the Spanish crown. No coast guard yet existed, and the system for levying customs duties was rudimentary. The Spanish king Philip III (known as "the Pious") aspired to maintain order in an empire that was more extensive than any the world had ever seen. The crown expanded throughout the new, seemingly endless continent. The new territories and discoveries leapfrogged each other in a kind of colonial race to infinity and beyond. This was an unofficial state of "last one in is a rotten egg" declared by the European powers, but the territories already annexed by each power left many openings on their coasts and borders, through which trade flowed as freely as the wind comes and goes on the high seas.

The way the overseas territories were settled often left a good deal to be desired, although Spain's uncompromising foreign policy was attenuated somewhat after Philip's ascent to the throne, in a period that history calls the Pax Hispanica. One of Philip's tactics for limiting the losses inflicted by the smuggling in Hispaniola was the forced transfer of the population in the north and east of the island into the interior, with the aim of containing it in a more enclosed territory that had no access to the sea.

This depopulation of the east of the island, ordered by the Spanish king, is known to history as the Devastations of Osorio, named after the governor of the time, who carried it out. It took place in 1605 and 1606, relocating the populations of Puerto Plata, Bayajá, Yaguana, and Montecristi to the interior, and collecting them in today's Monteplata and Bayaguana.

These displaced populations in the interior brought with them what little they could, leaving behind houses, lands, memories, history, and tradition. Among all their poor treasures, however, there was one they especially did not want to abandon: a polychrome wood carving, a little more than three feet tall, representing Christ crucified. It had been found not many years before on the beach in the now disappeared Bayajá, where it is thought to have turned up as a floating vestige of one of the Spanish shipwrecks that were so common during those years.

So the deportation unpremeditatedly turned into a pilgrimage, and when the adventitious pilgrims arrived at their new home, they built among their houses a chapel for the Christ of Bayaguana, known today as the Holy Christ of the Miracles.

It is the custom today among Dominican Christians to make a pilgrimage to the Christ of Bayaguana at least once in a lifetime, or more often in order to make a plea to God for something very important. But for the faithful of Los Llanos, from 1998 to 2002 it became a tradition to make the pilgrimage annually: every Good Friday during that period saw the start of a pilgrimage by hundreds of men and women, both Dominican and Haitian, who came from the campos as well as the bateyes. Their parish priest led the way, and to this day they remember those Good Friday pilgrimages with the greatest joy. Their outbound journey was by night and their return by day, twenty-five miles each way. Many of them barefoot, in prayer and penance, they numbered not ten or twelve but six hundred to nine hundred, and sometimes more than a thousand. They were the poor of Los Llanos, who visited their Holy Christ of the Miracles every year.

By the summer of 1998 Doctor Noemí Méndez was Father Christopher Hartley's close colleague in the affairs of the residents of Los Llanos. One of the biggest problems they faced was the enormous number of undocumented persons who lived there. These included not only the Haitians who had crossed the border covertly but also the Dominican children of those Haitians. Those children had no papers because their parents had none.

The lawyer dealt with the bureaucratic issues, and little by little, like the father, she came to know the most isolated bateyes from the inside, slowly forming an idea in her head that would later become her work: to set the human dignity of the Haitian workers on a firm legal foundation.

Father Christopher meanwhile continued his evangelizing work, baptizing "anything that moved", proclaiming the joy of the gospel, and savoring firsthand the fruits of a labor in which he was not alone. He tells us in his fourth letter how he has recruited different groups of volunteers who support him in the catechizing preparatory to baptism and in other parochial tasks.

In this period of Easter and the Holy Spirit, he is noticeably happy and optimistic. The effects of his first exposure to what he found in his parish seem to have passed, and he is convinced that everything, with God's help, is going to change for the better. One example of this is the parish of Gautier, where, like a miracle of our times, the numbers of faithful and converted are growing by leaps and bounds. The father recounted all this at the end of June 1998, when he had been a missionary for nine months and things had not yet gotten too complicated.

$\sim$

"Spirit of God, come to my life, come to my soul with your power and fill me, fill me with your presence, fill me with your love, fill me with your goodness."

Dear friends of the mission:

With these beautiful words of praise and glory, which the young people in these lands sing to the Holy Spirit, I greet you from the mission of San José de los Llanos. A few days ago we were celebrating the great solemnity of Pentecost throughout the Church. Moreover, as you well know, our Holy Father Pope John Paul II has declared 1998 a year of the Holy Spirit in preparation for the great Jubilee Year of 2000, in which we'll commemorate the Incarnation and birth of the Son of God, made flesh for us and for our salvation.

God's spirit is also sweeping forcefully through these blessed plains of sugarcane, working prodigies of love; or, in the words of the Collect for that day, it is he who renews among us the wonders of Pentecost.

We've truly been privileged witnesses to God's wonders in this season, and I therefore ask that we all join in Mary's Magnificat to give thanks. A tremendous thanks to the triune God for these and so many other things.

Gautier, again

It seems that the good Lord has decided to pour himself out, with his love and provident grace, upon this part of the parish. The enthusiasm that has welled up among the Catholics in this community is extraordinary. The fruits are there, easily recognizable to anybody with clear eyes and a grateful heart.

Three weeks ago the faithful themselves surprised me by saying that the CEA (the State Sugar Council) had given a considerable plot of land so that the Catholic Church could build a place of worship and other buildings necessary to our pastoral work. It's almost a half-acre of land. This will no doubt be one of the projects into which we'll need to throw ourselves as soon as we have some funds.

Also in Gautier, the number of Catholics is growing nonstop. We now have considerably more than a hundred faithful at the monthly Masses. We still celebrate it outside, and we fervently pray at the beginning of each Mass that . . . it won't rain! It's the rare Mass at the end of which I'm not approached by a good number of young people, adolescents, and adults who say to me simply, "Father, I want to be a Catholic. What do I have to do?" Many of them have been baptized in other sects and need to be baptized validly.

Some of them are mothers, and they want to be baptized with all their children. Let us hope that, when the young lay missionaries come this summer, we can formalize many of these situations.

Lent, a time for walking

The Friday before Palm Sunday, the whole parish—villages, campos, and bateyes, and when I say whole, I mean children, young people, adults, the elderly—the whole parish community, without exception, made a pilgrimage to the sanctuary of the Christ of Bayaguana. It was over twenty miles through mud, mire, water, cane . . . We departed from the parish church at ten o'clock at night and entered the sanctuary at nine thirty in the morning. More than two thousand people made the pilgrimage. Walking all night. It had poured all afternoon, and the road was one great, long quagmire. Imagine this impressive spectacle, almost two thousand poor people, exhausted, without adequate shoes and clothing, out of breath, walking along dead tired. Yes, walking. Walking without looking back. Eleven hours of walking nonstop in the middle of the darkest night imaginable, an overcast, moonless night. Two thousand people, each one with his little candle and rosary in his hand. Singing, praying the Rosary, the Via Crucis, and so many devotions specific to this village.

Many pilgrims were fulfilling vows and made the trek barefoot. A display of faith that was simply incredible. Besides our group of pilgrims there was Father Antonio, who, by another route, and with a group almost as large, made the pilgrimage with his parish. After we went into the sanctuary at sunrise on Saturday, ground down with exhaustion, we went to the park nearby to celebrate a Holy Mass presided over by Monsignor Ozoria, our bishop. There was so much joy among us all that we were even more joyful than we were exhausted.

Only God knows the fruits of the evangelizing acts of love, but in his infinite goodness, and to strengthen our meager, feeble faith, he grants us an insight into the power of his glory. We saw one fruit of the pilgrimage during the pastoral visit. Monsignor Ozoria and I made a visit to a campo called La Jengibre. We met with those poor people and asked them about the Christian life of their community.

They all suddenly began talking at once, talking over each other, describing their participation in the pilgrimage. They began to tell us that God had wrought a miracle for one of the mothers in that campo. It turned out that her twelve-year-old daughter had been kidnapped two years ago. She had been taken and forced into prostitution, as hundreds and hundreds of other girls in the campos of this country are taken—with deceit, false promises, and even drugs. The mother was desperate and worn out with sadness and anguish.

When she heard about the pilgrimage, she decided to join the group and offer a sacrifice to God so that he would return her daughter. She was barefoot the whole way, crying and praying, praying and crying. She was absolutely sure that God would bring her daughter back to her. Hard though it will be for you to believe it, forty-eight hours later her daughter walked through the door of her house.

The girl didn't know where she had been during those two years because she never left the brothel where she was being held. She had had a child, whom they took away from her when he was born. One night, one of the brothel's customers asked her why she was so sad. She told him her story, and he said he would help her escape. Unbeknownst to the brothel keepers, she got her belongings together and gave them to this unknown customer, and when the guards weren't watching he escaped with her. The girl knew only that this man was a Canadian; he didn't tell her anything more. He took her to the bus station and said good-bye to her there. She arrived at La Jengibre two days later, which we realized meant that the girl was freed at exactly the same moment that her mother entered the sanctuary of the Christ of Bayaguana. Such is the power of the mother's faith; such are the miracles of God. Blessed be God!

The pastoral visit

For three weeks our bishop, Monsignor Francisco Ozoria, has with true pastoral spirit been visiting every corner of this very far-flung parish, affirming the truth of Christ our Shepherd: The shepherd knows his sheep. He leads them to pasture. He does not flee when the wolf comes. He lays down his life for the sheep. They know his voice. A stranger they will not follow, for they do not know the voice of strangers (see Jn 10).

From May 21 to June 14 the bishop was here to walk through the streets of this town and of the campos and bateyes, and he experienced firsthand the dust, the mud, the torrential rains, the enormous distances, the endless suffering, the despair, and the hopefulness of these blessed people, who have been put to such a test by pain and the cross. He has approached all of them and stopped with all of them. For all of them he has had a word of love, of hope, of consolation . . . With my own eyes, I've seen, in the person of the bishop, Jesus Christ, the Father's mercy, softening hardened hearts and healing wounded hearts. We prepared and waited with these people for this pastoral visit with great care and affection, and especially in a true spirit of prayer and sacrifice. So the children said to him, when they welcomed him at the beginning of the Holy Mass: "Blessed is he who comes in the name of the Lord."

Among the many wonderful moments that I have lived at the bishop's side, I would like to single out the hard work he put into visiting every one of the sick. We spent a whole morning going house to house, door to door, greeting and comforting every ill person. We went into unspeakable little palm-board houses thatched with palm fronds. He himself brought them Communion, and he heard the confession of anybody who asked him to. All of this was witness to pastoral charity, and it was a great lesson that my bishop taught me about the limitless love, even to the point of giving one's life, which should burn in the heart of every priest.

The day he went to visit Gautier was also unforgettable. It was the culmination of so many efforts and so many struggles, of so many prayers and petitions to God the Father. Children, young people, and adults were thronging the entrance to the town, and they received the bishop with placards and songs. He descended from my all-terrain vehicle and greeted all of them one by one. From there he walked among the people, stepping in the mud and muck and soiling his immaculate white soutane, on the very parcel of land that had been donated to us so we could build our church, where we then celebrated the Holy Mass under a canvas canopy that we raised on four poles held together by ropes. Imagine the extraordinary grace of the fact that this piece of land, donated two days before by the CEA, was sanctified by the bishop's celebration of the Eucharist in an open-air Mass.

Wonderful people

As the months have passed, the good Lord has placed in my path people of very high caliber and unbounded heart. I'm referring to the people here, good people of these lands, who offer of themselves humbly, silently, with no aspiration to do anything but serve. I won't name names because it would appall them, but I'm thinking especially of a lady who had the opportunity to visit a batey for no more than fifteen minutes. The ways of God are such, though, that the only person she could greet was a young Haitian woman, the mother of five children, who had the youngest in her arms. He was the only boy and had been born with his feet totally deformed. This visitor to the batey soon got in touch with me to say that she and her husband would pay the cost of surgery and other treatment for this child.

She even had an appointment to see a specialist. We've already had several consultations, and it seems that when the child's feet grow a little more, it will be possible to perform an operation that holds considerable promise of enabling him to walk. Do not fail to commend this intention in your prayers.

Another example of the caliber of the people here is a group of young professionals, all of them members of the same parish in Santo Domingo, the capital. They got in touch with me on the advice of their parish priest, who's suffering from a serious illness and to whom I was blessed to be able to administer the sacrament of anointing of the sick when he was hospitalized in New York last year. Now these young professionals come every Sunday to one of my most remote little villages, called El Manguito. There they divide into three groups to attend to the people of El Manguito and of the adjoining campos and bateyes, who've been gathered together beforehand.

The first group deals with the legal registration of the children, helping their parents with all the necessary paperwork. It's exceptionally important work, because the corruption that prevails at every level of society in this country is such that these poor people are charged, among the swindlers, lawyers, and civil officials, between six hundred and nine hundred pesos to regularize their status. Imagine what this means to families that don't have two pennies to rub together. It's estimated that, because of that problem, there are more than a million unregistered Dominicans—that is, Dominicans who don't legally exist and therefore can't go to school and can't get a driver's license or an identity card or a passport. Because we know the law and have the backing of the Church—with which no one dares to be at loggerheads —we help them solve the whole problem for forty pesos.

The second group's assignment is evangelization. The people who come to this little campo, while they are waiting to be attended to regarding their papers, receive catechism lessons. They are very grateful for them and participate very enthusiastically, to the point where many parents ask then and there for their children to be baptized, or for one or more other sacraments.

The third group works on the construction of a new church, since the one in El Manguito is so run-down that it is about to collapse. Some of those young people are architects and engineers. They draw up the designs and plans themselves, asking the suppliers to donate the construction materials and manual labor. As I have said, these are wonderful people who, living the "life of Riley", sacrifice their weekends and vacation time to give of themselves to others and take the gospel to heart.

The young people and the summer mission

The group that's going to come and work in July and August is ready to go. There will be more than forty to be shared between the parishes of El Puerto and Los Llanos. In the name of Christ and sent by the Church, they'll evangelize among the poorest of the campos and bateyes. They'll visit the families there, catechize the children and young people, and help in the registration of children and the undocumented. They'll work with the doctors providing medical services, and in no end of other activities. If there are more young people who would like to come, ask them to get in touch with me as soon as possible so we can see whether they can. We are convinced that it is the missionaries themselves who will benefit the most, that in giving they will receive a hundredfold.

The mission's grace

Notwithstanding all the plans we present to you in this letter, there's no doubt that the true wonder is being here, living among these people. It's not what we do that matters but rather being with them, among them, and much more important, being for them the living presence of God's love, of his mercy.

Every day I see more and more how important it is to know how to recount to them all the experience of Mary Magdalene on the morning of the Resurrection. To know how to tell them all, in the name of Jesus Christ: "Go to Galilee, and there you will see me" (cf. Mt 28:10). There's a Galilee in the life of every person. It isn't a matter of a geographical place, obviously, but rather of the place where the risen Lord wants to be with every person. The poor, too, have their private Galilee. They haven't yet been blessed with knowing it. Only the Church knows where the Galilee of every human being is. That is the place of mercy. Therefore, mercy is not a feeling or a judgment of absolution. It's the grace of an encounter with Christ who, just as he changed Mary Magdalene's life, wants to change the lives of all of us.

It's very important for me to stay true—come hell or high water —to this fundamental conviction of our faith. I've come here not to do things but to be with the people, and to be for them the living presence of the mercy that is God. To be the Galilee of these poor people.

We need your help

There are many projects that are being held up for lack of funds; it's as simple and sad as that. This letter is meant also as an SOS to all men and women of goodwill. Please don't put this letter aside. Do something; give whatever you can, as a sacrifice. This summer must be a call of conscience for all. We waste so much in the summer! We unnecessarily squander so much money, for which one day we'll have to account to God. I ask you one more time: Can't you give something? No matter how small, every little bit helps.

Continue to pray for the mission. We've commended all these works of love to the Blessed Virgin Mary, the star of evangelization. We want to run swiftly, with her and like her, to bring Christ to all men.

I promise you, as always, a prayer and a very special remembrance before the tabernacle of the mission.

Father Christopher

THE FIFTH LETTER

A Hurricane of Love in the Canefields

Summer is the harvest season, and it was at the end of his first summer in the Dominican Republic that Father Christopher seemed most elated, most optimistic, most blessed by the hand of God through no end of events that he describes in a letter written at the beginning of September 1998.

All by itself, the title that heads this letter inspires a longing to steep oneself in his story. "A Hurricane of Love in the Canefields" brims with the love that the missionary has received from priest friends of his who have gone to visit him and from a little group of volunteers, apprentice missionaries who have participated in the exhausting work of the mission.

Also present is the love that reaches the poor who live in the campos and bateyes, and everywhere else: the love of God, which the father describes as the Alpha and Omega of his presence there, a love that is born from no reality other than that of prayer and contemplation. Yes, during this period the father is immersed in problems and controversies, but these were of nowhere near the consequence that they attained later. There will come a time in this story when Father Christopher's sojourn in the Dominican Republic will be a question of state, a topic of national conversation in which the participants include the political, economic, and media elite, polarizing Dominican society between those who would give their lives for the father and those who would take his life—at least, according to the threats that he received—casting a shadow on a vast, monumental work of pastoral evangelization, which had brought the presence of the Church, the sacraments, to places where they had not been for years, and to other places where they had never been at all.

True, this missionary's personality and character have very often been controversial; but we will never know if his defects, which are thoroughly and widely known, as he himself recognizes, are used by

92

God in a well-judged plan for turning around a situation in which love can be brought to bear only through a compelling persona, which never leaves people indifferent. During our stay in Los Llanos, following in the father's footsteps, the poor of the campos and bateyes always reacted with an unequivocal smile when they heard his name. Everyone acknowledged having sometimes argued with or been scolded by him. That such recollections have survived the passage of time makes affection for the man all the more notable. The people he served must have recognized something beautiful in him if they remembered him less for his reprimands and arguments than for his dedication. It is that dedication that is mentioned most often by those who knew him best.

This letter bears eloquent witness to the fact that this man is motivated by a desire to give of himself and to manifest the Church. In following in the footsteps of the author of these letters, I have met all sorts of people who have either marveled at this man or called into question his way of doing things. What I have been able to absorb from his life and works—and what interests me the most—is that Father Christopher turns the mission into a personal matter, not for love of the spotlight but rather because of the impossibility of compartmentalizing his persona. The care he takes of his faithful and parishioners is personal, as is anything to do with a child who is the responsibility of any parent. Just as Christ took all of humanity personally, so does Father Christopher take his mission. This indivisibility of life, vocation, and persona, combined with the difficult, complicated, and competitive character mentioned by his family, bring the father to a place that others have not even approached and make him a man who gives the impression of always sounding the alarm in the presence of danger.

That was what Father Christopher did when he saw the real world of the people to whom he went, first and foremost, to proclaim Christ. Can anybody who goes to evangelize and knows this reality remain indifferent? One's manner of being and acting, and the reaction it elicits, will vary according to each person's makeup and manner, but we must ask this question: Would just anyone be prepared to evangelize in circumstances like those in which the people of San José de los Llanos, of its campos and bateyes, were living in 1997?

Before the combative, difficult times, there was a summer of great success in which the missionary shares his joy with us, as a man in love would do when his courtship is going very well. He pours out his tales of good things as though his hands were overflowing with them, and he sidesteps the bad things as though they do not exist. Here and there he lets slip a sign of annoyance, in the face of the poverty and the misery of these people whom he has for a while now loved as his own children, whose care the Church has given him as the pastor of the parish. But even in such things the father sees the great power of love, which is capable of turning the suffering and death of a poor woman, who in her agony has been rejected because she is a Haitian, into an occasion of praise to God for love given and received.

The father catechizes in this letter, through his witness to the discernment necessary to do something that truly matters. He puts a special emphasis on the relationship between love and prayer, wishing to make it clear that he sees his work in the Dominican Republic, first and foremost, not as a sacrifice on his part but rather as a gift from God that, transformed through prayer into an uncontainable love, he must himself give in order not to die with it locked up in a frozen heart.

The father wrote the letter after his first year in the mission had passed, and with it the deadline Cardinal O'Connor set for him to decide whether God called him to stay in the Dominican Republic or return to New York. The enthusiasm that wells up from his words makes it seem as though the father already sees the answer clearly, although the final decision will not come until a few weeks later. That decision is still gestating thousands of miles away, on the African coast, in the form of a tropical wave[1] that is heading toward the Dominican Republic. Its name is Georges. Yes, there will be those who see in it no more than mere coincidence, while others will see it as heaven's providence, but nothing and no one knew then, when Father Christopher wrote the heading for this letter, what was soon to descend on the population of Hispaniola.

~

---

[1] A meteorological phenomenon that can trigger the formation of tropical cyclones.

*"When the day of Pentecost had come, they were all together
in one place. And suddenly a sound came from heaven
like the rush of a mighty wind, and it filled all the
house where they were sitting. And there appeared
to them tongues as of fire." —Acts 2:1–3*

Dear friends of the mission:

God has recently done so much for this corner of the world that the
hardest part of writing this letter is knowing where to start.

The gift of friends

Since the last letter we've had visits from many very good friends, both
priests and lay persons, who've left behind them both the witness and
the inspiration of their love. At the end of June my good friend Father
Javier Serra passed through, and in his brief stay with us he helped
us immensely with the celebration of the Holy Mass in various little
campos, as well as in the parish church, and with his many homilies
before an assortment of groups and gatherings.

Father Ambiorix Rodríguez, a New York diocesan priest who was
ordained barely a year ago, spent almost the whole month of July with
us. Without a doubt, this turned out to be for me one of the greatest
blessings the mission has had. I met Ambbis—as we affectionately call
him—when he was an adolescent and had barely begun to take his
first steps on the road to a Christian life. Imagine the happiness I've
felt deep in my heart as a priest to be able to celebrate the Holy Mass
together with a young Dominican whom I met in the streets of New
York when I myself was taking my first steps as a priest.

Father Ambbis didn't have a moment's rest while he was in Los
Llanos. He celebrated Mass in almost all the campos, visited many
sick people, and held several retreats both in the parish church and in
the different rural communities, baptizing fifty-nine children in the
batey of Copeyito. But, for me, the greatest happiness was having a
brother priest with whom to pray the Divine Office and adore Jesus
in the Eucharist, in the morning and at night, in our little chapel. It

was truly a gift from God to have another priest here in the mission, which confirms to me that our first and most urgent need is for the good Lord to send us more priests. I beg you with all my heart to pray constantly for that intention.

Other friends have passed through here. With their presence, assistance, testimony, and enthusiasm, they have given me very valuable help in the task that has been entrusted to me. To them all, in the name of the people here, I give my deepest thanks. We are counting on you!

Father Leo Maasburg, a close friend of mine over many years, also visited us. He was truly a gift from God, because nothing does more for the inner life and pastoral ministry of a priest than other priests who are bosom friends, with whom to share "our things". Saint Teresa of Jesus said: "These are hard times, and God's friends must stand behind each other." Elsewhere she added, "Make friends with God's friends, who will take you to God."

The end of the pastoral visit

The bishop's visit to our parish had two peak moments. One was the first Communions of seventy-three children on Corpus Christi, with its very solemn procession of the Host in the monstrance as it made its way through flowers, songs, and humble altars in the doorways of the houses, the streets, the quarters, and the quagmires of our town. This was a procession that not even the oldest inhabitants remembered having seen, and it brought people of every class and condition out into the streets under the relentless sun that brightens our lives in these parts.

The other moment, which officially brought the pastoral visit to a close, was that of the confirmations. More than forty children received this wonderful sacrament and were forever marked by the fire of God that made them friends, disciples, and the vanguard of the Church in these grim trenches. In the same Mass the bishop named sixteen men and women in our parish extraordinary ministers of the Eucharist. So, from that day on, all the sick, the elderly, and the disabled in our parish receive Holy Communion immediately after the end of Sunday Mass. In addition, the extraordinary ministers can celebrate the Word and administer the Eucharist in the different campos and bateyes to which I regularly send them.

The month of July

In July all my plans fell through. The missionaries I was expecting didn't arrive, and I found myself alone with Father Ambbis, so we had to improvise a series of apostolic projects that turned out to be a true blessing from God for the whole parish. With some seventy volunteers from the parish, young people and adults, we organized a summer camp for all the children in the town. More than 340 signed up, and they did all sorts of things. Each of them had catechism class every day, at one of the four levels into which they were divided according to age, and after that the program varied between crafts, folkloric dances, a first aid course, etiquette, and protocol!—which basically meant, "Children, the fork is for eating, not for poking out the eye of the person next to you." They had a sports period, some educational films were shown, and we made three excursions to the capital, a city to which most of the children had never been. For them, visiting the aquarium, the zoo, and the colonial quarter was like taking a trip to another planet.

We also organized a camp for Haitian children in the batey of Contador, the biggest batey. About a hundred children came every day. This project was made possible by the participation, with great sacrifice, of four missionaries from El Puerto who are with Father Antonio. The children learned to sing, to pray, and to make the sign of the cross; they learned the commandments and the sacraments, and they had time to play games, to paint . . . They couldn't understand why these missionaries came, why some white people would come every day for a month, just to be with them. In the end, when the missionaries explained it to them, the children understood: out of love for Jesus and out of love for them.

Particularly moving was the case of a girl these young Spanish missionaries found in the batey. She was about nine years old, and she was barefoot and very dirty. She had half-open sores and scabs all over her body, from head to toe. She didn't complain, never said anything. The only notable difference between her and the other children, who were happy and noisy, was that she never laughed.

We took her to the little hospital—for lack of a better term—in Los Llanos, where a truly unpleasant doctor, who didn't deign to rise from her chair, attended to the little girl only because she was with me. The girl, terrified, clung to the missionary who brought her. When they took off her ragged clothes the scabs came off, and her wounds began to bleed. When the doctor and nurses saw our dedication and commitment to getting her the kind of treatment that was due to any human being, they had no choice but to treat her case conscientiously.

We ourselves took care of getting the prescriptions filled. If you could see the grateful expression of that little girl, completely abandoned but now in our hands . . . To her we were strange white people whom she had only just met but who exuded confidence, the confidence of our love for her. It was pathetic to see during our visit to the hospital that this girl's poor mother, a Haitian, couldn't understand a single word of Spanish and that her other daughter had to translate everything for her.

A few days ago I returned to the little hut where they live, and the little girl showed no trace of the sores or of any illness. Do you see what love and a minimum of medical care and hygiene can do?! And there are thousands and thousands of men and women whom no one attends to, for whom no one has any concern. How much, dear God, how much could be done if there were more hands ready to serve and more hearts ready to love!

Missionaries with a troubled heart

The restless wind of love that marks these summer months is still gliding back and forth across these lands, burnt by the implacable Caribbean sun, flooded by the torrential tropical rains, and, above all, blessed and sanctified by the strenuous labors of a handful of lay missionaries, young people of indomitable spirit and a burning heart. Young Spaniards who have taken life seriously, ordinary people, ordinary Catholics, men and women with ordinary lives. Real people with names—among them three seminarians from the Archdiocese of Madrid who are on the verge of being ordained. Most of them belong to the Cursillos de Cristiandad movement and come from various parts of Spain: Seville, Madrid, Toledo . . .

They arrived in August, prepared for anything, to leave a piece of their hide and an enormous part of their young hearts in canefields and roads, bateyes and campos, streets and neighborhoods of this vast parish to which Christ the Good Shepherd has sent me in his name and with the strength of his Spirit.

The days were getting long, very long, so long that it seemed as though they would never end, and the nights and periods of time off were short and far between, considering our fatigue. From the moment we got up, around five thirty in the morning, when it was still the darkest night, until we finally went to bed, we went nonstop. We sweated as we've never sweated in our lives. The heat was searing; it rained almost every afternoon; the humidity clung to us like a blanket of water that soaked everything. We got up tired, we stayed tired, and we ended the day so exhausted that we hardly knew our names. There were days when even our hair hurt.

The average day's routine started out getting out of bed to be at the parish church at six thirty. The Blessed Sacrament was exposed, and morning prayer began with Lauds. We prayed slowly, with the seminarians commenting on the psalms and putting them in context, which was a big help to us. We then had a long period of silence, with Christ the Eucharist, before we ended at seven thirty with the benediction and the Angelus. We then went to breakfast, and at eight we had the meeting of preparation for the apostolates of the day, and at the same time discussed the events of the day before.

At eight thirty we were on our way to the various places where we would be evangelizing. For the mornings, we chose six bateyes that, for lack of time, I hadn't been able to visit at any point during my entire first year at the mission. Places that were spread around an immense area but had actual names: San Ildefonso, San José, Batey Nuevo, Brujuela Norte, San Felipe, and Yabacao.

We were accompanied by several volunteers from the parish, whose role was doubly important because, besides being of help to us in our work, they would continue from then on to evangelize in the Haitian bateyes throughout the year. No missionary, whether a priest or a layman, had been to these corners of the parish, according to what the local elders told us. Nobody had ever been there to evangelize, catechize, or otherwise prepare these people for a sacrament. Nobody had ever come to pronounce the word Jesus. The honor, grace, and privilege of being the first to make Christ present to these people were ours. Everybody's enthusiasm was extraordinary. There was so much happiness, so much joy in the hearts and faces of these poor people, weathered and worn by pain, hunger, abandonment, affliction, sweat, exhaustion, sun and more sun, illnesses, oblivion . . . The faces of the children were so full of tenderness and innocence . . . Every day, when it was time for us to leave, they looked at us as though to say, "Will you be back tomorrow?" As if having such a good time couldn't last long, as if it were all a dream that they were afraid to wake up from.

The people were divided into groups of men, women, and children, which were assigned to different missionaries. The time was devoted to teaching them the sign of the cross, the simplest prayers, religious songs, games for the children, reading and writing for the adults . . . and anything else that was within the reach of each missionary's imagination. Since we didn't have anywhere to gather, we made use of the shade of a tree, an arbor, the yard next to a house . . . We brought our school supplies, such as chalk and a big blackboard that had been given to us and that we cut into three pieces. The thousand scenes and unforgettable moments that would certainly be etched deep in the heart of every missionary from then on are, without a doubt, the greatest recompense and treasure that the Lord could have given us.

How could one forget the moment when, during a prayer of thanksgiving in one of the bateyes, a woman who had never in her life prayed out loud said: "Thank you, Jesus, because we have always lived like animals, but now we know we are children of God"?

We planted a big cross in every batey, in the most visible and busiest place, to show that the victory of the crucifixion had come to this place and that these people were now bathed in the precious blood of Christ. We began the day in prayer before the cross and ended it there, approaching the cross one at a time to kiss it and to bid Jesus good-bye until the following day. I've been back there, and in all the bateyes they still gather every night to sing and to pray the simple prayers that they learned during the days of the mission. And I wonder: What does God feel when he hears these songs and prayers? Is he moved? Is he moved when he hears a child in filthy shorts, his face covered with mucus, or a woman worn out with suffering and troubles, or a man with calloused hands, hard as leather, singing with his eyes closed and his hands raised to heaven: "God's love is wonderful . . . so great . . . so high . . . so broad . . ."? Our God isn't blind, nor has he a heart of stone. You friends who read this letter in other parts of the earth: How many surprises are awaiting us in heaven! How near are these poor people to God and the kingdom of heaven!

Tina

Tina wasn't so much a Haitian woman as she was a human ruin whom the missionaries found in the batey of San Felipe. Completely naked, she was confined to a revolting cot. Unattended by anybody and badly fed. The hut where she lived with a daughter and two strangers was indescribably dirty and squalid.

We learned that afternoon at the hospital in Los Llanos that they had diagnosed her with terminal tuberculosis, among other illnesses. When we went back in the afternoon, we baptized her, prayed with her, spoke to her about God's love, about the importance of repentance and the hope of heaven. To the surprise of the whole batey, which was crowding in at the door, we wrapped her in a sheet for what had to be, unbeknownst to us, her ultimate calvary, a calvary that opened all our eyes to the horror and hell in which the poor live.

We arrived at the "hospital" of Los Llanos, where they didn't want to receive us and attended to us badly. Pleading inadequate facilities and resources, the doctor didn't condescend to get near Tina, much less accept that she should stay there. We saw that she was going to die in our hands. We got the town ambulance. They wanted to charge us for it, but we emphatically refused. This taught me that only those with sufficient economic means have access to the luxury of an ambulance. Tina was taken in it to the tuberculosis hospital in San Pedro de Macorís, but they didn't want to admit her there, either, saying they had no space.

They gave her first aid and sent her back to Los Llanos. Her condition deteriorated. In Los Llanos the nurses and doctors wouldn't even open the door. When I arrived it was agreed that the ambulance would take her to Santo Domingo. The waste of another hour of travel time. They didn't admit her there, either. After midnight the missionaries were back in Los Llanos with Tina, who was by this time in agony. They had to give her a little space in the corner until dawn broke and we could bring her back to her wretched batey to die.

The worst part is that she was fully aware of what was going on and just kept repeating, "If I'm going to die, why don't they want to take us in anywhere?" Nevertheless, the bond of love that was forged between Tina and the two missionaries whom she didn't know at all was extraordinary. They gave her all the love, affection, and care they could. They brought her a new mattress with clean sheets and clothes, so she could die with a little more dignity. She died the next day, after having wandered halfway across the Dominican Republic in one night, searching for a little relief and mercy. But they slammed the door in her face everywhere. For being poor, for being black, for being Haitian, for being tubercular, for being a miserable human remnant. They slammed the door on her as life had done since the day she was born. Deep down, she died as she had lived, treated by this society as a parasite, as a black woman. Worse still: a Haitian woman. She only knew, for a brief instant, the unfathomable love of some apprentice missionaries who, with no medical or professional training, gave her something with which their hearts overflowed in torrents, the only thing that this poor woman truly needed, as you do and I do: love.

Like the first Mass, the last Mass, the only Mass

The mission reached an unambiguously clear peak moment that embodied and made sense of all our tasks and efforts: the celebration of Mass in these six bateyes for the very first time. It took us a month to prepare for it, explaining every day one aspect or another of the Mass. Those men and women didn't have the slightest idea of what the Mass was, and in all the bateyes we taught the same songs and the same responses to the various parts of the ceremony.

The big day arrived. One afternoon, at the end of the mission, we gathered everybody together in the biggest batey, San Felipe. We organized transportation with a tractor and a cart used to haul cane, besides making several trips in our vehicles, gathering them all under the bower. The happiness of the people from the different bateyes was indescribable, and even more so, if possible, was the joy of the young missionaries at seeing them arrive. There was an outpouring of enthusiasm. The songs followed one another to the rhythm of clapping and the guitar. Despite the deluge that was falling, and the quagmire in which we found ourselves bogged down, there was nothing that could dampen so much happiness.

The Mass finally began. The first Mass. The people were amazed, they followed every step and every gesture with amazement, they sang and sang, and there was no way to stop them. When they said amen, they shouted so loudly that they seemed to pierce the clouds and reach heaven itself. Only one person had been baptized, one man, who was the only one who could receive Communion.

I talked in the homily about the simplest things, the really important things. Holding high a crucifix in my hand, I explained the love of God the Father, who gave his Son to the world, and how he, the innocent, had died for our sins. I talked about the Church, about how we are called to be the Body of Christ in the world, and emphasized that there are no strangers in the Church. I talked about the Virgin Mary, about her maternal love and her constant presence at our side. The Mass ended when darkness fell, and after singing, singing, and more singing they finally got back into their wagons to go back to their different bateyes. They had all come in their Sunday best. They returned up to their ears in mud but happy, radiantly happy. They had all participated in their first Mass. And I had the odd feeling of having celebrated my own first Mass all over again! If it was the first Mass for them, it was also the first one for me.

When we missionaries arrived in Los Llanos, completely exhausted, sweaty, and covered with mud, we understood that we had lived something utterly extraordinary, impossible to explain in words. Our happiness poured out of our every pore. Never before had exhaustion been so worthwhile.

Time devoted to God alone

The mission wasn't always work, work, and more work. There were also times of solitude and communion with God. Twice we went on retreat. The first was with the community of El Puerto, with Father Antonio and Father Manuel leading us. During these two occasions for our renewal in the Spirit we had time alone with God, to allow us to grow in our love for him, to open ourselves to his plans for our lives, and to ask for the light and grace necessary to respond to him as generously and radically as possible. These were moments of intense prayer with Christ in the Eucharist, moments of inner peace and tranquility in which to thank the good Lord for the undeserved gift of serving him in the men who are our brothers.

These two retreats helped us all to recall yet again that to pray is to love, that he who doesn't pray does not love. And what help to me, or to the poor, are missionaries who are incapable of love? Only love bears apostolic fruit. These poor people need the love of Christ in which we are steeped when we pray. It is only when we allow ourselves to join the school of the great practitioners of prayer that we are capable of understanding the profound meaning of the mission. There has never been a single saintly missionary in the history of the Church, man or woman, who has not been deeply contemplative. Only prayer can make us authentic witnesses of Christ's Resurrection, and it's precisely that witness that is the root of apostolic fruitfulness and, in the case of priests, pastoral charity. A witness has seen, personally knows, has tasted, and speaks with the same authority as Christ.

Prayer moves the soul to love, impassions him who prays with the ideal of the gospel, opens our hearts to the love of God and inspires us to want to give our lives, with Christ and like Christ, for whomever. Prayer merges the lover with the beloved. When we pray we realize that for all eternity we've been created by God to be sought and found by him.

God searches for us, is always searching for us, night and day. It's terrible that we should be so unaware of the fact that God loves us so much. The missionary's vocation, in this sense, springs from contemplation. The more contemplative the missionary, the more viscerally he feels and the more urgently he wants to run, to fly, to the farthest reaches of the universe, to be a living witness. The true missionary is one who, as a result of his contemplation, has the experience Moses had when he came down from the mountain with his face so aglow that, although he had been struck dumb with awe by his vision of the mystery, everyone knew he had seen God. The missionary is a true contemplative, and he produces abundant fruit not because of the eloquence of his words or his other natural gifts, but because he has the spirit of the living God; he carries the fire of God in his soul.

For the young missionaries, the true fruit of this mission isn't in the many things they did for others, but rather in the meekness with which they allowed themselves to be kindled with God's fire. That fire will never die out, and they will carry it within them wherever they go. During this period in the mission, including the days of the retreats, they are called to prompt young people to have a fully developed experience of God's love. In doing so, they too will be capable of saying with Saint John: "We know and believe the love God has for us"

(1 Jn 4:16). He who has known the love of God can thereafter proclaim: "That . . . which we have heard, which we have seen with our eyes, which we have looked upon and touched with our hands . . . that which we have seen and heard we proclaim also to you" (1 Jn 1:1, 3).

The summer mission, and specifically these days in the retreats, have also served to foster their vocational discernment. It has been a time for them to ask themselves the questions that truly matter: What do you want from me, Lord? Where will you send me? When? These moments help immensely in thinking about the seriousness of life and the consequences of our decisions. For that reason the mission helps us think anew about God's light in prayer throughout our life—about doing something worthy with our lives, and not living just to live. All in all, it involves discerning to whom our indivisible heart belongs, in such a way that, when we dedicate it, we dedicate ourselves forever; in such a way that we belong entirely, all our life long, to the one to whom we dedicate our heart. This is a magnificent opportunity to discover to whom our indivisible heart belongs.

In the afternoons

The afternoon activities began after lunch and a brief rest. We divided ourselves into three groups that were joined by a group of volunteers from Los Llanos. One group worked in La Palma, perhaps the poorest and most neglected neighborhood in the town of Los Llanos. The missionaries accomplished an extremely difficult task that had never been accomplished before. Going from house to house, they visited hundreds of families in the neighborhood who were struggling to make ends meet. The people were amazed that some young white people would spend the afternoon with them, that they would approach them and treat them as equals. These visits are important for the people, because they help them realize that the Church hasn't forgotten them, that God has come to visit them and show them that his face is a face of mercy. This task of home visits was especially important and required the missionaries to have an adult faith, enabling them to keep on acting with enthusiasm even when they didn't see specific results from their efforts.

This group also organized a camp for children, attended by almost a hundred of them. They were very poor children, some of them brothers and sisters by different fathers, some with mothers in other religions, many with alcoholic parents, many from homes where there's no love and a great deal of domestic violence, where the mother changes husbands as she does her shirt. They prayed with these children, sang with them, taught them handicrafts, played games with them, performed little evangelizing plays . . . The work with these children was especially important because we harbor the hope that they'll all be able to join the catechism course that's now beginning in the parish.

Another group worked in Gautier, about which most of you have already heard. We did house visits there, too, which for those people was unheard of. One of the outcomes of those visits was the formation of a group of almost forty young people. Very few of them have been baptized, and they aren't very educated, but they radiate enthusiasm and a desire to know Jesus. They participated in a retreat with all the other young people in the parish that ended with a Mass celebrated by our bishop, Monsignor Ozoria.

This group also organized a camp for children. So many of them showed up that we had to ask for permission to use the school's classrooms, since we couldn't accommodate them all anywhere else. Another part of the mission consisted of preparing a very big group of children and adolescents for baptism. The first baptisms performed in this community in years and years. The little course was given to the parents and godparents, and the other preparations were made. Altogether we baptized eighty-two children. Eighty-two new children of God, new, living building blocks in the Body of Christ that is the Church. It was one of the most beautiful days during my time at the mission. We were all overcome with joy. We also worked with the adults, whom we gathered together for catechizing, lessons in reading and writing, prayer, learning songs, and even encouraging them to prepare themselves to receive the sacrament of marriage.

The last group worked in the community of La Victorina, a mixed campo of Dominicans and Haitians that we chose because it was surrounded by other campos. Just getting there was a heroic achievement in itself. The roads were actual swamps, a sea of muck that defied even the most skillful driver. We got bogged down several times and had to be rescued by tractors.

It was wonderful to see children, adolescents, and elders arrive every afternoon, materializing from the cane and the mud, from little campos such as Los Santana, La Jengibre, La Rinconada, El Guayabal, Paña Paña, El Coco . . . It felt like a page out of the Acts of the Apostles! Whether we were drowning in rain or broiling in the sun, they were there to hear the Word of God, learn their ABCs, sing at the top of their voices, learn simple educational games . . . In all this they sought the love of God, which filled the missionaries' hearts to overflowing.

At the end of the day the missionaries went back to Los Llanos just in time to take a bath, change their clothes, do a little washing by hand, and head for the parish church to celebrate the afternoon Mass. Lived that way, the Eucharist truly had another flavor, another meaning. The words, the liturgical rites—everything had a different value. As when in the liturgy the celebrant said, "Blessed are you, Lord God of all creation, for through your goodness we have received the bread we offer you: fruit of the earth and work of human hands, it will become for us the bread of life." Hearing those mysterious words at the end of the day, feeling absolutely exhausted, gave a new and deeper meaning to our Christian life in a way that was completely new to us. Those words brought home to us the greatness of our vocation and mission. They made us realize that it had been worthwhile to give of ourselves to the point of exhaustion, without complaint and with a smile on our lips. To think that our exhaustion, our sweat, our poor efforts, placed now on the altar and offered up in the hands of the priest, would be converted into the very Body and Blood of Christ: the bread of life for the world and the chalice of salvation for all men.

We then went to dinner, and there, as at other meals, the general tone was set by a stream of festiveness, healthy humor that recalled the amusing aspects of the thousand curious incidents of each day, aimed at sharing with the brothers so many beautiful things that had happened to each of us during the day.

Sevillanas

It will seem strange to you that a letter like this would tell you about such a thing as sevillanas. It happened that in the mission of El Puerto, as well as our own, there was a group of brothers from Seville, and you can imagine the rest. Any excuse would do to prompt people to get up and dance. They danced in the most picturesque and unexpected places, as, for example, in the *locutorio* (parlor) of the Discalced Carmelites, in that of the Missionaries of Charity, and also in Los Llanos, wherever. But the most picturesque was clearly when they began to dance in the middle of a highway, in the open bed of my pickup truck.

It was a day when we were returning from Santo Domingo to Los Llanos, and we had the bad luck of getting stuck in a spectacular traffic jam caused by Fidel Castro's arrival in the Dominican Republic, as you may have seen in the news at the time. Between being bored with waiting and roasted by the heat, as the midafternoon sun beat down on us mercilessly, and with the idea of making the best of a bad situation, some of them began to clap rhythmically and sing *bulerías* (fast flamenco rhythms), and, in the blink of an eye, the first couple had stood up in full view of the throng of drivers and passengers, who couldn't believe their eyes: a priest and a band of who knew what class of people, putting on a show . . . With alarming ease and freedom, they sometimes went from being missionaries to being pilgrims on the El Rocío pilgrimage or at the *feria* (festival) in Seville. But don't let what I'm saying surprise you. Humor, healthy happiness, kidding around, jokes, and anecdotes were the best, most relaxing medicine at the end of the day, or to alleviate the momentary bad humor or annoyance that could arise in a traffic jam. The result was magnificent!

Baptisms and more baptisms

As the fruits of our labors and the apostolic work of all of us in Gautier, we baptized eighty-two children, adolescents, and young adults. It was a memorable afternoon. No one could recall such an event in that community's history, after so many years of being a victim of neglect. It's impossible to put the happiness of those people into words. There was such a to and fro of godmothers in their very best clothes, and of parents and godfathers as proud as peacocks. Not a one failed to help or to try to put his best foot forward.

Since we didn't have a building where we could celebrate the day, the young people put up a canopy in the middle of the dirt road. It began to pour, and we all had to run to the public school to take shelter as best we could. The whole team of missionaries pitched in to help in various ways. The Lord had given us eighty-two living build-ing blocks for this his Church, "a building from God, a house not made with hands, eternal in the heavens" (2 Cor 5:1). May the good Lord will that such a gift, such love, such grace, so undeserved, not be wasted.

Thanks to all

If it hadn't been for all of you, who've given me so much financial support throughout my first year of missionary life, it would have been impossible to bring all this apostolic work to fruition. The house where the girls live has been repaired with your help, and we bought the all-terrain vehicle that made it possible for us to go to the remotest bateyes.

But, again, many projects are being held up for lack of money. It's that simple and sad. This letter is intended as a cry on behalf of the poor people who've put all their trust in the Church. We can't disap-point them. I ask you, beg you, to help as much as you can, even as I say at the same time that you've been extremely generous. Do not tire of helping, because Christ and the poor deserve it all.

When I was on my way to the Dominican Republic, I asked the Holy Virgin to come with me, and as soon as I could, I made a pilgrimage to lay myself at the feet of Santa María de la Altagracia.[2] I confessed my poverty, told her that I was coming to her unaccompanied, again leaving everything behind, and begged her to send me companions for the journey. There's nothing that these people need more than other men and women who want to dedicate themselves, with an undivided heart, to Christ her Son on behalf of the poor. To be poor with them and in their midst, thus showing them the face of the Father's mercy.

No day goes by when I don't remember you all before the tabernacle of the mission. Do not forget me in your prayers to the Lord.

With my most loving and grateful blessing,
Father Christopher

---

[2] Patron saint of the Dominican Republic.

What Even the Hurricanes Could Not Bring Down

The blue light of the sky permeates everything that surrounds you in the little campos of Los Llanos, as though night were never going to fall. The people here are poor, but not as poor as they are in the bateyes. The houses here, little wood cabins, are painted in vivid colors that delight the eye and invite you in to chat with their inhabitants around a cup of coffee that they pamper you with, its flavor as sweet as an embrace. You may be in the Dominican Republic, but when you drink coffee in a little campo with these people, you have a feeling of having come home.

An elderly lady with a perpetual smile welcomes us with a boiling pot of freshly filtered coffee. Her face, once the envy of all who knew her, is worn with the wrinkles that time has etched in it. She goes barefoot, and she wears a threadbare violet dress and a bobby pin holding back bangs that are turning white. We are in the village of El Manguito, and her name is Altagracia. Her ninety-five years seem like a lifetime and a half to her, and life has treated her accordingly. She has seen her fifteen children grow up and go elsewhere, leaving behind the little campo in the hope that they will not end up being forced to work in the sugarcane fields.

Some hens cross Altagracia's sitting room, along with an ingratiating dog that smells the chocolate cookies that we brought in our backpack as a snack. We do not give it even one, but it sticks to its purpose and silently stays next to us. In the end, the dog contents itself with a caress. The dogs here are poor, like their owners, and they never in their lives have tasted biscuits in the shape of a bone or dry kibble or anything like them.

The house is clean and tidy, demonstrating that poverty does not have to be at odds with elegance. With its woodstove and unglazed windows, it could be a dollhouse. But, nevertheless, the house of a poor doll. Among all the rooms in the house, Altagracia shows us one with tears in her eyes. It is the one where they kept the Blessed Sacrament for eight years, after Hurricane Georges wiped out the little chapel in El Manguito. In fact, when that brute force of nature roared through San José de los Llanos like a derailed train, Altagracia's husband rescued the tabernacle from the chapel and, clutching it in one arm, lived through the hurricane hidden under his bed. Can you imagine the scene? A category-4 hurricane determined to blow away his house with a deafening roar, and the man, scared to death, hiding under his bed for hours, holding on to a little tabernacle for dear life. That is the faith of the poor. That is how they regard the things of God and of men, matters of life and death, with the conviction that God himself, hidden in a tabernacle, needs the protection and care of a poor man in Los Llanos.

Hurricane Georges crossed the Dominican Republic during the night between September 21 and 22, 1998, leaving not a single board or stone on top of another. With winds of up to 125 miles per hour, Georges devastated everything in its path. The inhabitants remember the sound of the wind as a brutal roar. It rained in buckets—horizontally, not vertically—and many people saw their houses smashed to smithereens and their lives flying away on the wind.

As we will see below, Georges marked the end of many things and the beginning of others. The inhabitants tell us that a hurricane is terrible, but that it offers the opportunity to pull up weeds by the roots, which would otherwise be impossible. And Georges—besides bringing poverty and destruction—brought new winds to the island, for it was in its terrible trail of pain that Father Christopher realized that his heart belonged to these people, that he had put down roots with them, and that what he wanted was to share their fate, whatever it might be.

Among the rubble of the bateyes Father Hartley found the foundations of a faith that was very poor in education and means, but extremely rich in authenticity. It is curious to see how the poor do not blame God for their misfortunes, but rather bless him for having spared them from something worse. Their life was already complicated enough, and Georges put to the test, to the breaking point, their faith in a God whom most of them do not know, but whom they intuit. The poor of these campos and bateyes know that God is there. They believe in him with a conviction that defies hurricanes, hunger, and social injustice. That is why the poor of these lands, who have lived and still live through the worst disasters, dramas, and miseries, do not commit suicide. I myself asked boldly why they did not end a life of hunger, hunger, and more hunger, of injustice, of sickness, of misery and death, and the reason they gave was simply that they hope tomorrow will be a little better than today, that the next harvest will give them more work, that the work will be better paid, and that their children will be less hungry and will not get sick or die. They have hope because they know about a God to whom Father Christopher has given a name in the person of Christ, but it is from these poor that the father, doctor of theology though he is, is going to learn, as he has from no one else, about this God in whom the poor place their faith, their hope, and their trust.

There are thousands of anecdotes that illustrate this lesson. One of them is about Father Christopher's companion Father Antonio Diufaín, rather than about Father Christopher himself, but it may be the anecdote that he most frequently recounts when he recalls the events that followed in the wake of the hurricane. It is about how Father Antonio, bent on delivering every kind of aid in his truck a few days after Georges' visit to the island, was reproached by an elderly lady, weighed down with her possessions, carrying her whole life on her back, for having forgotten them. In reply he asked her how she could say that, when he was delivering material aid everywhere. Imagine his surprise when the lady gave him a great lesson: "It's been a long time since you've come to celebrate Mass." That is the faith of the poor who know Father Christopher in the bateyes: the faith of an elderly lady whose house has flown away in a hurricane and is waiting, more than for material aid, for the priests to celebrate Mass.

~

"Who then is this, that even wind
and sea obey him?" —Mark 4:41

Dear friends of the mission:

I want to assure all those who've read the most recent letter from the mission that I wrote it before Hurricane Georges literally went through San José de los Llanos, and that the title I gave it—A Hurricane of Love in the Canefields—was purely coincidental with the devastating atmospheric phenomenon that was about to demolish, a few days later, the Dominican Republic and other Caribbean islands. I believe that the letter from the mission for which that title would be fitting wasn't that one but this one. It's true that the hurricane has truly been a horror for all the inhabitants of the country, especially for the poorest among them, but the storm has also fostered an extraordinary surge of love among so many people of every origin and condition. How much good, and how much love, has spontaneously sprung from the pain and suffering of these our brothers! I have no doubt whatsoever that today—as always—suffering is the handmaiden of God.

Heartfelt thanks

I would like above all to give thanks in this letter to so many marvelous people who have given with such spontaneous generosity, not from their excess but rather from "what they live on", for the love of their neediest brothers. What I wish for from the bottom of my missionary's heart is that all those who've been moved to generosity by the suffering of these poor people will be drawn by that generosity nearer and nearer to God. May it help them discover existentially that there is a living God. The God who has touched their hearts to be generous and share what they have, and their love, with the poor, is the same God who one day touched my heart and gave me the blessing of leaving my house, my family, my people, my things, to go with him, to go alone with Jesus to distant lands. How true it is what the

Gospel says, that he who forsakes everything for Jesus will receive a hundredfold! I've just seen it unmistakably with my own eyes in the days that I spent in Madrid.

The lessons in love that all these marvelous people gave me throughout these days of my stay in Spain were beautiful, but no less so were those taught by the people in the mission who lost everything in the hurricane. The hurricane took me by surprise in Haiti, the next-door neighbor with which the Dominican Republic shares the island of Hispaniola. The effects of the wind there were also terrible. I was there preaching spiritual exercises to the mothers superior of the Sisters of Mother Teresa of Calcutta in the Caribbean. When I learned of the destruction caused by the hurricane, I quickly returned to the mission. I arrived at night. It was such a spectacle of devastation that I barely recognized the parish. There was nothing left of Doña Isabel's house, and that's how it was—that simple and that horrible—for house after house, family after family. There was no electric light, no telephone service, no running water. There were only people wandering through the streets like shadows with no apparent destination, or looking incredulously at the rubble of their houses, the rubble of their shattered lives.

I quickly armed myself with a powerful spotlight that I connected to the battery of my pickup truck and, together with some young people from the parish, set about exploring the town street by street, house by house. I tried to think about the help that I would want to offer the next day to the neediest, in the name of the Church. Very, very early, as dawn was breaking, I went to the neighboring parish of El Puerto, because at the time its parish priest, my friend Father Antonio, was in Spain. The situation there was similar, with little campos that had disappeared or of which one lone little house was all that remained of the sixty that had been there before.

I went back to my parish and began to organize the refugees who were in the parish church. There were more than thirty families who had lost everything and were living there. The church was their home, their only roof, where they slept, cooked, ate . . . It was truly their house. Almost a hundred more refugees had taken shelter in the children's dining hall of Christ the Redeemer, which the parish has in the poorest and most marginal neighborhood in the town. Because it is adaptable for the purpose, we fitted out the dining hall so that anyone who lacked food, potable water, or shelter could take refuge there. I got hold of four tanks with a capacity of almost a hundred liters each, and, with the help of a seminarian from the parish, I went to the batey of Cánepa, where they had told me that there was still running water. Having obtained potable water for many people to drink and cook with, we made our return by the end of the morning and started looking for food for them.

With two of El Puerto's lay missionaries, and some volunteers from my parish, I went to the capital to get food and to call our families to reassure them. Fortunately, a good friend who owns some big supermarkets took me immediately to his warehouses, where we filled up the trucks with the essentials. With that we went back to the parish.

The next day, a Sunday, I celebrated Holy Mass in Los Llanos in the parish of El Puerto. At midday Father Antonio arrived on the first plane (in the cockpit) he had been able to find. I went to visit the campos in the afternoon. It was an indescribable odyssey. No one had been to visit the rural communities since the hurricane. We had to negotiate around huge trees that had fallen in the middle of the road, cross veritable lakes of muck, and sometimes drive a quarter of a mile or more through the middle of the canefields until we managed to arrive at the first villages: La Rufina, El Coquito, Paña Paña, Gaviota, El Guajabo . . . These settlements practically no longer existed. The people there, with the remnants of the palm-wood walls and crumpled sheets of zinc, were trying to reconstruct at least one small hut in which people could take shelter and begin to remake their lives, their families.

What surprised me most when I went from campo to campo was that nobody complained, nobody protested, nobody pointed an accusatory finger at God. Nobody asked me why God had wrought or permitted such a tragedy. On the contrary, to my surprise they gave thanks to God for having spared them anything worse, and for having miraculously saved their lives.

If in all these villages they lamented anything, what in truth they told me with genuine pain in their voices and faces was: "Father, the little church has collapsed." Of the sixty villages in my care only twenty had chapels, and those twenty all fell to the ground.

Witnesses of the faith

The witness borne by these poor people was extraordinary. In one village, when I was saying good-bye, I said, "Don't forget to pray", to which one lady responded, "Father, we've never stopped praying. I know that God always hears all our prayers. What happens is that when we pray to him, he sometimes says yes and sometimes no." To hear a poor woman surrounded by small children bear witness to her certainty that God always hears her prayers, when we were talking in front of the ruin and rubble of her house, gives us all something to think about.

In our circuit from one campo to another, we finally arrived at El Manguito. It's a special campo because its little church is the only one that has the Blessed Sacrament. I now confess that I was moved when we got there, and I cried. I went by myself into what was left of the church, jumping over bricks, boards that were every which way, and fragments of benches, and I saw that the tabernacle wasn't there. I hadn't realized that a lady had come into the church behind me. She had taken care of it for years. Her house had been destroyed, like all the rest, and without ado she said to me, "Don't worry, Father, the Lord is all right. When we saw that the church was falling down, my husband went out into the hurricane and brought the tabernacle home. It was hidden in his arms under the bed. Nothing happened to the Lord. We made a little room for him as best we could . . ." I simply couldn't believe it. There, in a corner of what had before been her house, they had put up some boards with a curtain. I knelt for a moment to pray; I got up again and stood there looking. The lady said to me, "You're not going to take him away, are you? Because if you take him, we'll be left with nothing." Sometimes you feel so small, so unimportant, so sinful, before a faith so great, so pure, so true. That's where the title of this letter comes from. This faith, this unconditional love of God, is what the hurricane could not uproot and destroy.

On Monday I returned to the campos to bring more food and clothing. The catechists in the other villages came to get it and distribute it in their own communities. In the afternoon I went to visit the Haitian bateyes to see how they had ended up. The same devastating spectacle. Some of the bateyes were now ghost villages. All that was left standing were the ruins of the few brick structures that dotted the awe-inspiring plains of canefields torn up by the roots.

The next day—leaving Father Antonio in charge—I flew to Spain, where I found an extraordinary response from so many people who, sometimes not knowing me at all, offered me their support and financial assistance or put themselves at my disposal for whatever we needed. It would be impossible to list so many people who truly shared, like the widow in the Gospel. I must mention the unconditional support of my family—I think my swift passage through my parents' house has already been described as the passage of Hurricane Christopher! My brother and sister-in-law's house suddenly became a warehouse filled with more than four tons of used clothing. The generosity of cloistered communities has been admirable, as has the help of the lay missionaries who had been in San José de los Llanos this past summer, and so many, many more who, with their quiet love and anonymous charity, responded by giving until it hurt, as a sacrifice, depriving themselves of something for the benefit of those who have nothing.

A town's generosity

My participation in COPE's program *El Espejo* (The Mirror) deserves its own chapter, thanks to Father Gago, who invited me to be interviewed on it.[1] I fortunately had the idea of giving out my home telephone number so people could call me. They've been calling ever since. Wonderful people. Extraordinary people of impressive human and Christian fiber. Rich people, average people, and very poor people, but all of them with the same eagerness to find out how they could help. They called from all over Spain and ranged from a rural parish priest who had taken up a collection from his faithful, who didn't know me at all, to a cleaning woman whose husband and children were unemployed but who wanted to help in any way she could. These are the good people of Spain, with the tender heart of a missionary.

Truly I have to confess that I can't explain to myself how people, without knowing you at all, without ever having laid eyes on you, with just the telephone number of a private home, could have been so generous. Blessed be God, who works such marvels among his people!

---

[1] COPE (Cadena de Ondas Populares Españolas) is a radio station that is indirectly owned by the Spanish Episcopal Conference, Spanish dioceses, and religious orders such as Jesuits and Dominicans.—TRANS.

Thanks to our good friend Father Ramón Tejero, we now have a pump for collecting water from wells or rivers, with its purifying plant and generator. This is vitally important, because in the town of San José de los Llanos—not to mention the campos and bateyes—we've been without water, without electricity, and without telephone service for two months now since the hurricane. This donation is extremely useful, especially for the nutritional center operated by the parish, where we feed and educate 120 children every day.

An SOS for our most urgent needs

With the help of what we've already accumulated and what we hope will continue to be offered us, we are undertaking a series of specific projects.

First of all, we are feeding and clothing the population. In the wake of the hurricane, with the help of two nuns and a good number of laypeople, we are conducting a detailed census to give us as precise an idea as possible of people's needs. We have succeeded in reaching twenty-seven of the campos, most notably the most far-flung ones, where no one except the Catholic Church has come to offer even the most minimal help to these people. So far we have a census of 1,300 families—that is, more than 5,500 people—receiving aid from the parish. Each one has been given a card produced by Father Antonio, indicating the number of family members and what they need most urgently. So they receive little bags with a few pounds of rice, beans, tins of sardines, tomato paste, concentrated milk, pasta, chocolate, oil, and anything else we can get our hands on. We also distribute clothing when we have it.

Imagine a pickup truck filled with these supplies, roaming the muddy roads from one village to another and from batey to batey, under the relentless sun or torrential rains. Sometimes you are chewing dust, and sometimes you have got mud even in your hair. The unanimous cry of these people never varies: "Only the Church has remembered us." The food we distribute to the population comes largely from you, who have helped us generously with your donations. Most of the funds raised in October on my trip to Spain are being converted into food for these people. We've also received food from the Dominican Cáritas and from some private donors here.

One of the most important lessons I've learned in this period was taught me by Mother Teresa's Missionaries of Charity. At the end of the day, few people are more expert than they are in the matter of aid to the poor. No sooner had the hurricane hit than everyone wanted to help the victims, but then enthusiasm quickly waned, making our current task more urgent than ever. Famine is now beginning, bringing with it malnutrition in the general population, diseases . . . Quite a few children have already died of things as simple as diarrhea. The crops have been destroyed, almost nobody has even a minimal steady income, and as the days go by the situation is becoming more and more unbearable for these people. Nor do we know how long the available resources will last or how long we can keep up this pace. From the moment we get up, at five in the morning, until the end of the day, we never stop for a minute. There are countless trips back and forth to Santo Domingo to get the food we need, or because we learn of a donation that we need to collect. We've provided the neediest people with building materials, things like sheets of zinc, nails, and lumber, so they can put a bit of roofing on their houses. We've also authorized them to take the remnants of the chapels that have collapsed so they can use them in repairing their houses.

Therefore, the most important assistance takes the form of money. Supplies are available here, but we don't have the economic means to meet the most basic needs. To give you an idea, some friends in the capital collected samples of the drinking water in the villages for analysis, and the laboratory results showed that the water was so filled with bacteria that it must have been polluted with feces. Money is the most urgently needed and useful aid for the people who are suffering so much.

We've also decided that we have to build chapels to replace the ones that have collapsed and also to build them in other villages that don't have them. The people need God before any other aid that the Church can offer them. Besides, the chapels or little churches would be the only buildings of brick and mortar that could serve for community meetings and children's catechism classes, and, of course, as a shelter for the population the next time a hurricane hits. I'll provide a detailed budget as soon as I can get in touch with the architects and engineers, so that everybody who wants to sponsor a chapel can do so.

We also need another all-terrain vehicle, a minibus, for the use of volunteer missionaries and the evangelists working with them in the same parish, so they can reach the remotest settlements. We are having many transportation problems in evangelizing and providing aid to these people. The young people and adults of the parish are extraordinarily enthusiastic about evangelization, especially in the Haitian bateyes, but we have great difficulty getting to the sites. To give you an idea of how eager they are, while I was still in Spain there was an occasion when, since they had no way of getting there, they asked for the garbage truck from the local government, cleaned it, and went out there in it!

On behalf of all these people, I offer you yet again our wholehearted thanks. You can't imagine what it's like to be in the trenches every day, alone in the mission, and realize that you have the backing of so many people who are praying for you, remembering your people, and wanting to share what they have with those who have nothing. Above all I pray to God that those who give do so for love of God, as a sign of their heartfelt conversion. That they deprive themselves of something, remembering that it is Jesus whom we are helping in the person of the poor. I don't care how much people give, urgent though the assistance is. What I truly care about, as a missionary priest, is that people, both here and there, find the love of Christ in their lives through the Church's mission.

Christmas after the hurricane

We've been so focused on distributing food and medicine that, without our realizing it, Christmas is upon us. The thought that this prompts in me is very simple. Because everybody here on this blessed island is poorer this year, surely we'll be granted a greater abundance and presence of God, who made himself a small child, fragile, needy, indigent, at the mercy of the avatars of history—and of climatology! Despite the hurricane, Christmas here won't be very different for children or adults from the Christmases of other years. Here they've never had Christmas presents or special feasts or celebrations. The lady who works in our house told me that when she was little, she believed in the Magi,[2] and her father told her on the night of January 5 to put

---

[2] In Hispanic culture, the Magi (the three kings, or wise men) correspond to Santa Claus, and Christmas gifts are usually given on Epiphany, January 6.—Trans.

her sandal in the doorway of the house, with those of her siblings. In the morning the sandals were empty, and their father would tell them that the Magi were poor this year and that maybe next year they would bring something for them. That happened every Christmas of her life. She never ever found a gift in her little sandal.

This child born in poverty is "the center of the universe and of history" (*Redemptor hominis*, no. 1). Jesus Christ, actually present in every poor person, continues to be the center of history; therefore, to be able to experience his rule, it's imperative that we welcome into our lives the values reflected in the Incarnation of the Word. It's essential that we return to read with simple eyes and innocent gaze the pages of Christ's infancy. He was unknown to all, persecuted, with nowhere to be born other than a manger, threatened with death from the first days of his life, rejected by almost everyone before he said even a single word, and he had to flee and live like a foreigner and refugee in Egypt. He was unknown even to his countrymen for most of his life.

Through the mystery of the Incarnation, God has effected a kind of union among all men (cf. *Gaudium et spes*), declaring his solidarity with the lot and destiny of every one of us. Thus, in a very real sense, we all become a part of the Body of Christ.

This couldn't be truer or more dramatic here in Los Llanos than it is during these days. In these poor people, Christ has lost everything. He has declared his solidarity with them by suffering in them and with them. These poor people, whom I've come to love so much, truly have nothing, absolutely nothing, and all the same I think about other people's Christmases, maybe your Christmases, the Christmases of those of you who've helped me so generously. Shouldn't we resolve to live Christmas in a more consistent, more evangelizing way? Aren't we perhaps responsible for the fate of our brothers? God-made-man is born in the poor hearts of all who want to receive him with love. To receive him with love means to receive him with love for men, our brothers. Our brothers in the Dominican Republic, Honduras, or Guatemala, or those whom we have every day right in front of our eyes, in our doorways, in our lives, if we but want to see them. This Christmas, why not resolve as a family to forgo all the profane folklore with which we've loaded up Christmas? Why not make a true Christmas present to the poor? Perhaps some of you write a Christmas list and send it to the Magi, and I, as father to the poor whom the Mother Church has confided to my care, also have a Christmas list for those poor children.

We need solar panels of 75 to 125 volts, to produce light and to pump water. We need water-purification plants, with a pump and a generator, because many villages have no water, or it's totally contaminated. We are trying to get a small truck to transport food, because the pickup trucks we have are quite inadequate. It would also be very helpful to have imperishable or preserved foods, because when we run out of food for the neediest people, we spend a great deal of money buying it in the capital, even though we haggle with the wholesalers.

My Christmas present

The Lord has given me, too, a present during this period just before Christmas. A few days ago we found our first leper in one of the bateyes to which we are bringing food and clothes. She is Haitian; the man she lived with died two months ago, and she's crowded into a tiny shack where a whole family with several small children is living. Nobody knows that she might have this disease. If they knew it, she would be cast out as though cursed by God. How many times Jesus approached lepers! How many times he identified with them!

For me, in this time of Christmas, the face of Jesus will evince an infinite variety, in kind and degree, of poverty, but Jesus will be born —he has been born already!—with the face of a leper. Jesus the leper.

With my most affectionate blessing, and assuring you of a very special prayer before the crèche and tabernacle of the mission,

Father Christopher

~

Not long after Hurricane Georges Father Christopher went to New York to meet with his bishop, Cardinal John O'Connor. In their meeting, the cardinal was very interested in Father Christopher's work in the mission, and especially in how things stood in the aftermath of Georges. Regarding the subject that they were there to discuss, the cardinal asked the missionary what he wanted to do, return or stay there, and the father had a clear answer. He couldn't leave, especially not at this moment of extreme necessity in which the hurricane had left the island, so they agreed on another trial year and another meeting between them in twelve months.

In just one year almost a thousand people had been baptized in the parish of San José, and they had also had confirmations, first Communions, and marriages. Many had been catechized in subjects that ranged from such basic matters as who Jesus is and making the sign of the cross, to training to administer Communion. A dining hall for poor children had been established, summer camps had been organized, and the groundwork had been laid for the construction of as many chapels as possible. With the help of his contacts in Spain, the father had established a foundation through which it was very simple to make donations. All this work was carried out at the same time that he was going out into the Haitian bateyes of the private sugar industry, getting to know the people there, working with them. The father had the choice of looking the other way or playing a role in what had to be done, and as he had explained in his letter, his vocation of service and dedication to the Church was indivisible.

Let the Canefields Proclaim the
Glory of the Risen One

Looking ahead now from the beginning of Father Christopher's second year in the mission at Los Llanos, we will be covering all of 1999 in just three letters. In them we will be able to examine the maturing of the missionary as he moves from learning about the problems in the mission to suffering through them together with his parishioners. The work increases this year, the experiences overlap, and what with one thing and another, it is evident that the father's happy enthusiasm dims somewhat from one letter to the next.

The year 1999 is brimming with good news and positive experiences, but above all it is purified in the fire that tested the father's resistance, his ability to navigate a course shaped more by conflict than by necessity.

The first symptom is that he wrote only three letters, half the number that he wrote in his first year. And each of them is shorter than its predecessor, as though his desire to write them diminished with each passing letter. Perhaps the father does not have time to write down his experiences, or he finds them uninteresting; or perhaps bad experiences begin to take up more time than good ones, and he is reluctant to recount them.

The father who came to San José de los Llanos like a hurricane, and decided to stay though he could have left, began to show signs of being diminished, as shown by the fact that each letter is tinged with evident sadness, and with anger over the injustices he sees all around him. He continues to see God in everything, but perhaps more with the eyes of the apostle of Holy Thursday, with doubts and questions, than of Palm Sunday, elated by his arrival in Jerusalem. He looks around him at so much suffering, searching for hope, and he finds it in small details and incidents.

None of this prevents the parish from reaching cruising speed by the end of the year. With the support of an enormous number of collaborators, catechists, and backers, the Liturgy of the Hours is prayed, mornings and evenings, in many little campos and bateyes in the parish. Every Sunday, after celebrating Mass, a team of properly trained extraordinary eucharistic ministers line up to bring Holy Communion to the sick and the handicapped in their communities. Adoration of the Blessed Sacrament is held every Friday, and the catechists for baptism, first Communion, confirmation, and marriage roam the nearly six hundred square miles of the parish of San José de los Llanos, proclaiming the gospel to the poor, the workers, the mothers, the married or separated couples, the orphans, the starving, the naked, the addicted . . .

Every hamlet and batey knows, weeks in advance, where Father Christopher will celebrate Mass every evening. When he arrives at the place whose turn it is, they have everything ready: the altar, the altar cloth, the corporals, the missal. The congregation gathers in the chapel, if there is one, and if not, in the shade of a coconut or mango tree. Rain or shine, not a day goes by on which he does not celebrate Mass in those campos and bateyes in the parish, in many of which Mass had never been celebrated before.

Baptisms are performed at an impressive rate. The father's helpers maintain the register to perfection. The preparatory formation is a kind of juggling act of catechization, because coordinating the meetings among parents, godparents, and godchildren is no exercise for the faint of heart.

The volunteers in the parish are ordinary people, laypeople with families and jobs, who decide to help the father in his pastoral tasks. Most of them, even though they are from San José de los Llanos, are completely unaware of the situation of the Haitians in the bateyes. Their ignorance reveals the isolation in which these people lived, enclosed in a kind of open prison where the most important guard is fear —a horrible fear of doing anything except cutting cane and following the rules of the game. They were Haitians, and the script of their lives called only for cutting cane for a pittance and living in unspeakable conditions. And so their lives unfolded day after day, generation after generation, in an endless loop about which their neighbors in San José had not the slightest idea. This next letter is written during Lent, a perfect time to catechize about the liturgical season of the Church through the specific situation of those campos and canefields. The missionary perspective shines a different light on this prelude to Holy Week.

Perhaps the priest's daily work and routine have gradually left surprise and novelty behind, but he did not stop marveling at the blessings bestowed by God around him, to which he was a privileged but somewhat imperfect witness. The lesson taught by this period is that wherever the Church makes her presence felt, with all the defects in her members that come with it, life opens the way to concrete, though not necessarily material, results. Material results, when all was said and done, would be the collateral benefits of evangelization, and what the father teaches us in his letters is how, wherever a missionary raises his flag, life becomes more civilized, structured, edifying, organized, ordered . . . But those benefits are still collateral, as the first and most important place belongs to the invaluable benefit of evangelization. Anyone who hears and accepts the story of Redemption finds that Christ changes his life from black and white to color, from night to day. In Christ, God is made one of us; the seeming senselessness of suffering acquires value, and injustice is compensated with justice. Christ does not banish pain, but he does endow it with hope, which is impossible without him. What is awaiting us after death if there is no Resurrection?

That is why these poor people, theretofore untouched by gospel, convert and are baptized. They do so because somebody has told them that their lives do not end with their earthly existence, but rather will go on after death in another form—in the person of Christ crucified and risen. This belief they have harbored in their hearts always. Perhaps the father takes the occasion of Lent in Los Llanos to remind us, men of the West, of the blessing we have in Christianity and have been losing, for whatever reason, in various corners of our lives.

This Lent is also a time of ripening for a friendship and partnership that will become critically important from the year 2000 onward. Noemí Méndez continues to work with the father this year, more and more closely, in the legal matters involving the Haitians in the bateyes. There will be a story this year about the father's kidnapping two children. In this and thousands of other instances, on occasion at the most inopportune times, the lawyer will receive an unexpected call from the father that requires her to come to grips with an enormously complex and difficult situation.

The father often follows his heart more than his head, but that is why the lawyer Méndez is there for him. And on no small number of occasions, such as the one about the kidnapping, things turn out well.

In this next letter the father tells us, too, about the most recent events in Gautier, the batey in which there had been only five Catholic women and that has taken giant steps that have turned it into the bastion of the parish.

These three letters from 1999 trace a passage in the life of our missionary from Palm Sunday to Holy Thursday, the forerunner of the passion and death of his mission, a period that will begin in January 2000 and end with Father Christopher's departure from the country in October 2006.

～

"Be mindful of your compassion, O Lord,
and of your merciful love, for they have
been from of old." — Psalms 25:6

Dear friends of the mission:

Lent has begun here, too. Throughout these campos and bateyes the ashes and the broken hearts show that something new is being born, in the same way that the cane has miraculously begun to grow again after the hurricane. Through very humble, almost imperceptible signs, God the Father wants to prepare us for the sacrifice of his Son in the Golgotha of the redemptive Passion.

Wherever you may be when you read this letter, it may occur to you, as it does to me, that the evil in the world sometimes makes it seem as though the Cross had accomplished nothing. We look around us and ask ourselves if this was God's plan for mankind, for the Church, on the threshold of the third millennium.

This holy time invites us to bring to fruition our baptismal faith, whose promises we'll renew during the Easter Vigil. We are called to examine our theological virtue of hope. In what or in whom have I placed my hope? It wouldn't hurt any of us to undertake a soul-searching examination of the hope we had at our conversion, our hope of attaining the holiness to which the Father has called us. Do I truly believe that I'm called, here and now, to holiness? Am I capable of seeing every person as he's seen by God, who created him to be holy? Whether we believe or don't believe that we've been called to holiness, whether we believe or don't believe that every passing person is called to holiness, is fundamental to whether the redemptive cross of Christ, rather than remaining a barren branch, will become a fertile tree that bears the fruit of eternal life.

Water and more water!

The need for water was already a genuine problem for these poor lands, but it became a true nightmare after the hurricane. Those among you who've read previous letters will perhaps remember that from the start we've spoken of the tragedy caused by the scarcity of drinking water. The hurricane, because it flattened the windmills that brought the water up out of the ground, aggravated the problem to the point of intolerability. It was so sad to see the multitude of children, young people, and adults carrying buckets of water for miles and miles. In particular, the campo of El Manguito took in people from ten communities, from dawn to dusk. A group of friends who came from Santo Domingo to see the situation for themselves took a sample of the water from Manguito's well to be analyzed in a laboratory, which showed that, because of the bacteria it contained, it was more of an aquarium than a well.

Through a series of providential contacts, I was able to get an interview with the executive director of INAPA (National Institute of Potable Water and Sewers), which is the government office for anything relating to water in the whole country. He promised us that he would send a team of engineers to evaluate the situation. I was able to accompany them on their visits to the different campos and bateyes. To my great surprise, they said to me: "Father, the orders we have from our director are that you take us to every community that needs a water well, that you make a list for us of all the wells you want, because it's been decided that we will remove all the windmills and install submersible pumps, an electric generator, and a tank for fifteen hundred gallons of water in every campo." I couldn't contain my happiness!

INAPA's investment in the campos and bateyes of our parish will amount to five million pesos. About a dozen wells have been completed, and they are working on the rest of the thirty-five that they are going to install.

You cannot imagine the happiness of the people at the prospect of having well water in their own communities!

"He began to send them out two by two."

During the Ash Wednesday Mass, as Jesus did in sending his first disciples out to evangelize, we undertook a great mission for the whole town of Los Llanos. The parish council designated the evangelization of the town as a priority objective for this liturgical season and solicited volunteers for it in the Sunday Masses leading up to it. Sixty volunteers, young people and adults, stepped forward.

There was a coordinating team that took charge of dividing the town into neighborhoods and streets. Every pair of volunteers was assigned a sector and, when the Eucharist was over, they were sent out two by two. The goal is to turn Lent into a large mission. They'll spend the first two weeks visiting every house in town with a syllabus of evangelization, a little catechesis with every family, making a note of the sacraments that each member needs, and an invitation to become part of a community. The third week will coincide with a novena to Saint Joseph, the patron saint of our parish, in which we have a different priest for every night with a set theme. The new communities will thus be established. We've already established five communities in the town. People from the same neighborhood meet every Thursday night with their own leader, and a series of parallel conversations are carried on in all of them. We pray that five more of the more marginalized neighborhoods will emerge as a result of the mission.

The mission will end with an act of penitence on the Friday before Palm Sunday, for which we are counting on priests in the surrounding area to help us hear confessions, as we expect there will be a great many who will benefit from that sacrament. I ask you to commend this mission in your prayers and sacrifices.

"Let us walk." [1]

With these words of Saint Teresa of Jesus we announced to the whole parish that, as a result of the great parochial mission, we are going to repeat last year's pilgrimage to the sanctuary of the Christ of Bayaguana. Recalling the great pilgrimage of the people of Israel through the immense desert to the promised land, we too want to make this ascetic practice a part of our Lenten mission. As you'll remember from earlier letters, we made the pilgrimage last year, and, by popular demand, we want to repeat it this year. The parish of El Puerto will join us, led by Father Antonio, and we'll celebrate the Holy Mass together when we arrive in Bayaguana.

---

[1] Teresa of Avila, "On the Way to Heaven" and "Embracing the Cross" in *Collected Works*, trans. Kieran Kavanaugh, O.C.D., and Otilio Rodríguez, O.C.D., vol. 3 (Washington, D.C.: ICS Publications, 1985).

God has given me two children

As you'll remember, a product of last year's mission was the establishment in the bateyes of a group of thirty evangelists to work faithfully on Wednesdays and Fridays. In one of the bateyes, the evangelists found an abandoned nine-year-old boy who was living alone with his stepfather. He wasn't being fed, he was being beaten to a pulp, and he was dressed in rags. Out of pity, the neighbors—who were destitute themselves—were giving him what they could spare from their own very meager food. They repeatedly insisted that I go to the batey of Contador to see him.

I finally went, and when they brought him to me, he said simply: "Take me with you." I didn't think twice. I put him in the van and brought him to Los Llanos.

The next morning, they advised me that there was a little girl in identical circumstances living in the batey of Paloma. The same story: a seven-year-old girl who was living with her father in similar misery and neglect. Her mother had died.

So, again without thinking twice, I brought her to the parish. This was another occasion on which I could see the greatness of the poor. I had only to ask one humble family in Los Llanos to take in the girl and another one to take in the boy, and they were welcomed immediately in both homes. There's always room in the house of the poor for one more child, food for one more child, love for one more child.

The next day I called the lawyer for the diocese to tell her, among other things, that I had brought two children out of the bateyes. She was stunned into silence, and then she said, "Father, under Dominican law you've just abducted two children." To this I replied, "I don't care. Tell me what I have to do, because these children are not going back to the bateyes."

The next day we went to the Palace of Justice in San Pedro and presented the case to the judge, who simply told me that he trusted me, that I should look for two responsible families, and that he granted me custody of the children.

As I said at the outset, I have two children: Alberto and Marina. We hope to baptize them at the Easter Vigil.

My greatest happiness

Gautier. When you go from Santo Domingo to Los Llanos, Gautier is the first town you come to. I've told you many times about this community and ought to continue doing so, because it continues to bear extraordinary fruit.

Gautier is the biggest town in the parish after Los Llanos itself. It has a population of three thousand, it's constantly growing, and it was completely abandoned by the Catholic Church for many years. Until I arrived it had been more than ten years since the Holy Mass, or any of the other sacraments, had been celebrated regularly.

We started building the church at the beginning of February. When we began we didn't have a penny for it. We hope it will be a big, beautiful church. It will have a seating capacity of three hundred. Think about how, when I celebrated the first Mass at the end of 1997, there were only five women there who were still practicing their faith. Now we have more than a hundred people who come to Mass on the first Sunday of every month. To me, it's simply a miracle. I don't have any other word for it. Besides the church, we are building a little house for when we will need to house a priest or a group of evangelists. We do not at this point have even a quarter of the funds we need, which is why I ask all of you to make in this Lent of 1999 a much greater effort to help us complete this project. If we get the funds, we expect to complete it by the end of May. I have not turned to any international organization because I want it to be your charity that, brick by brick, raises up the house of the Lord. I've also asked friends here in the Dominican Republic who are willing to lend a hand. For starters, the engineer who is managing the work is doing it completely free.

It's impossible for me to describe the people's happiness. It fulfills the psalm: "May those who sow in tears reap with shouts of joy!" (Ps 126:5). We wanted to give Jesus "living building blocks" before beginning construction, so the day before we started, the first Sunday in February, we had first Communions of children, nineteen in this case, for the first time in many years. They took place on the same plot of land on which work on the church began the next day.

Moreover, as if all that weren't enough, it's now the laypeople of Gautier who are going out to evangelize in the bateyes and the campos around them. I went with several ladies to visit some new bateyes. I say *new* because I just found them, and no one had ever in his life seen a priest, a Mass, a catechism, or a baptism there. We promised to send them a group of evangelists every Thursday. To my great joy, last Thursday there were eleven adults and young people who walked for an hour along a road through the cane to get to the batey. It was such a success that, from next week on, I'll send them one of the vans so the whole team can go.

Many of you have asked about the name of this new church. I want to dedicate it to the Blessed Virgin Mary as a sign of our love for her, the star of evangelization and Queen of the Americas. It will be called Saint Mary, Mother of Mercy. I owe her everything that I am, and the gifts of my Christian life and my priesthood. I've consecrated my life and humble apostolic efforts to her ever since I arrived at the mission of Los Llanos.

The truck

Thanks to some of my brother's wonderful friends, we are awaiting the arrival of a truck with four-wheel drive and a fourteen-foot bed. We need it urgently, because it's indispensable for the many projects we have going. And we have a second need for it—to transport the evangelists to the remotest corners of the mission, for which we'll convert it into a passenger vehicle. That's why it has to be a four-wheel-drive vehicle. After a lot of research, I've found out that four-wheel-drive buses don't exist, so I've thought that the truck could sometimes serve as a bus for the missionaries. The ones who were here last summer know that, given our numbers, there was no way for everybody to fit, and many of them came and went hanging off the truck and covered with mud.

Again with all my heart, to all of you who are trying to find the funds that we need for the truck: a thousand thanks! God bless you.

The Mission of Mercy Foundation

Since the end of last summer we've been working to establish a legal framework for many of the activities that we're engaged in to further the mission of Los Llanos. To that end, there's a group that's organizing the establishment of a foundation. It's a very simple structure that will channel material assistance and staff in support of the mission. It will be called the Mission of Mercy Foundation. The most important thing is that we're hoping it will unleash a movement of all sorts of people in all kinds of circumstances who'll feel called, as an act of spirituality, to dedicate themselves to participating in the mission. Many people won't be able to come here, of course—at least not more than once—but there's a very great deal that you can do to help. You'll be the first to benefit.

In that sense, it's very important to stress that we need more than economic support, and that the Foundation is meant to be a meeting place of prayer and sacrifice for the mission. The Foundation can help us all discover that vocation and baptismal spirituality are essentially missionary. All of us can do ourselves immense good by committing ourselves to the mission, because, although we may never go to visit missions, it will help us live our call to holiness with a truly missionary consciousness.

The missionaries

I would like to urge everybody who is considering coming here during the summer not to be discouraged by the difficulties you may encounter. There's no substitute for enthusiasm. We have to motivate each other. We may know others who are interested and whom Jesus is inviting to be, with him, "fishers of men". I hope we may come together in Madrid at the end of May, all of us who are going to participate this summer in the mission of Los Llanos, on a retreat that will help us get to know each other, understand each other, and join together to pray for each other.

"And I will give you shepherds . . ."

With these words from the book of the prophet Jeremiah (3:15) I'm announcing to you a great joy. Since the end of November we've been four priests from Toledo instead of two, now that Don Francisco, the archbishop of Toledo, has authorized Fathers José María Cabrero and José Zarco, two very good friends of ours and fellow students at the seminary, to come work in our Diocese of San Pedro.

They were originally assigned to Cuba, but because their visas were delayed, we asked that they come to work with us instead of waiting for their visa in Toledo. Our bishop here has immediately assigned them both to two huge parishes that were unattended because of the shortage of clergy. The city of San Pedro has well over two hundred thousand inhabitants, and until these two arrived it had only three priests besides the bishop.

The four of us meet weekly, which is of very great benefit to us. We confess to each other, pray together, celebrate the Holy Mass together, and exchange experiences. These two priests are a wonderful gift to this part of God's people, and may he will that they stay a long time among us. I told you in my first letter that what we most need here in the mission can't be bought with all the gold in the world, because we needed priests more than anything else. Continue to pray for this intention: we still need many more. I myself urgently need one for this parish.

Lent, begging God's forgiveness

There's no doubt that Lent is a very special time of grace between God the Father, who searches for man, for every man, and the man who allows himself to be pierced by the arrow of his wounded love. This period helps us live what Saint Teresa of Jesus asked of her novices: "I am not asking you to do anything more than to look at him."[2] I make so bold as to ask of you simply that: that you behold Christ in the poor. That you look upon every poor person with the same gaze and tenderness with which God the Father looks upon him, contemplating the disfigured face of his own crucified Son. I ask you to have the maternal heart of the Blessed Virgin Mary. To ask yourselves, what will the Virgin think when she sees the suffering of the poor? What will she feel in her maternal heart?

The pope has highlighted this in his Lenten Message, with a truly dramatic cry. He has said that there is no place at the tables of the rich

---

[2] Teresa of Avila, *The Way of Perfection: A Study Edition*, trans. Kieran Kavanaugh, O.C.D., and Otilio Rodríguez, O.C.D., (Washington, D.C.: ICS Publications, 2000).

for so many of today's Lazaruses who have nothing. In the name of the poor, abandoned Christ, I ask you not to spend more on yourselves than is strictly necessary, so you can give to others that which we do not own but rather of which we are custodians, and thus for which we will all be called to strict account.

You see, poverty is horrible. The misery of these people and of whole sectors of mankind is unacceptable. Neither you nor I have the magic formula for its eradication. Let's not waste time theorizing about the virtues and imperfections of market economics and collectivism. That, my friends, may have circumstantially eased somebody's troubled conscience, or filled a few hours of comfortable discussion after a sumptuous dinner, but it has never put food on anybody's table or solved anything.

The evil lies in man's selfishness, in his inability to allow the baptism we have all received to make us such that we "may all be one" (Jn 17:21), as Jesus asked the night before he died for love of us. But explain to me how a person of average goodwill can believe that we Christians think that in the Church we all are one, when some of us feast in splendor while others die of hunger, often working for employers who presume to call themselves Catholics!

"We thought you wouldn't come back anymore"

If some naïve reader of these letters thinks that the missionary work of the Catholic Church in San José de los Llanos goes from crest to crest and success to success, let me tell you that nothing could be further from the truth. Here is quite a sad example, and it is what gives this section its title.

One of the many Haitian bateyes in our care is called Sabana Tosa. It comes from *sabana*, without an accent mark, like the savannas of Africa, and from Tosa, the name of a river that passes nearby. Well, it had been some time since I had been there. I recently was able to go there, and I learned that practically the whole batey had become "evangelicals"—"converts" is what they call them here—and when I asked why, this was the simple and emphatic explanation they gave me: "Because we thought you wouldn't come back anymore. It had been a long time since you came to give us Mass and baptize, and these 'brothers' come all the time and bring us things." They were right. I had been away for a good while, and they had the right to complain about me. I know that the reason I stopped going was not that I didn't want to or was lazy. I hadn't gone because with the little love I still have to spare, my body couldn't do more. My conclusion is simple: I need help not only in the form of financial support but also in the form of people, laypeople who want to come and evangelize, not just for a month or two in the summer, but for a longer time.

I've learned that being a missionary is being in the trenches. Just as a starving man cannot wait until morning to eat, because he's hungry today, people also hunger for God and for the truth revealed in the Gospels, and they can't wait until tomorrow. If the priest, the Catholic Church, doesn't come today, maybe tomorrow it will be too late for they will be taken away by the sects, which I call "soul thieves" and also "faith merchants", because they are literally buyers, offering these people food on the condition that they come regularly to their services.

My last request is that you pray very hard for the Lord to move the heart of some priest to come work with me in this parish. It covers hundreds of square miles: San José de los Llanos and sixty small villages, between campos and bateyes.

All of us are making our way together across the desert of Lent; we are one in this pilgrimage of faith and grace. Let's pray intensely for each other, so that on Easter Eve, the mother of all vigils, we may together renew the promises of our baptism and sing and proclaim together around the paschal candle: "The Lord has risen indeed. Alleluia!" Together with all the saints may we celebrate with Mary: "Be glad and rejoice, O Virgin Mary, for the Lord has risen indeed. Alleluia!"

I assure you, as always, of my prayers and a very special remembrance before the tabernacle of the mission.

Father Christopher

How Beautiful Are the Feet of Those Who Preach Good News!

There is no news from the father from Lent to September 1999. To find out more about his comings and goings during this period, we met in San Pedro de Macorís with Reina, a Dominican woman who, through her marriage to a man from Salamanca, is familiar with the Spanish character, and who decided to work with Father Christopher in a new mission: a prison pastorate at the penitentiary in San Pedro de Macorís, which in 1997 had a capacity of some six hundred inmates.

The father began his periodic visits to the convicts at the beginning of the year, and Reina joined the group of volunteers who accompanied him. According to her, the prison was ruled at the time by the law of the jungle. Corruption was the order of the day, there were daily beatings, and there were as many crimes committed inside the prison walls as there were outside.

The work of the penitentiary's pastoral team was to evangelize in the prison. The father celebrated Mass and heard the confession of anybody who wanted, and his presence in the prison wrought quite a revolution. First, in form: when he arrived he started to play baseball with the prisoners. He talked to them as though he were one of them. He was not afraid of them, but rather had a profound respect and compassion for their past history, no matter what it was. Murderers, rapists, drug dealers, and robbers were Father Hartley's friends on Saturday mornings.

Second, he set right many conditions that had become the norm even though they were unjust, no matter how you looked at them. The father confronted the prison authorities quite a few times. Though in most cases he was right to do so, in others he acted out of pure pigheadedness, as, for example, when they changed the gate designated for gaining access to the prison and he insisted on bringing in his all-terrain vehicle by the old one, thinking that what they wanted was to keep him from entering at all. The chief guard and warden had to be called, and in the end they let him come in through the unauthorized gate, though for the last time. From then on he followed the rules.

Third, the father's presence was for many prisoners an inner revolution, the end of a punishment much more significant than the one symbolized by the bars and the walls of that notorious prison. Forgiveness, hope, love. Reina tells us that "the father reached these people in his homilies, knew how to speak their language, knew where they were coming from. He brought Christ home to their hearts. Many of them burst into tears when they asked for confession, like the man who had killed his brother. He had had an awful childhood, full of violence and pain, and nobody had ever offered him a word of hope or love before. The father gave it to him through the gospel, telling him the story of Christ, and the man repented of what he'd done. He stayed in prison, but the father freed him of his hatred."

His helpfulness to the prisoners earned the father the antipathy of quite a few prison guards. In fact, on one occasion when he celebrated Mass, a lieutenant sat down to listen to everything he said, disrespectfully, to provoke the father and see if he could get a reaction from him. The father realized it, and, although his blood boiled at the guard's lack of respect, he kept on celebrating the Mass without paying any attention. When he finished, dressed in his alb and stole, he read the lieutenant the riot act.

Another time the father was with his team of volunteers when a truck full of people pulled up at the door of the "slammer". They had been arrested on the orders of somebody who was very powerful. They were workers in a quarry, extracting stone for a private project of this person, who, in order not to pay them the wage he owed them, asked the army to raid them on the grounds that they were undocumented. By pulling strings, he got them arrested. That is how things worked.

When the father saw the truck and learned what was going on, Reina says, he furiously and loudly ordered the detainees not to get off the truck, while the soldiers, of which there were many, tried to get control of a situation that had gotten out of hand.

The father was glued to the telephone for hours that Saturday, facing a truck that was filled with workers who had been unjustly arrested. What the father feared was that, once they entered the prison, anything could happen to these unfortunate men, who should never have been arrested.

He secured their release after hours of negotiations, and he did not go home until the last of the detainees had left. Reina tells us that she had rarely seen anybody so angry as the father was during the incident with the truck. Asked why she thinks he acted that way, Reina has a clear, ready answer: "He lives his priesthood to the utmost. He doesn't control himself when there's an innocent person, a poor person, who's being treated unjustly. I remember that once a young fellow came out of the prison. He'd been there for murder, but he had nowhere to go, and the father took him home. He slept there, a complete unknown, a killer. The fellow had been in prison for several years and, once he was free, didn't know what to do with his freedom. So the father brought him home and later gave him money for a bus ticket."

Another time, somebody warned him not to spend much time with prisoners because they were dangerous criminals, to which the father replied in front of everybody: "Here, playing baseball with them, I'm as safe as I can be." Then he pulled down his cap and resumed his batting stance, as though the courtyard he was in, ringed with walls and barbed wire, had been a school playground.

Where did this way of looking at life, and this behavior, come from? "They came from God," Reina tells us, "from outside him. And he doesn't do it to get attention. What happens is that he does get attention. It's impossible for it to go unnoticed when you take a murderer to your house or when you put in his place a guard who gets carried away. Nobody throws himself into it that way out of self-interest. It's an enormous vocation combined with a very strong character."

Reina wants to testify to what she learned from her days working with the father: "He taught us to be unafraid, that when you involve Christ in whatever you may be doing, you need not be afraid. The father reminded us that you needn't fear anything that might kill your body, and that with Christ the soul lives forever. He wasn't afraid of anybody, which is why he called out the guards and rebelled against injustice: he knew that Truth was on his side. He's left the country, but the most important thing is that he left behind a seed that has borne a good deal of fruit in the hearts of these poor people."

It was a fundamental rule of the penitentiary pastorate never to take any material thing to the prisoners. Not even food or clothing. That

was how the father avoided having people come to Mass to get something. When he finished his prison pastorate, a chapel had been built
there that is still standing today, a great many prisoners had been baptized, and a prayer group had been organized for the days that he was
not there. But it is better to leave to his letter of September 1999 the
description of how the father lived during this period of the mission
of Los Llanos.

∼

Dear friends of the mission:

I'm getting in touch with you once again to share the wonders that God the Father is working among his people. So great are the goodness and mercy he grants us that I barely know where to begin. Perhaps the best way would be to resume this chronicle of the mission where the last letter ended.

Holy Week

One clear sign of the spiritual growth of the parish and the growing commitment of our evangelists is that this year we were able to reach even the farthest corners of the parish in these three holy days. The extraordinary ministers of Communion in each of our parish communities were authorized to take the ciborium with the Holy Eucharist. Each community was assigned a specific number of campos. It was their responsibility to organize the celebrations of the Holy Triduum.

It was beautiful to see them leaving every afternoon in their vans, with rain, with mud, with the relentless sun of the Caribbean, ready to take Christ to all the souls, especially to the most distant ones. The people responded in masses, a true festival of faith. That's the heart of my vocation and mission for this land: that all of them experience Christ and his infinite love for men. All the rest is incidental, important only to the extent that it helps the men, our brothers, receive Christ and his saving power in their lives.

The prison

This is the new mission that my bishop has entrusted to me: to coordinate the penitentiary pastorate in the diocese, especially in the military prison of San Pedro de Macorís, popularly known as La México, after the name of the neighborhood where it's located. It's a dreadful spectacle, where no priest has set foot in years. The Protestants, however, are involved there at all hours.

I announced in a Sunday Mass in Los Llanos that the bishop had assigned this new task to me and that I needed volunteers to help me in the evangelization of these brothers. Imagine my surprise when no fewer than thirty lay members of the congregation stepped forward and made themselves available to come with me every Saturday morning. When the eight o'clock morning Mass ends, they are all in the doorway of my house, with their Bibles, their song books, and their rosaries, ready to climb into the vans. You have never seen a happier or more smiling team than these people. They give the impression that they are going to spend the day in the country, rather than in a prison. On the way there we pray the Rosary and sing, and on the way home we share the events of the day that we have lived with the prisoners. It's a real pleasure to live the faith with a group of brothers who truly carry God in their hearts.

The prison is a revolting place. It bears no more than a coincidental resemblance to the prisons that we might have seen in our country. It looks more like a pigsty. Almost six hundred fifty half-naked prisoners, spread among modules of fifty each. Many of them do not have beds in their cells, or even standing room, and they spend their days without running water. Only 5 percent have been sentenced, with the rest being in preventive detention.

This means that many have spent years there, have not even been tried, and do not have a lawyer. They hold them as though they didn't exist. They do absolutely nothing all day long except stay there behind bars, watching life go by in idleness, forgotten by everyone, stewing in hatred and resentment, and totally dehumanized. They take them out to the sunlight a half hour per day, and the other twenty-three and a half hours they are kept inside doing nothing, wasting their lives.

We didn't begin visiting them until seven months ago, but we've developed an immense affection for them. We know every one of them by name. The soldiers trust us very much, and I walk around among them as if I were at home. When we are a quarter mile away and they see us coming, they all begin to shout from their modules, "Father, Father, today's your turn to be with us." For now, we do not bring them many material things, in order to keep it clear that our mission is one of evangelization. But if we can do something to improve their living conditions, we are obviously delighted to do it.

We've already taken some steps in that direction. There's a team of lawyers supported by the Conference of the Dominican Episcopate who have begun to offer free legal advice to those who cannot afford to pay a lawyer.

The summer mission

We've been blessed again this year to have among us a big group of lay missionaries, who in July and August have given the best of themselves, moved by their love of God and their fellow men, their brothers. Over those two months there were sixty missionaries who, together with the volunteers from the parish, went out along the roads and paths, mornings and afternoons, in search of the neediest souls.

Don Juan Esquerda Bifet

It was a delight and truly an enormous gift from heaven to have a great priest with the whole July group of missionaries, both of El Puerto and of Los Llanos. Don Juan Esquerda Bifet gave us talks and days of retreat and shared with us some unforgettable days of mission work. He came from Rome, the true heart of the Church, where he has given the best efforts of his priesthood to encouraging missionary work throughout the world. His presence among us served to confirm us in the faith and motivate us to keep giving the best of ourselves for the glory of the Lord. Thank you, Don Juan!

Camps

We've had four summer camps for a total of a thousand children and young people, who engaged in a great variety of activities: catechism classes, sports, journalism, poetry, preparation of the Sunday liturgy, puppets, and so forth. One of the most wonderful fruits of this activity has been the number of children and young people who've received the sacraments of baptism, first Communion, and confirmation. Specifically, we baptized more than four hundred children and young people in the two summer months.

The camps have also yielded a great number of adolescents and young adults of the parish who have engaged in these activities and have already committed themselves permanently to pastoral work. They're now totally available to continue volunteering in many other activities for the benefit of the neediest.

A mission with two headquarters

Last year's mission convinced me that the parish of San José de los Llanos is too big for all of the missionaries to be concentrated in just one place. We were spending as much time going to the various parts of the mission as we were spending with the people, so this year we decided to send a group of missionaries to live permanently in Gautier, seventeen miles from Los Llanos. Traveling those miles twice a day, round trip, meant more than sixty miles a day for the missionaries.

I drew an imaginary line around the area and assigned the missionaries thirteen campos and bateyes, in some of which we had never evangelized, celebrated the Holy Mass, and so on. These missionaries must have been the first people to bring the name and love of Christ to these most forgotten brothers. I am truly proud of the work accomplished by these evangelists. They have freely given a great deal, receiving nothing in exchange. They've given and dedicated themselves generously. They have withstood the broiling Caribbean heat, the torrential tropical rains, the dust and mud of the roads. They have lived day after day without electricity and running water, with a smile on their lips, without one complaint or the smallest protest.

These missionaries have been a word of love and peace in the middle of so much desolation and suffering. The risen Christ and the power of his redemptive cross have been made present with all their power where, until then, there was nothing but despair. Their presence has shown these people that God the Father has not forgotten them; that he nourishes and feeds them in their spiritual and material needs; that the Mother Church attends to them. These two months have truly seen an explosion of love in the middle of these immense canefields. My parish, thanks to God's glory, has been inundated with happiness. We can do no more than unite in the Magnificat of the Blessed Virgin for the extraordinary wonders that the good Lord has achieved through these humble helpers.

In agony, and in joy that runs over

I can find no other way to describe the experience we've been blessed with in the company of Marta in the batey of Copeyito. Both the July and August missionaries undertook with great dedication to relieve the pain and suffering of this Haitian woman. Let me tell you about her.

Marta is twenty-eight years old and has five children. She's paralyzed and stretched out on a miserable cot, abandoned by the last man she lived with. Her mother and some sisters live with all of them. They have no source of income at all. They live off the charity of neighbors and what the missionaries have been able to bring them. Marta's body is covered with sores and wounds; she's a human ruin. I met her some time ago. Some friends had gotten a wheelchair, but she can no longer sit in it. She doesn't have the strength to sit upright, and it exacerbates the pain of her sores. But here's the thing: the fundamental illness of this family is simply hunger, and this hunger is the cause of all their other misfortunes.

This year our missionaries include several doctors and medical students, who, with the help of others, visited Marta often, trying to relieve her pains, cure her wounds, and help the family with the food they need. They were working a miracle in Marta's house.

Thanks to their care and the missionaries' great love, Marta's body was healing bit by bit, but what was truly healing was her heart. We saw with our own eyes that love had given Marta a new heart, an inexpressible and uncontainable joy. A desire to live that imperceptibly transmitted itself to us, so that in the end we had the strange sensation that it was she who was giving us happiness with her smile and unearned gratitude. The missionaries nourished not only the bodies of Marta and her family, but also and especially their spirits. One missionary gave her a little missal so she could read the daily readings, with the Ten Commandments written in the missionary's own handwriting on the last page. Imagine her surprise when she came back the next day and found that Marta had memorized them.

The climax of the miracle came when we went to baptize and confirm Marta. Two missionaries served as her godparents, and there were many people there in her hut. It seemed impossible to me that there should be so much happiness in a face that was so deeply worn by the traces of Christ's Passion. The missionaries had dressed her in a new dress and given her clean sheets. We were all deeply moved, and I'm sure that at that moment the very angels were crying in heaven.

I simply marvel at what love, the charity of these missionaries, can do. We had found Christ in Marta, face-to-face, and it is this encounter with Christ—in whatever guise—that is always so transformative. May God will that the face of this blessed woman, whose days in this world can't be many, internally transform all of us who have the undeserved privilege of knowing her.

Witness to the impossible

Never have so few been able to accomplish so much. What the missionaries in Gautier were able to achieve in this mission was truly extraordinary. This batey of Gautier, which two years ago received me with five women for the first Mass that had been celebrated there in ten years, has now overflowed with generosity for the Lord. They had a summer camp that ended with a fantastic field trip by the children to the aquarium and various places in the capital. As in the previous year, for many children it was the first time they had been up or down stairs, crossed a bridge, or seen the sea. They learned about all sorts of things in the camp, and, with the help of the missionaries, the number of volunteers in Gautier has grown enormously.

It was such a success that the pastors of the evangelical sects were indignant. They first tried to start their own camp and boycott ours, but after the resounding failure they had when not a single child attended their camp, they came to ask us to join our efforts with theirs. Even the children of the Protestant pastors were coming to our camp behind their parents' backs!

They began the day praying Lauds at six thirty in the morning, and the number of attendees grew every day by leaps and bounds, to the point where, in a few days, they had to go outside and sit on the bricks, the boards, and the scaffolding of the construction project, because they no longer fit in the building. We organized a suitable place in the little house of the missionaries, and soon we were even able to put Jesus in the tabernacle, to live there for the first time in Gautier's history. Every morning, with the help of a seminarian, the Lord was displayed in the monstrance. The number of helpers kept growing until there were more than a hundred of them, who, with their psalters in hand, adored and praised the Lord.

Every day the missionaries went out into the campos and the bateyes on their assignment to evangelize door to door and to gather the children and adults to organize catechesis and classes in reading and writing. The people welcomed them very happily and awaited them with real eagerness, as the true presence of God among them. They prepared the adults and parents and godparents of the children for the sacrament of baptism, which had to be celebrated at the end of the mission in each of the campos.

It was a true blessing to have among us, living with the missionaries in Gautier, Father Francisco Barrionuevo, from the Diocese of Getafe. He spent the last two weeks of August with us. In anticipation of his arrival, the missionaries had already prepared people for the various sacraments.

During this time, mornings and afternoons, he celebrated baptisms and first Communions in all the campos. There were hundreds who received baptism at his hands. His presence as a priest was a very great blessing for all these people, many of whom had never attended Mass.

The bishop in Gautier

Twice we had our bishop with us in Gautier. The first time was a surprise visit to pray Lauds with the whole community and for adoration and benediction. Afterward he had breakfast with the missionaries. The second visit was the Sunday Mass. It was the first Mass celebrated by the bishop in the church in Gautier, which, although still under construction, was wonderfully decorated by young and old so that the three sacraments of Christian initiation could be administered to a large number of adults. Among them were six couples who celebrated the sacrament of marriage.

Monsignor Ozoria was awestruck by the work that had been done by the missionaries and the very enthusiastic response of the people, even hinting that, in the future, the church in Gautier could become a parish. God will tell.

It's impossible to recount everything that these intrepid missionaries accomplished. They did it all with the greatest love in the world and gave it their all, to the point of exhaustion. Let Christ Jesus be their only recompense, and let the grace of God multiply the seeds of the gospel that they have sown in this little corner of the Church with such love and generosity.

From the heart of the parish

Most of the missionaries were concentrated in Los Llanos. The group was so large that this year they had to be housed in three places: the boys in the parish dining hall, some of the girls in classrooms at the school that the secretary of education made available to us, and the other girls in the former parish house. The living conditions were quite primitive, but they all accepted them with great happiness.

I never imagined that we would be able to reach places in the parish that were so remote from Los Llanos. In the morning the truck and the pickup truck would deliver the missionaries and volunteers to nine Haitian bateyes. The distances were huge; the last ones took almost an hour to get to their mission and also were the first to begin the return trip. The people received them with immense happiness, especially because they knew some of them from when they had worked there the year before.

The missionaries and volunteers helped by giving first aid to many sick people and even transported them to the hospital when the seriousness of a patient's condition required it. They organized camps for the children among the Haitians and, above all, prepared a large group for the sacrament of baptism in each of the bateyes. They were able, moreover, to conduct a census of the most urgent needs in each batey, both material and spiritual, so they could be addressed later on.

Horrors emerged sometimes, when the missionaries and volunteers discovered terrible cases of abuse of minors.

Living among the poor

One of the innovations this year was that several of the missionaries went to live for a few days in the campos where they were evangelizing. It turned out to be a marvelous experience of living together in friendship with these poor people. The missionaries were able to experience the life of the poor and at the same time evangelize them "from within". It also enabled the missionaries to teach them to pray Lauds and Vespers every day. Imagine how happy it makes me, as the pastor of this immense parish, to know that every day there are brothers who gather to pray the Divine Office at six in the morning and six in the afternoon, in such places as Rinconada, La Jengibre, El Manguito, Mata Caliche, Gautier . . .

In the morning, the missionaries would gather the community together to teach them to pray the liturgy. After breakfast, with some volunteers from the little campo, they would go out to visit the sick in all the campos and bateyes, bringing with them a little portable medicine chest. They would dress wounds, look after the most urgent cases, and give them medicines that the sick could not buy. But above all, they would always evangelize in any way they could. The missionaries have filled even the remotest places in the parish with love. Wherever I go, the people ask after them by name. These young people will never know the good they've done and the love they've sown. May God himself be their recompense.

The great pilgrimage to Los Llanos

The culmination of all the work of these two months was a great pilgrimage from all the campos and bateyes to the parish church in San José de los Llanos. Each missionary organized the people in his campos and bateyes in such a way that, when they got going, they began to merge with one another.

In the end, more than a thousand people walked to Los Llanos. The communities there organized themselves to welcome the walkers with cold water, a plate of food, and, above all, the warmth of the love that unites us all in a single faith, in a single Church. It was a huge mass of brothers who joined together around Christ in the parish tabernacle. We had an afternoon of retreat, of thanksgiving to God for two wonderful months of evangelization, received from the hand of the Blessed Virgin Mary, Mother of Mercy. We wanted to lay at the feet of the Lord the humble efforts of all the evangelists. For this effort we invited our bishop Francisco Ozoria, and during the thanksgiving Mass almost a hundred young people received the sacrament of confirmation. We were so many that we had to bring recipients of the sacrament up to the presbytery and fill the church with many additional benches—and even then many had to follow the Mass through the window that looks out on the parish garden.

It's hard to express the happiness we all felt, the immense gratitude to God for so much love and goodness. Though it was true that the afternoon also left us with the bittersweet taste of saying good-bye to the missionaries, our eyes were fixed on the words of the song that was so beloved, and so often sung, by the missionaries of Los Llanos: "Nothing will separate us . . . nothing will separate us from God's love."

My greatest happiness

Let me repeat to you here what I said in my previous letter. We began the construction of the church in Gautier at the beginning of February. We got underway without having any funds at all for it. We hope it will be a large, beautiful church. It will have a seating capacity of three hundred. Many of you have asked the name of this new church. I want to dedicate it to the Blessed Virgin Mary as a demonstration of our love for her, the star of evangelization and Queen of the Americas. It will be called Saint Mary, Mother of Mercy. I owe to her everything I am, the gift of the Christian life, and the gift of my priesthood. It's to her that I've consecrated my life and the humble apostolic efforts I've made since I arrived at the mission in Los Llanos.

My final word is necessarily one of boundless gratitude to the Good Lord for the wonders he has allowed us to behold. And also of gratitude to so many people who've been of enormous help to us, with their support, prayer, sacrifices, donations . . . Our thanks go to many cloistered communities who, from their monastic silence, are the heartbeat of the Church. And to all those who have so promptly come to our aid on the many occasions when the well of our economic resources has run dry.

I assure you, as always, of a prayer and a very special remembrance before the tabernacle of the mission.

Father Christopher

The Story of Bubona: The Other Face of Christmas, on the Eve of the Year 2000

On the eve of Christmas 1999, Father Christopher began his last letter of that year. He had not written his benefactors since September, and this letter to them, which arrived in February, was his shortest so far. In it we see that the father is tired, annoyed, outraged. He is not the father of two years ago. He has matured, having learned how to translate in his head a situation that he thought was one of poverty into one of humanitarian conflict. But at the same time he is almost incapable of displaying in a letter any reason for happiness, except for a brief mention at the end of the letter of the progress in building the church at Gautier.

We can see how, in the missionary's evolution, an interesting circumstance emerges. Father Christopher had known poverty before he arrived in the Dominican Republic, from working with the Missionaries of Charity on the margins of society and in extreme deprivation. But the situation that he came to know in the bateyes was something else, and the father had never seen at such close range the divide between the rich and the poor, where men pay a pittance to workers living a wretched existence.

This situation is dangerous, because it can turn the priest and missionary into an overzealous social activist. The father sees, however, in the teachings of the Church, a demanding and authentic principle regarding workers' rights. These writings, if they had not been signed by the likes of Leo XIII or John Paul II, could have resembled workers' manifestos in Bolshevik Russia. But, above all, there are two extraordinary reasons that bring the father to develop a new dynamic. The first is the poor and the situation that generates their poverty. The second is the homily John Paul II gave in Valencia, on the day he ordained the father a priest together with 140 deacons from all over

Spain, in which he said: "Commit yourselves to all the just causes of the workers."

The father's mission is no longer driven by the delivery of sacks of food, such as are given out in the desert or after a natural disaster. It is driven by social justice, in the form of a demand on behalf of the poor that they receive what they have earned by their labor. In other words, the father did not go out looking for trouble; the trouble was there, right in front of him.

The tone of the letters therefore takes on a different shade, a different cadence, denouncing more than announcing; and yet, what we continue to hear in them is a cry torn from a suffering heart, which sometimes confuses us so that we cannot always recognize whether it is the cry of the poor, the cry of the father, or the cry of God himself that comes from the poor through the father. The following is the ninth letter from the mission, written in February 2000.

~

Dear friends of the mission:

We were on our way to the batey of Yabacao, where Haitians make up the overwhelming majority of the inhabitants. It's the last among a multitude of bateyes. Access to it is almost impossible because of the constant rains, but we reached it by chance one morning while we were conducting a little census in the surrounding bateyes. We happened upon a small house that was revolting, filthy. A good number of children were splashing around in the mud that surrounded the hut. They were wearing nothing but rags.

Suddenly, when we first appeared, we saw her there inside the hut. She was lying on the floor, completely naked. This is the appalling story of a woman, a mother, a family that was preparing—like the rest of mankind—to enter the year 2000 of the Redemption. I say *enter* because *celebrate* isn't the appropriate word in this case.

Her name is Bubona. She's thirty-four and has seven children, and she's epileptic. She was lying on the floor because she had suffered one of her frequent attacks and had fallen into the fire, burning her whole body and being scalded by the water boiling in a pot. We don't know how long she had been that way. Her whole body was an open wound and had suffered third-degree burns, and pieces of her skin were falling off.

Pedro, one of the missionaries who's with us for the whole of this year, picked her up with the help of other volunteers, wrapped her in a sheet, and set out on the endless and tortuous road back to Los Llanos, amid puddles, lakes of mud, numberless potholes, through an unending sea of cane.

They arrived with this poor woman at the small, rudimentary hospital in Los Llanos. When the surgeon saw her, he didn't think twice before taking her to the little room where he performs his operations. To call it an operating room would be a mockery of his noble profession. He amputated almost all her fingers, and the nurses applied dressings to the huge sores on the rest of her body. They admitted her to the hospital.

For several days we went to visit Bubona in the hospital, morning and afternoon. I was able to bring her Communion on those visits. Every day, she received Jesus, the Bread of Life, with great joy. Some of the evangelists in the town started visiting her regularly, helping to meet her needs, praying for her, and taking care of her seven children left in the batey.

So great was her change of heart that she began to get up and visit the patients in other rooms. Bubona prayed beautifully in Creole, and she started a true apostolate with the other Haitian patients. With the stumps of her fingers wrapped in bandages, and with the other wounds and burns on her body wrapped in gauze, she went from bed to bed, praying with the others, encouraging them, and talking about God's love.

One morning, when we went to visit her, we discovered that she wasn't in the hospital. We asked the nurses about her, and they told us that, the night before, she had had another attack of epilepsy and had dislocated her jaw. We looked for her in the hospitals of San Pedro de Macorís, until we found her. There she was, abandoned, supposedly discharged—that is, no one was doing anything for her. Her face was still disfigured, and the stumps of her fingerless hands were suppurating. She was a living Christ. She was the abandoned Christ. The only thing she asked was to be taken back to her revolting batey. The only thing she wanted was to be with her seven children and her husband. After we had prepared some sacks of food for her and the children, we took her there and, with a mournful heart, we left her in her batey again.

Brothers, Bubona is still there, in the batey of Yabacao. In a remote corner, lost in a vast sea of cane. A little hell on the threshold of the year 2000 of the Redemption. Bubona, her husband, their children, and the other Haitians who live in this miserable batey are also God's children. The Word was made flesh for them as well: Jesus Christ, of a Virgin Mother. Jesus wants to be born in Yabacao, too. Would it be very different from the manger in Bethlehem, a stable of animals, where the Son of God was born for the first time? Perhaps today God the Father would choose the misery of the batey of Yabacao to bring his Son into the world.

Do you know? It is an honor for me, a priest, to live with and share in the pain, the cross, the exhaustion, the humiliations, the illnesses, the hardship, the discrimination. I'm their father; they're my children. I love them with all my heart. Bubona and all the Bubonas in this land are my children. The God who is within me loves every one of them. Tell me, what good does it do them if God loves them but they don't know it? How can they believe in this love of God if no one goes to them in the name of Christ to give them credible signs of it and make it visible? This, brothers, is the inspiring task of the Church, which is to say your task, and mine.

Most of you will never have the privilege of coming to and experiencing Yabacao. I do have that privilege, but it will mean nothing to me if you don't help me. We urgently need your prayers and your financial help. Please give generously, because the poor cannot wait until tomorrow.

Some news

Rejoice with me, because the church in Gautier, which is called Saint Mary, Mother of Mercy, is now almost completed. Rejoice, too, because we have already begun the construction of the house for the missionaries here, in San José de los Llanos. It will be called Saint Mary of Galilee. May God will that it be the first of many other "Galilees", that is, places where men, our brothers, can personally find the risen Christ.

The poor and I wish you the healthiest and happiest Christmas. I assure you that in the midnight Mass we will pray for all of you before the mission's crèche representing the birth of Christ. Our thanks to the many of you who have helped us throughout this time. Without you, I could have done nothing.

With my most loving blessing for all of you, and commending myself to your prayers,

Father Christopher

If a Child Could Be Crucified

The whole Catholic Church greeted the year 2000 with immense joy as a Jubilee Year, a period of special grace and celebration declared by Pope John Paul II to mark mankind's entry into the Third Millennium of the Redemption.

While the Church is decked out for a festival, she also addresses new challenges, many of which are related to the work of the new evangelization of the West. As she does so, black storm clouds are approaching the little diocese of San Pedro de Macorís and will take over the parish of San José de los Llanos, unleashing upon it all the fury of a tornado. This period sees the beginning of the true test of what Father Christopher has been preparing for during these two years. In any case, the events happened in such a way that they seemed inevitable. Perhaps it would have been a sin for the priest to stay silent in the face of the opportunity that providence offered him, in the form of a campaign visit by President Leonel Fernández to San José de los Llanos.

It was January 2000, when presidential elections were being held in the Dominican Republic. At that time, the constitution did not permit a president to serve two terms in a row, so Leonel Fernández actively supported his party's candidate, Danilo Medina. The candidate's campaign manager had the bright idea of a visit by President Fernández to one of the bateyes of San José de los Llanos, where no one could remember any high dignitary of Hispaniola having visited since the time of Columbus.

The place that was chosen was the batey of Gautier, and the date, January 28, 2000. As part of the event they asked the parish priest of Los Llanos, a Spaniard with an English name whom no one knew beyond the campos and bateyes, to give his blessing to the presidential party, which, in the eyes of Father Christopher, amounted to nothing less than lending divine approval to the political initiative of the moment.

The father decided to reject the idea out of hand because he felt he was being manipulated. But Noemí Méndez tempered his hot-blooded reaction with a cooler one, appealing to his reason to see what he could not see with his heart: a historically unique opportunity to give the Haitians in the bateyes a voice before the president of the Republic. "Father, they'll never ask them, so you have the chance now to tell the president what's going on in the canefields."

Noemí went to sleep as usual at her house in San Pedro, unaware that she had sown in the father's heart the seed of a storm whose thunderclaps are still echoing today in San José de los Llanos. As he himself recalls, several things that were atypical of his life happened that night. The first was that he woke up in the middle of the night with an uncommon lucidity, after he had fallen asleep very peacefully. The second was that, for the first time in his life, he sat down to write a speech. He had never written a speech before, because he had always relied as much on his charisma and inspiration in the moment as he had on his God-given way with words. The third was that he wrote something which he confesses he is now ashamed of and would not write today, that is, he would write the same substance but not in the same form.

After a couple of pages the father went back to bed convinced that what he had written was what the cane workers would tell the president if they had the chance. In the speech, the father gave a detailed description of what he saw as the facts, attributing the ills of the poor to the family that owned the bateyes. That morning of January 28, the whole Dominican media was focused on the baseball field in Gautier. As the political meeting unfolded, the various speeches that were given did not generate even the most trivial headline in the press. Everything was unexceptional and unexceptionable.

By the time his turn came, Father Christopher's awareness of the seriousness of what he had written was such that his hands and legs began to shake, but not to the point at which he would limit himself to stepping up to the podium, praying an Our Father, and getting out of there.

The speech was very possibly the harshest speech a foreigner had ever addressed to his host country's own president. In fact, as the father read on, he became aware of the recklessness of what he had written, and he started skipping paragraphs at random to lower the tone, while

the reporters were waking up, trying to sort out the name of this foreign priest who was lecturing their president, and the whole country,
with blunt truths about their home.

"Mr. President, you are here in hell's waiting room." That was the
sentence with which Father Christopher welcomed Leonel Fernández,
in the presence of the country's mainstream media, going on to give
a detailed description, mincing no words and pulling no punches, of
what he had seen with his own eyes in the more than two years that
he had been there. We can read the entire speech below, from which
he excised some paragraphs but which he unthinkingly distributed,
uncensored, to the president as well as to the press.

~

January 28, 2000

His Excellency Dr. Leonel Fernández
President of the Dominican Republic

Honorable Mr. President:

I invoke the blessing of God the Father, Son, and Holy Spirit upon you and the great responsibility that divine providence and the Dominican people have placed in your hands.

Because of the greatness of your responsibility on behalf of all of us who have the honor to live on this blessed island—citizens and foreigners—so great must be the stream of grace that we implore the good Lord to shed on you this afternoon.

Mr. President, you may not know it, but you are in hell's waiting room. Look around you at these endless expanses of sugarcane. Cane that has flourished by being watered in the blood, the sweat, and the tears of poor Dominicans and Haitians alike. The sufferings and neglect of the people who roam these roads of mud, dust, and mire every day, seeking a miserable crust of bread, are as immense as these canefields. The municipality and parish of San José de los Llanos where we are now cover a geographic area of about 580 square miles. Scattered through the length and breadth of these fields, conveniently tucked away behind the parapets of cane, there are more than seventy bateyes, about half of which belong to the CEA (such as the sugar mill of Boca Chica, Quisqueya, and Consuelo). Most of the other half belongs to the all-powerful and ubiquitous Vicini family, from whose bateyes, paradoxically and inexplicably, no undocumented Haitian worker has ever been deported, but in whose bateyes the cane cutter's wage is a pitiful thirty-five Dominican pesos per ton of cane, or two American dollars and fifty cents, so small as to be the equivalent of slave wages.

Mr. President: God, whose blessing we invoke upon you, knows that these bateyes are fit more for animals than for men.

—Many of these bateyes, to this very day, have not received a single visit from an official or governmental entity since Hurricane Georges. They themselves can tell you that only—and I repeat, only—the Catholic Church has come to their aid.

—When we have asked the managers of the sugar mills and bateyes why they do not even have a few poor latrines, the only answer we have received is that that is what the cane is for.

—More than half of these bateyes lack a public school, which means that thousands of children either lack schooling or have to travel distances that are superhuman for a small child, under torrential tropical rains or the merciless Caribbean sun.

—More than 40 percent of the children have not been registered in our municipality and have no possibility of being registered, either because their parents are not registered or because the swindlers who act as agents charge the poor at a prohibitive rate.

—There isn't a single doctor in any of the bateyes from Gautier to Los Llanos, and judging from the outside of the health stations that appear now and then, the only medication they have is the condom.

—These people are so poor, Mr. President, that in their want they have no place in which to worship the living God. Not a single batey in this municipality has even the humblest chapel. We haven't been able to get a single palm's width of barren land on which to worship God, a place to weep over our pain, to find a little relief and hope in the middle of so much pain and neglect. You will see behind you the only Catholic church in all these bateyes. Mr. President, not even God has a house in these bateyes, not even a humble hut in which to live and accompany these people in their exodus. God's only place is in the poor hearts of these marvelous, suffering people.

—Little more than a half mile from where you are now there is a batey called La Luisa. Last week it was practically emptied without notice, as has happened and continues to happen in other bateyes. The overseers and representatives of the CREP (the Commission for the Reform of Public Enterprises) required them to leave their huts immediately. Here before you are families who were given seventy-two hours to leave what had been until then, and for generations, their humble home. These families have either been crowded into a single room, with the lack of hygiene and the disarray of all kinds which that implies, or they simply lack any roof over their heads other than the starlit sky.

—You, Mr. President, are turning these bateyes over to the private sector. The private sector, in the case of three sugar mills I've mentioned, has a name. It is a Mexican monster called Conazúcar[1] that devours everything. Why was it necessary to evacuate hundreds of huts at the point of a bayonet and rifle if you repeatedly say in the media that no more Haitian manual labor will be brought for the harvest? Where do those hundreds and hundreds of young Haitians who are flooding into those huts come from? Who brings them, if they are coming from the border with a certificate of the Public Health Service of the Dominican state? If they did not intend to bring new manual labor from Haiti, why was it necessary to evacuate the huts and expel humble families who were living there? Why have they abandoned us, through privatization, in the hands of the most ruthless and cruel capitalism, which has so many times been condemned by His Holiness John Paul II throughout his pontificate?

Mr. President: if you want to be our president, that is, our servant of the public good, please do not forget or abandon us. We poor are not an audit or a statistic or a percentage. We poor have a name and a face, that of Jesus of Nazareth nailed to the wood of the cross, a cross made of cane, of mire, and of mud. Being poor is horrendous. Never forget it, Mr. President. I repeat: being poor is horrible.

The proof that the good Lord our Father's blessing has descended on you lies not in official speeches but in concrete acts that will help us escape from our poverty.

In the name of the entire community in the municipality and parish of San José de los Llanos: may God bless you.

> Father Christopher Hartley
> Parish priest

---

[1] A corporation capitalized in Mexico that at the time leased sugar mills in the Dominican Republic.

Father Christopher's speech was followed by more speeches, and after the event was over, life seemed to go on in Gautier as if nothing had happened. The cane cutters went on cutting cane. Those who had houses went back to them, and those who did not went on without them. That night nothing seemed to have changed in San José de los Llanos, and yet nothing went back to what it had been before.

Overnight, Father Hartley became famous in the Dominican Republic. All the media led with the father's brutal denunciation of the conditions that sustained the sugar industry. In his speech he called out by name the Vicini family, a clan of Italian origin that had established itself on the island in 1860, amassing an enormous fortune and building a powerful business empire based on the cultivation of sugarcane.

In his speech, Father Christopher denounced the Vicini family for being the owner of the Cristóbal Colón sugar mill, which is located on the highway between San Pedro de Macorís and San José de los Llanos and owns all the sugar plantations and bateyes within the boundaries of the parish of San José de los Llanos. So the father's objection to the family was nothing personal but circumstantial, rooted in the fact that it owned the bateyes where the priest evangelized.

His denunciation was extremely harsh. Only the word *slavery* could describe the conditions in which the Company kept the Haitian workers. In addition, he had rubbed salt in the wound of suspected human trafficking, which involved the absence of the rule of law among a very large population of illegal or undocumented immigrants. It also involved the state's utilitarian treatment of the workers when it evacuated them days before from the huts that belonged to the sugar mills of the CEA, which had been privatized that same year.

The father also denounced the approach to cultivating sugarcane taken by Conazúcar, and he accused the Republic, in the person of its president, of making untamed capitalism the basis for the exploitation of the cheap manual labor of the poor.

Inevitably, the reaction of the Vicini family was swift. But what seemed to foreshadow a day in court turned into a proposed meeting at which what was going on could be explained. Seen in hindsight now, years later, it gives the impression that nobody had understood that the working and living conditions of the cutters in those canefields were out of the nineteenth century, and that nothing about them had changed by the beginning of the twenty-first.

The Vicini family reacted in two ways. The first was to publish in almost all the country's media a full-page color advertisement contradicting, point by point, the parts of the father's speech in which he had made his accusations. The second was to get in touch with Father Christopher to seek a meeting at which their disagreement could be resolved amicably. The father agreed to meet with them on the condition that his bishop would approve and attend the meeting, and that the meeting would be held in the bishop's house. The representatives of the Cristóbal Colón sugar mill made no objection and agreed to sit down with Father Christopher and Monsignor Francisco Ozoria, bishop of San Pedro de Macorís.

For the father, the Company's contradiction of the accusations he presented to the president was the worst thing it could have done. Besides considering the Company to be responsible for what was going on in the bateyes, the father also saw it as having made him out to be a liar. So he decided to prepare himself for the meeting by going out with Father Antonio Diufaín, carrying a digital camera, into all the bateyes that displayed the conditions he had denounced days before.

Father Christopher showed up at the meeting in the bishop's house with a collection of photographs that seriously undermined the position of the Company's representatives, who decided to turn things over to the owners. They set up a second meeting with Father Christopher, the bishop, and the others at the first meeting—among them, Noemí Méndez and Father Antonio Diufaín—but this time with the owners of the Company.

And so war had broken out. The Church, in the person of the bishop and his priests, hoped it would be resolved. There was in their opinion a very simple way to do that, which was just to bring the living and working conditions of the workers into compliance with the constitution and Dominican law.

For the second meeting, which was held on March 16, 2000, Noemí Méndez and Father Christopher had prepared a report titled *The Situation of the Bateyes and Their Inhabitants*,[2] in which they detailed the respects in which the living and working conditions of the Haitians who lived in the bateyes failed to comply with Dominican law as then

---

[2] See the appendix for the complete text of the report.

in effect. The atmosphere during the meeting, which some members of the Vicini family attended, was cordial considering the seriousness of the situation, and it ended with firm proposals from both sides on how to resolve the conflict.

Father Christopher's next letter was written in Lent 2000. In it he relates the true story of two small children who, in a sense, have already been crucified. The story is uncommonly harsh, and it outlines how the Church should behave in extreme situations, what is to be expected of her even if she has yet to meet those expectations in so many situations.

$\sim$

Dear friends of the mission:

This is the Holy Year 2000, the Jubilee of the Incarnation of the Son of God, the God who made himself man to die and be resurrected by the love of the Father, for love of men. We're reaching the end of another Lenten exodus. All of us are walking, whether we realize it or not, toward Golgotha. There are many at our side who are on the verge of being sacrificed. Christ has an infinite number of faces. We've all seen many of these semblances of the crucified Christ! I see so many every day! I would like to kneel before every one of them and ask forgiveness. Wiping away a tear, sweat, blood . . .

Let me present two very small Christs, their skin as black as night, who are just children, two small children. Here, in these lands of cane and sun, we've crucified two little Christs. Just nine years old, they've experienced everything. Only God's love can resurrect them, can redeem so much cruel, unnecessary, unjust pain and suffering.

At the end of December the local radio station broadcast a report that the police had found a child nine years old who was lost in some bateyes in the municipality of Consuelo, in the province of San Pedro de Macorís. He had been "detained" in the local police station three days before, waiting for somebody to come and reclaim him. The radio said over and over that the child was from the batey of Gautier, in the municipality of San José de los Llanos. After the police talked to him for a long time and earned his trust, the child told them his name was Jonathan, that everyone called him Chiffchaff, like the bird, and that he wanted to go to "the father's house".

The police finally turned him over to the guardianship court in San Pedro. Fortunately, Doctor Brugal, with whom I had worked in the prison at San Pedro de Macorís, had just been appointed there.

The child repeated to her over and over, "I want to go with the father of my church." When she asked him the father's name, he said Christopher. Not content with that, she asked him to tell her something about this father, and he replied, "He has a blue pickup truck that's always covered with mud, and I clean it for him."

The doctor was finally able to get hold of me, and I went with several members of the Gautier community to fetch the child. When we went in to see him, the eyes of this very dark child of Haitian descent lit up. We gave him something to eat that he wolfed down in two mouthfuls, and after I signed the necessary document, the judge granted me legal custody of the child.

We went back to Gautier to return the boy to his mother, and, much to our surprise, we learned that his mother had gone to the capital. That's where she was when Jonathan told us the details of why he had escaped from his house. He told us that his mother had gone to Santo Domingo, and she had tied him up with a chain so he wouldn't go wandering in the streets. Desperate to get free, and inflicting more and more damage on himself, he decided to get help. Tipapí, a friend of his who was equally Haitian, equally abandoned, and just as much of a stray as Jonathan, arrived. He asked Tipapí to urinate on his foot, and with that he was able to slide off the chain and escape.

He convinced a passing driver—such things happen in these parts —to take him "to the father's house", and he turned up, lost, in some very faraway bateyes, no one knows how.

I found this Tipapí, Jonathan's fellow sufferer, about whom I had been told several times in Gautier and whom I had seen hanging around near the church. He was living in a tiny room of an appalling barracks for cane cutters, with an old invalid who they said was his father, which seemed to me to be biologically impossible. The old man begged me to take the boy away.

So before I knew it, I had two boys, nine and ten years old, and I didn't know what to do with them. I knew I couldn't just leave them in Gautier, so I got them into the famous "blue pickup truck covered with mud" and went to San José de los Llanos.

The arrival of these two boys was like an apparition for us. They had never taken a shower or put on clean clothes. It was already night. We fed them dinner, and it seemed that their stomachs were bottomless pits. They ate and ate without stopping until they could eat no more and then asked, "Are you going to feed us again tomorrow?" We got some clean sheets from the neighbors and finally got them to go to bed. I gave each of them a small image of the Virgin, and Jonathan put it on his little night table. He put a couple of little coins in front of it and said, "This is so the little Virgin will take care of my mother in Gautier." It was his mother who had chained him up. That's how children are . . . Ah, if only we were like them!

In less than a month we found a couple who decided to take Tipapí to their house and adopt him. And finally, a week ago, a wonderful couple in Santo Domingo took charge of Jonathan. He has found a family, a home, a ton of affection, respect, and the dignity that had been denied him since the day he was born in this vale of tears.

So a new life in Los Llanos has begun for both of them. In the morning they go to the parish's preschool and nutritional center in the La Palma neighborhood. There, besides studying, they have breakfast and lunch. They bathe and put on a school uniform and go to the public school until five in the afternoon.

Jonathan and Tipapí had experienced everything: several adults had sexually abused them so brutally that we even had to test them for tuberculosis and AIDS. They've been subjected to the most degrading abuse that the human mind can imagine. They've been hungry since the day they were born. When they were six years old they were sent to Boca Chica with their little shoeshine box, and the last cent they had been able to earn had been taken away from them. It will be hard for you to believe, but they were arrested by the police many times, in the raids that they carry out to clean the tourist areas of "local people" who detract from the image of the zones reserved for foreigners who have dollars. How rarely do they take away the prostitutes the tourists look for like a piece of meat to devour!

Let us kneel before these modern calvaries where so many of our brothers are crucified. Today, in the Golgotha of Gautier, two little Christs had been crucified, two Christs with the faces and bodies of children. Yes, through the humble work of the Church, these two have now been brought down from the cross, but there are so many more like them! Pray for us, that the charity of the Church may continue to make the presence of the mystery of Redemption felt. Jesus Christ ascended the holy wood of the cross on the afternoon of Good Friday so that no one would ever again have to be nailed to it. Why were these two boys crucified? Because the Church still hasn't been able— two thousand years later—to take the redemptive power of Christ to the farthest corners of the earth. It's precisely for that reason that the Church's missionary work exists today, so that the Redemption, the Resurrection, may reach all men.

Other news

The church in Gautier is almost completed, finally and thanks to all of you! Soon the bishop will come to consecrate the church. The missionaries' house—which we want to call Saint Mary of Galilee—is moving forward under economic pressure and anxiety about the scarcity of funds. Even so, the second floor is now up, and we hope they'll come this week to pour the concrete of the roof. We're trying to complete at least the first floor for the arrival of the missionaries in July. We'll put two bunks in each room if necessary, depending on the number of people.

We need many missionaries this year, to be able to respond to the challenges that the mission throws at us, and more people who want to commit themselves to helping us economically to complete the missionaries' house, rebuild the chapels that fell during the hurricane, and open two new dining halls in which to feed malnourished children.

That is all. Pray and pray again for us, that we may do everything with immense joy. That is what *Jubilee* means! With all the love in our heart, with unswerving hope, and a very great desire to please God in all we do.

This Holy Year is all about Mary, whose consent given to God made the Redemption possible. To her we commend these small apostolic efforts. I promise you, as always, a prayer and a special remembrance before the tabernacle of the mission.

Father Christopher

I Was Glad When They Said to Me, "Let Us Go to the House of the LORD!"

By the summer of 2000, Noemí Méndez, the lawyer, had been working on countless projects, reports, and laws relating to the Haitian workers in the bateyes. Cocola's seventh child was now doing the work she was born to do—just as a Haitian woman from an unknown batey had predicted to Noemí's mother years before, without any idea of what was going to happen.

At the time, relations between the parish and the Company were in a state of tense calm, of anticipation. Some expected a concrete, positive reaction from the Company, in the form of improved working conditions, while others adopted a wait-and-see attitude. All in all—and this is what interests us in reading these letters—that was the situation. Parish life went on, and when the first summer of the twenty-first century had ended, the father wrote another one of his missives, this time both with joy, when he recounted how the church in Gautier had been consecrated, and also with unsuppressed sadness, when he described another event—yet another one—over which his missionary heart cried out, through prayer, seeking explanations but finding no comfort.

～

Dear friends of the mission:

What had seemed like an impossible dream has finally become reality. On August 30 of the Holy Year 2000, our bishop Monsignor Francisco Ozoria consecrated the church in Gautier under the patronage of Saint Mary, Mother of Mercy.

It was an unforgettable afternoon, a page out of the holy Gospels. During his pastoral visit in May 1998, our bishop told the tiny group that had gathered there: "One day we will build a church, but the temple that the Lord truly wants is made of living stones." Well, brothers, living stones we have given him, to build not a small chapel but a true cathedral!

That ceremony saw 150 baptisms, 80 first Communions, and 85 confirmations of children, young people, and adults who came from the four corners of our immense parish. You should have seen the crowds of people arriving from the remotest bateyes and little campos to participate in the consecration of the new church and accompany the young people as they received the sacraments. There were so many who received the sacraments that day that the bishop had to authorize Father Manuel Homar and me to join him in the baptisms and confirmations.

That day was the climax of a long journey of evangelization made by many people: the missionaries who came from Spain for three consecutive summers; the catechists and evangelists who went out from Los Llanos one afternoon after another, riding in whatever transport was available; and so many wonderful people who went forth to sow the seed of the gospel of Jesus in the hearts of the people of Gautier and the surrounding campos and bateyes.

It was impossible not to be reminded of the beginnings of the Catholic Church in that community. When we began, it had been more than ten years since the Holy Mass or any other sacrament had been celebrated there. Five heroic women, the only Catholics who were left there, came to the first Mass, celebrated in the school, and when their poor means permitted, they went to the villages of the neighboring diocese where they had heard there might be a Mass.

The open-air Masses in Doña Justa's yard were behind us. How many times we had to run to take refuge from the rain in the middle of the ceremony! There were also the gatherings in the street, with candles, oil lamps, and lanterns to encourage the little communities in prayer, in the beginnings of catechesis, the groups of young people who came out in force . . . What a wonder and what happiness it was to see how every night more and more were coming to join the faith and our little communities! So much enthusiasm amid so much poverty! So many beautiful reminders of the birth of the Church! Might it have been the same in the Acts of the Apostles, in the birth of the communities of Corinth, Ephesus, Thessalonica . . . ?

I think of so many people who dedicated themselves and worked with the greatest generosity, who couldn't be present to see this un-forgettable afternoon. I think of the first young Spanish missionaries, who plowed and broke the earth to make the first furrows for the sowing of the Word of Life; I think of the "ladies" of Los Llanos, who, with their Bibles under their arms, came every afternoon to share their faith with those who had received less of it. Some of them had gone home to the Father, and there they will surely have tasted the beauty of the crowning of their efforts. How true it is that "one sows and another reaps" (Jn 4:37) . . . In little more than three years, these small seeds of the gospel grew like wildfire, burning with the fire of the Spirit.

These people, who at first had been afraid and cowardly, immedi-ately went out on the roads and lanes of dust and muck and mud, and they themselves, the ones from Gautier, began to sow the Church and form new communities that were being born in the surrounding cam-pos and bateyes. La Luisa, La Redonda, La Mula, Magantillo, San José, Cayacoita, Peso en Medio . . . Every Thursday and Sunday the pickup truck went out from Gautier, crowded with young people and adults, full of an irrepressible joy, singing and laughing with their Bibles and catechisms, ready to proclaim the living Christ and his love for men. It's true that they returned at the end of the day drained, exhausted, sweating, spattered with mud, and feeling even in their hair the pain of being bounced around in their trips back and forth, crowded into the bed of the pickup truck. These people were happy. Experiencing God's love had made them happy, with a happiness that could come only from the presence of Jesus in their lives.

Blessed be God, who works such wonders with such poor helpers! Thank you, thank you, thank you a thousand times with all my heart for having helped so generously in your prayers, your sacrifices, and your donations!

Dying of hunger

It goes without saying that jumping for joy isn't all we do in the mission. During the time that the missionaries from Spain shared with us in these months of the mission, we've had the chance to live very close to the mystery of Christ's Passion, together with the abandoned Jesus.

In the batey of Sabana Tosa, a young Haitian mother had given birth to twins. The living conditions in this batey are truly disgraceful. By the time the missionaries went to help this mother, there was very little they could do, and there was even less in our rudimentary hospital in Los Llanos. It was heartbreaking to see this poor mother with the twins in her arms, desperate, searching for food, medicine, and help.

Although we did all we could to help her, it was already too late. One of the babies died on a Sunday morning. The medical diagnosis: malnutrition. Which is merely a more elegant way of saying, simply, hunger.

As soon as they heard about the death, they came to let the missionaries know. They went immediately to the batey and saw some poor men disassemble a dilapidated table from which, with other boards that had been discarded there, they improvised a little box for the poor baby. It was raining in torrents in Los Llanos. We all went to the cemetery. There we found some poor Haitian men, barefoot, digging the little hole for the box. We stood as if paralyzed, immersed in our thoughts and prayers, trying to comprehend the incomprehensible, searching for the sense of something that simply had no explanation. Soaking in the rain, it seemed to all of us on that Sunday afternoon that even the heavens themselves were crying.

Dying of hunger! There are things we have heard about but never thought we would see. To have witnessed the increasing anguish of a mother who went from one place to the next seeking a cure for such pain. First the hunger of the mother, who had not a drop of milk in her body with which to nurse her children. The missionaries even saw how, in her desperation, the mother tried to feed these newborns some spoonfuls of cold noodles. It was also agonizing to see the impotence of the missionaries who tried to do the impossible in order to save them. They managed to save one. They ran to the hospital in San Pedro de Macorís, where he was rehydrated. The pediatrician couldn't believe what she saw when she asked how many days had passed since the child was born, and the mother said five months. Brothers, no one should die of hunger! The Christ child died of hunger on a rainy Sunday afternoon in San José de los Llanos. We saw him and will never forget him.

Thank you

Although the mission's construction projects are temporarily at a halt for lack of financial assistance, I would like in the name of the mission to give our wholehearted thanks to so many wonderful and very generous people who have helped us with what has been built so far.

As you know, we depend completely on divine providence, which is the tender and merciful love of God the Father, who touches the hearts of men and women of goodwill. We have no resources on which to subsist other than yours. We place our confidence, yet again, in the fact that God never abandons his children.

What has already been achieved

As most of you know, we've now completed the first floor of our center for retreats, where this summer we lodged our missionaries. There are thirteen rooms, in each of which there are two bunks and a bathroom. The house is called Saint Mary of Galilee. Although it's only a small part of the whole project, we want to start using it for the spiritual renewal of the poor of our parish. To that end, we'll have our first retreat this weekend for girls, who'll be coming both from the town of Los Llanos and from the campos and bateyes.

The girls have taken up the idea with so much enthusiasm that we've had to ask those from Los Llanos to sleep at home, so we can have fifty beds for the girls from other places in the parish. Since we don't yet have a kitchen, we've asked the people of Los Llanos to cook at home and bring the food to the church. We're beginning on Friday, and we expect to end at five on Sunday. We ask you most wholeheartedly to commend in your prayers this new program of activities in our parish. The poor, too, have a right to go on retreat and have a time of prayer and reflection to hear the Word of God, experience his mercy, and discern his will for their young lives!

Help us!

Remember that the projects we have under way are: to complete the house of Saint Mary of Galilee, which lacks the second floor of rooms, the kitchen, the dining area, the chapel, and the conference room; to renovate the barracks that the batey of Paloma has donated to us to make another dining hall for malnourished children, like the one we have in Los Llanos (this one will also be for a hundred children); to build the batey's chapel in this same barracks; and to build the chapel in El Manguito that fell down during Hurricane Georges two years ago. Since then, we've kept the Host in a little room made of palm-wood boards and a zinc roof.

Our thoughts fly to the Blessed Virgin. You will, perhaps, have noticed that all these projects are named for her. This humble mission and the poor seeds that we've so far been able to sow for the sake of Christ, to help build his Kingdom, would never have bloomed so beautifully without the virginal presence of Mother Mary. She has guided us all like little children in the faith. She is truly Saint Mary of the road. We are never alone. She is by our side, encouraging, motivating, correcting, raising, awaiting, cradling, and carrying all of us next to her heart. This work belongs entirely to her, the Lady of the missions and Mother of the Church.

We remember all of you before the tabernacle of the mission. Do the same for us.

With my most loving and grateful blessing,
Father Christopher

Love Is Carrying You; Do Not Ask It Where

In the year 2000, the government finished its privatization of the CEA's sugar mills, so the mills, like the plantations and bateyes that had belonged to the state, passed into private hands, either under lease or by direct sale.

This left a good part of the population homeless, since the workers in those bateyes were evicted and given no choice but to look out for themselves wherever and however they could. The evacuated bateyes would be used to house the workers who would be arriving for the next harvest, when the sugar mills to which the bateyes belonged would begin operations.

The Church stepped forward to ask the government for land on which to build houses for all those who had ended up in the street. The agreement that was reached had some conditions attached. The land was not put in the Church's name but was granted her for the sole and exclusive purpose of building, at the Church's expense, housing for the Haitians who had been left homeless. This was a real bargain for the state: in return for the grant of a piece of land, the Church stepped in to solve the major problem the state would have had of taking off the street a sizable number of homeless Haitians who could have otherwise created a lot of difficulties. At the same time, the Church could take satisfaction from the agreement, seeing it as a step forward in her evangelizing mission of charity and human advancement. Each parish in the diocese of San Pedro de Macorís received a piece of land, which, in the case of San José de los Llanos, was in Gautier. All in all, though Father Christopher's defects—his failure at times to observe the niceties of protocol—are known and even notorious, it is also clear that his virtues and gifts include the ability to attain a seemingly impossible goal when it serves a cause in which the poor have an interest.

The next letter is the first one in which Father Christopher publicly describes his confrontation with the sugar industry. Anyone following his actions solely through these letters would be unaware that the father had now entered a period of constant tension that would sometimes bring him to the limit of human capacity to tolerate such conditions as fear, loneliness, betrayal, and suspicion. These conditions are not necessarily the lot of a missionary surrounded by poverty but are characteristic of a conflict such as the one in which he finds himself. Add to this a character that sometimes makes him lose his composure and patience, even with his closest volunteers and associates. If we had to judge, these factors add up to a picture with many shadows among the bright spots.

But—and this is what gives this story its greatness—the overall result is an example of God's greatness in a human heart that is dedicated to him, despite its unhappiness and failings. It is true that there are quite a few volunteers who, knowing Father Christopher during this period, never want to see him again. Proximity to him during these months of the mission was not pleasant, either because they expected something else or because the father was not as kind as they hoped. At times it was clear to them that this man, who put his all into attending to and loving the poor, was taking out on them the tension built up by the collision of adverse events with the character of a man pushed to his limit. The problem is that the father does not hide how he is. There is not time in the mission for dissembling or appearances, nor do the extreme situations leave room for human respect. There everyone —the poor, the missionaries, and the volunteers—completely expose themselves. Make no mistake, that is the truth about the mission.

This is the time to record an important observation: the mission, any mission, is not a summer camp or a theme park for Catholics looking for adventure. The mission—I have seen it with my own eyes many times—exposes everyone's shortcomings to the light of day, as do all extreme situations that we confront in our lives. I have known a good number of them in my work, and no mission is a Bambi movie. The greatness of a mission is that, next to the shadows cast by those missionaries, there is a much greater light that shines through the fruits of their labors and reveals the presence of God in the imperfect love that the missionaries have for him. I mean the imperfect love of a man made of dust who has been called and has said yes, and this case serves as an example. The mission has its miseries, as does every house, but if we permit, it also has, hidden among them, the surprising veiled messages of that God who resides in so many hearts wounded by sin —their own sin and that of others.

One of those messages is the story of the village of Gautier and the Company that the father tells in his next letter. The father knows it is no accident that the land granted by the state on which to build the Haitians' housing is in the same batey where the new church is being built, and he celebrates that to the skies.

∿

Dear friends of the mission:

I'm writing with great joy to continue sharing with you the wonders that the good Lord continues to work, with the power of the Spirit and for the edification of the whole Church, among these magnificent people. Wonders to which we missionaries should never allow ourselves to become accustomed. I pray God to sustain our capacity for wonder and adoration always.

Overcome with emotion in the presence of God's goodness, we are preparing ourselves, at the beginning of one more liturgical year, to enter Advent, a new time of God, who, through his Son, wants to celebrate the Incarnation and Redemption among us. Yes, friends. Here, too, among mud roads and a great ocean of cane in flower, we are preparing ourselves to celebrate the mystery of Christmas: of God made man, as we are men. He comes to live among his people as one of them, he comes to save us; he comes to give all men a reason to live.

The birth of a new village

It has been nearly a year now since the voice of the Church was raised like a trumpet, loud and clear, before the president of the Republic and the powerful oligarchs of this island. As a result of the Church's prophetic voice on behalf of those who don't have a voice, we were able to end, at the national level, a perverse program of massive repatriation of Haitians. The government euphemistically called it a "relocation" of Haitian workers and whole families, by the thousands, in all the bateyes in the country. It actually took the form of the arrival of the military security forces at the bateyes and the eviction, at the point of a bayonet, of thousands of families from what had been their homes, in some cases for generations. Thus, with nowhere to go, whole families with little children were sent wandering aimlessly, in a new exodus with no promised land in sight.

All this led to negotiations that we initiated with the government to make the relocations more humane, with the Church as the true guarantor of the process. As a result, the government donated very extensive lands to the Church so that housing could be built for all these families.

This affected numberless very poor, undocumented families who were dying of hunger and terrorized by fear, by panic over the possibility that the army would come and separate the men from the women and children and take them all to the Haitian border. It was a human drama of massive proportions. The drama of countless people living in conditions of true slavery.

Very soon, perhaps next month, we'll begin construction of almost two hundred housing units, each with its own parcel of land for a vegetable garden, in the batey of Gautier, which, as you know, is part of the parish of San José de los Llanos. More than a thousand people will come to live on this land, which is right next to the batey's new church that we've just finished building with everybody's help.

The road has been arduous, the heartaches innumerable, but the Lord has never abandoned us. Christ has been the Good Shepherd of these poor people in all the efforts that Mother Church is exerting for them. They bring Jesus' words in the Gospel to life: "Come, O blessed of my Father, . . . I was a stranger and you welcomed me" (Mt 25:34, 35).

The government intends to evacuate most of its bateyes so the new owners of the canefields can bring and house their own workers. Our task is to offer a place worthy of these very poor Haitian families, most of them undocumented, so that they can have a little house on a little lot to grow their food and raise their animals. These people are the abandoned Jesus; they are Saint Joseph and the Virgin Mary on the road to Bethlehem, with nowhere for their Son, Jesus, to be born. It seems to me an extraordinary grace that, after the enormous effort all of us have made to build the church in Gautier, dedicated to Saint Mary of Mercy, the good Lord should will that an entire village emerge around it, that these houses we want to give to the poor be born, that the Church be like a mother to all these houses, to these people who are going to take refuge in their shelter.

You can't imagine the arduous work that was required from the evangelists in the parish who went from one batey to another, from one little campo to another, taking a census family by family, filling out forms, listening to the pain and suffering of one person after another. Only God knows the extraordinary effort that these young women made to bring this project of decent housing into existence!

Rejoice with us, for we'll be bringing the most indigent families out of the bateyes, where they have been lost and sunken in the most absolute material and human misery, and we'll be able to make of all of them a whole new village, a large family, that will take refuge around the church you helped to build. How impressive Christmas will be when it's time for this new neighborhood of the Gautier batey to be born! There will be people, mostly Haitian, whom we will immediately begin to evangelize and whom we will invite in Christ's name to come and be part of our huge Catholic family. Could we perhaps call this village Bethlehem?

A new nutritional and educational center in the batey of Paloma

In our eagerness to bring Christ's charity to the farthest reaches of the parish, we've obtained from the relevant authorities quite a large piece of land on which to renovate a barracks and build a school and dining hall for children, in addition to the batey's chapel.

We desperately need your help for this project. We've chosen this batey because it's in a central location among the parish's canefields. Hundreds of children walk miles and miles, and we would be able to give them food at midday before they go back to their huts and shacks, under that sun of righteousness, which here they call the "Caribbean sun". This batey is famous for the number of cases of AIDS and tuberculosis that the secretariat of state for public health has found there, and absolutely no one does anything at all for them.

Just this morning a sixteen-year-old girl visited me to say that her mother had died of AIDS, leaving her and her five little siblings behind as orphans. Their house is falling down around them, and they have some very dirty sheets of plastic as their roof. The grime and filth are dreadful, and, above all, there are the unmistakable faces of children with hunger, sickness, and neglect etched deeply upon them.

We urgently need your help. Let us not walk indifferently past so many abandoned Christs whom we would see crossing our paths every day if we would only open our eyes a little. Let us not live Christmas as though Christ didn't want to be born in so many hearts through the generosity and open-handedness of those who have the means. I beg you to deprive yourselves of something in this season to give it to someone who has nothing.

We remember you all before the tabernacle of the mission; the poor pray for all of you every day, and you will know that God never turns a deaf ear to the prayers of those who have him as their only treasure. May Saint Mary, Mother of Mercy, teach us all to love Jesus.

With my most loving blessing,
Father Christopher

The Bitter Taste of Sugar

Luis Narciso lives in a dark hut in San Felipe, a property of the Vicini family. He is a sixty-four-year-old Haitian who came to the Dominican Republic looking for work when he was thirty-five. Since then he has cut cane nonstop, except for when they fired him for working with the father. Luis is one of the many hands with which the father has reached out to the campos and bateyes.

One fine morning a tractor, pulling a wagon with a field guard in it and a group of other workers walking alongside, appeared in front of his house. Together they emptied Luis Narciso's house, put all his things in the wagon, and took them out to the road, outside the plantations. They put a lock on his door right under the noses of this helpless Haitian and all the inhabitants of the batey. They then announced to him that he was fired and that, because the house was the sugar mill's property, he could no longer use it. His crime? Having participated the day before in a meeting of workers in which he publicly denounced the abuses to which they and their families were subjected. When Luis Narciso refused to abandon his home, one of the field guards fired into the air, in an attempt to intimidate him. That is how things were done in the bateyes of Los Llanos.

Luis fled in fear through the canefields until he reached the father's house to tell him what was happening. The father, as he had been advised to do by the lawyer Noemí Méndez, drove to the headquarters of the national police. There he reported what was going on to Colonel Burgos, who was upset by what he heard and told him that only the national police had the authority to carry out such an operation, and then only pursuant to a judicial order. When the necessary formalities had been completed, the colonel told the father to go calmly back to his parish, because he himself would order the lieutenant in Los Llanos to "unseal" the house, in the company of the justice of the peace and the lawyer for CEDAIL assigned to the San Pedro Diocese. That same afternoon the judge and the lawyer appeared at Luis Narciso's house accompanied by a locksmith, who proceeded with the unsealing, thus allowing Luis to go back to his humble home, under the astounded gaze of his neighbors, the field guards, and the overseers.

The Company had dared not only to punish Luis but also to set an example of what could happen to the others if they continued to help the priest. But it was the rule of law that set an example that day, through its legitimate representatives, by showing that the authority of the law that applied in the batey was superior to that of the field guard on duty.

The lawyer tells us that the Company was tremendously clumsy, because if they had used the law and followed the right procedure, they could have evicted Luis in a few days. But they did things very heavy-handedly, as they had been doing since the nineteenth century.

Luis was rehired a little later on. In 2012 he is still living in this batey with his two daughters, nine and ten years old. He admits that he goes hungry and that what hurts him the most is to see his daughters doing nothing all day, waiting in the batey for their father to come back with something to eat after a day spent cutting cane.

"Look at them," he says, gesturing toward the two dark-skinned girls who are wearing a fearful expression, "I have to get them out of here. What kind of a future do they have?" Luis shoots us a look that is more of a lament, stops for a moment in silence, then goes on talking about his misery.

"Many things changed with Father Christopher. Before, there was no freedom; they did whatever they wanted with you. Now it's different; although in my case, for example, they still watch me. Today they know you're here. They're already investigating, and tomorrow they'll come and ask me who you are and what I told you."

"Aren't you afraid?"

"No. They killed Jesus for telling the truth. So we can't be afraid for telling the truth. I have Jesus."

"How can you possibly believe in God? Your life leaves the impression that if God exists, he's abandoned you."

"I don't think so. Look, there are times when I go to bed with an empty stomach and without a peso, and still, the next day I've eaten better than somebody who's gone to bed with four pesos. I know the God of the poor, and God appears suddenly because on that day that you don't have anything, somebody comes along with a little job for you to do, or to share something to eat."

"What did the father do here?"

"He changed a lot of things. He took away our fear; he brought Jesus to us. And he visited us in our houses; he visited the poor. He loved us and was interested in us. He was hot-tempered but he was a father; that's all I can say."

We leave San Felipe amid a sea of blank stares that light up their dark faces with fear. It is hard to concentrate on the next letter after you have smelled poverty, after you have seen the dirty, disgusting hut that Luis lives in with his two daughters. They share a room and a bed; they have no electricity, no kitchen. Just a small stewpot on the embers that they light every night to provide some warmth and to heat the food of a poor and miserable family who has nothing more than faith and is no longer so afraid.

～

Dear friends of the mission:

A few weeks ago we began a new season of grace and salvation in the Church: Lent. It's the season when we're invited to walk in the loneliness of the desert, trusting in the promise of God, who wants to bring us out of the slavery of our thousand Egypts and take us himself, by the hand, to the promised land, to Canaan, "the land of milk and honey". Here, too, in these wondrous lands of the mission, fields of cane to the horizon, where the desert is the green of the endless canefields, where the slaves in my parish say, "Father, they don't know it in your country, but the taste of sugar here is bitter, and not white, but red with our blood"—here, too, God's holy people have set out on their road.

We're a people on a pilgrimage, we're a people enslaved—like Israel in Egypt—to whom God has promised liberty. This is the mission of the Church in the whole universe: to liberate men through the victorious power of the cross of Jesus Christ. To spread the gospel of salvation and thereby move the hearts of all of us to conversion. To proclaim from every pore, with every fiber of our being, with the Virgin Mary and Saint Mary Magdalene, that God lives! Jesus is the Lord! The Lenten season is an invitation from Christ to discover him with his Mother in the poor, in those who suffer the most, in those whose painful lives are an icon and an embodiment of the Passion of Jesus right before our eyes. We can't ignore the drama of the poor, their voices silenced a thousand times by the world's powerful—their voice so often transmuted into a broken cry, into a desperate moan in the presence of so much pain, so much hopelessness, impotence, and oblivion. The Church is here with them, to cry out beside them, to relieve them, to comfort them, to assure them that they're not forgotten by everyone, because the Mother Church shelters and protects them the way a mother whispers sweetly to her heart's child in her lap. The only hope of the poor lies in the gospel of Christ proclaimed far and wide by the powerful voice of the Church.

Look, brothers. I've said it many times: The poor are poor because the rich are rich. Anybody who has enriched himself has enriched himself at the expense of the poor, because he has closed his eyes to their penury, hardened his heart before his brother as he passes him by.

God's Word leaves no room for deceit: "But if any one has the world's goods and sees his brother in need, yet closes his heart against him, how does God's love abide in him?" (1 Jn 3:17). There are too many poor people because there are too many rich people, greedy people, who don't share, who have hearts of stone. What are they thinking? That their life here on earth is eternal? That they're going to be buried with bags and bags of cash? That their money and power are going to open the gates of heaven the way they open doors for them here on earth? No, brothers. No, my friends. Not at all. The paradox of the evangelical life is that, in giving, you receive. That what you don't give, what you greedily keep, you'll lose in the hour of your death. That whatever you give out of the love of the Christ who is in the poor, you'll have received as alms for your soul in eternal life. "Truly, I say to you, it will be hard for a rich man to enter the kingdom of heaven" (Mt 19:23).

The teaching of the Church, of the saints, makes our hair stand on end in the presence of such a huge subject. The great Saint Teresa of Jesus—who I don't believe is likely to be suspected of being a Marxist —said:

> I often think about the matter and cannot understand how there can be so much peace and calm in persons who live very comfortably. (*Meditations on the Song of Songs* 2, 14).

> They [the rich] enjoy what they have. They give alms from time to time. They do not reflect that their riches are not their own but given by the Lord so that they, as his stewards, may share their wealth among the poor, and that they must give a strict account for the time they keep a surplus in their coffers while delaying and putting off the poor who are suffering. (*Meditations on the Song of Songs* 2, 8)

> We must not want as much as those who give a strict accounting, as any rich person will have to give, even though he may not have to do so here on earth but receives it from his stewards. And how strict an accounting he will have to give! If he understood he would not eat so happily nor would he spend what he has on vanities and trivialities. (*Meditations on the Song of Songs* 2, 10)[1]

---

[1] Teresa of Avila, *Meditations on the Song of Songs* in *Collected Works*, trans. Kieran Kavanaugh, O.C.D., and Otilio Rodríguez, O.C.D., vol. 2 (Washington, D.C.: ICS Publications, 1980).

Lent is a time of true conversion; it isn't about just giving from what you have left over. It's about reliving, ourselves, the life of Zacchaeus, the miserly little man who climbed a tree to see Jesus as he was going by (see Lk 19:1–10). Jesus stopped in front of him and said to him, "Zacchaeus, make haste and come down; for I must stay at your house today." Today, too, Jesus is passing by us—we, too, are small people, small in love, small in compassion, small in generosity—and he is telling us that he wants to enter the house of our life, the house of our heart. The Gospel says that Zacchaeus "made haste and came down, and received him joyfully". So today, too, Jesus Christ wants to generate the same happiness in us, entering our life, exposing himself as an object of ridicule and mockery as he did when he entered Zacchaeus' house. "And when they saw it they all murmured, 'He has gone in to be the guest of a man who is a sinner.'" Christ hasn't minded suffering people's scorn for wanting to enter me, my house, my life, my heart.

May the good Lord will that, like that little man whom Christ set out to win over, we, too, may proclaim with a heart brimming over with delight and the presence of Jesus: "Behold, Lord, the half of my goods I give to the poor; and if I have defrauded any one of anything, I restore it fourfold." That's how it is, brothers. When Christ enters the darkness of our hearts, he moves us to be converted, and an obvious sign that Jesus has entered our heart is the delightful and spontaneous desire to share what we have with others, our material possessions, of which we're no more than stewards.

Our uncontainable happiness will therefore be to hear Jesus say, "Today salvation has come to this house, since he also is a son of Abraham. For the son of man came to seek and to save the lost." Wouldn't it be wonderful to hear it from Christ's lips, as he says to each of us: "Today salvation has come to this house"? God spends every day at our side and says to us what he said to the Samaritan: "Give me a drink" (Jn 4:7). He will repeat it again on the cross: "I thirst" (Jn 19:28). These are the moans of Christ's heart, which are repeated in so many places on earth today. Here, too, the cruel taste of sugar, which makes these people's lives so bitter, calls us to account at the same time that it animates us to do something, to look at ourselves and not to pass by, indifferent to so many brothers whose lives are crushed by the overwhelming weight of the cross.

How good is God

I need not say that, among so many sorrows that these people have to endure, God the Father is working wonders, true miracles of love. For example, during the last three months, we've baptized in practically all the bateyes more than four hundred children and adults, with intensive catechizing and a short preparatory course for the parents and the godparents. It was truly moving to see a mother herself baptized with her seven children; to see old, illiterate cane cutters, prematurely aged from so much hardship, and their cup of joy and enthusiasm running over at being baptized! We now have fourteen villages in which Lauds are prayed every morning, wherever the villagers can pray: in a lady's yard, under a palm tree, or in an arbor. During Holy Week the Divine Office will be prayed in six villages, more than in any previous year, with the help of the missionaries who've come from Spain and the number of impressive evangelists who are emerging from our own parish. In addition, the number of those who come to the adoration of the Blessed Sacrament, exposed every Friday in the parish church from two to seven in the afternoon, keeps going up.

The great news this year is the youth Easter. We've had the idea this year of celebrating a retreat of more than two hundred young people, from Holy Thursday to Easter Sunday. We want to give them the opportunity truly to live the Easter of the Lord. You can't imagine the enthusiasm this has generated throughout the parish. The bishop will be coming on Sunday afternoon to celebrate Mass. For the Easter Vigil we have more than 130 people prepared to be baptized and to receive the other sacraments of initiation. In the church in Gautier we've begun a second nutritional and educational center with 120 children from this batey. We have six splendid volunteers who spend the morning teaching reading and writing, catechizing, and serving food to their respective groups.

We're working with a government program for the distribution of bags of food to the bateyes. We distribute food to 2,500 families a week. You have no idea how much work this is. Loading the truck and the pickup truck, going from batey to batey, conducting the census of each village . . . Also, we're continuing to evangelize every Saturday in the military prison in San Pedro de Macorís. We also help the prisoners manage their documentation, and we give them legal counseling.

We're working with the secretariat of state of public health on the transfer of the former hospital of San Pedro so the Catholic Church can establish her own hospital and thus offer better medical care, particularly to the very poorest.

Let me tell you about some of the projects we have under way. The first is to complete the missionaries' house. We've been able to complete the second floor, which will also be useful for retreats and other parish activities. On the other hand, we still don't have the kitchen, the dining area, the chapel, the laundry, the store rooms, and so on. We hope to be able to complete all that little by little.

Since Hurricane Georges we haven't had a single chapel in any of the campos or bateyes, and we want to start building them in all those rural communities, for liturgical celebrations and also for catechizing and other community meetings.

As I've also told you, we're trying to build two hundred houses in the batey of Gautier so we can relocate the poorest families of other bateyes, especially the ones that are farthest from the most basic services or other sources of jobs. Every house consists of three bedrooms, a living room-dining area, a bathroom, and a kitchen. All in all, 450 square feet on a parcel of 1,600 square feet.

Missionaries

The taste of sugar in these lands is horribly bitter, as I said at the outset, but thanks to so many wonderful missionaries that the good Lord has sent us, this taste is sweetened by the goodness and generosity of these young people who come with boundless enthusiasm and a fireproof faith to give of the best of their lives. It's impossible to measure the amount of good they do, because charity isn't a matter of numbers. They give all, and they give it in exchange for nothing, out of their love of God and of these people who for this world are nothing more than "pieces of flesh with eyes". That's how so many people here describe the Haitians in the bateyes, but for them, the missionaries, through the mysterious grace of baptism, they're friends and brothers: "One faith, one baptism, one God and Father."

That is all. Remember us always in your prayers. Through the Blessed Mother, the Virgin Mary, place our life and works for the

Kingdom on the altar, like the drop of water that's mixed in the chalice with the redemptive blood of Christ. We remember you every day before the tabernacle of the mission.

> With my most loving gratitude, and my blessing,
> Father Christopher

~

In the light of this letter, it should be mentioned that the day after we met Luis Narciso, they in fact came to ask him who those foreigners were and what he had told them.

Saints in Hell

Between March 2001 and November 2002, the father sends only two more letters, and in them he reveals between the lines, in the intimacy that writing affords him, that he has begun his personal Good Friday. Life in the mission becomes a dark, silent tomb, only barely relieved by a little light. The daily incidents of his life, a life immersed in poverty and misery, seem to be whittling away at his heart, so sensible to everything around it. The father begins to taste the loneliness of the missionary who would like to reach everyone, calm everyone, satisfy everyone, but who, in his overpowering apostolic zeal, reaches the limits of his capacity. He wants to and cannot. He wants to and fails. And all the while, the negotiations with the Company go on and on without yielding specific results that will better the life of the workers in the bateyes. As the father and his team of associates see it, the meetings that unfold one after another are full of good words but empty of intentions.

All of this erodes the morale of a priest who wants to be an evangelist rather than a social worker, but who, on the road of the gospel, finds again and again a starving Christ, a sick Christ, an exploited Christ, a Christ who is dying for four miserable pesos that support no more than a minimal subsistence.

The father feels that Spain and his contacts there are very far away. In fact, he reveals his anger in this next letter. He is angry at the world, at the missionaries, at those who do not give money, or who give what seems to him to be too little. He is angry at the industry, at injustice, angry about all that could be done but is not, because of greed, the love of comfort, selfishness. This next letter is the loneliness of his priestly heart, an agonized cry like that of Christ nailed to the cross. Like him, the missionary says yes, but it is a yes in which his last hope lies in the Resurrection, not in the glory of this life.

The father becomes embittered in this period. He argues with everybody, judges many, makes enemies of some. So much so that, for a time, a smile appears only in the company of the poor. In the loneliness of his writing we see a father who rebels against the little that is left of the proud missionary who arrived on the island with no idea of what he would find there. The only thing he sees clearly is that he is not going to leave unless his bishop tells him to. He is not going to give up. He is not going to throw in the towel. In fact, he confesses that it is his dream to be buried in the secret cemetery when he dies, in a piece of land where room is found for the bodies of Haitians who die without any family, whose bodies nobody claims. They are graves without headstones, without names, without a past or remembrance. Anonymous in the sugarcane, secret even in death.

In this extreme situation, in which the father can take refuge only in daily prayer—something he will never abandon—there will also be an event that triggers the last battle, which marks his limit. One morning, while he was visiting a batey with Noemí Méndez, her telephone rang. She received the sad news of the death of a ten-year-old Haitian girl named Roberta, whom the father met a few years before and for whom he had a particular affection.

The affection between the father and Roberta had been born in a setting of illness, because the girl had had AIDS ever since she was very small. Neither her mother nor her father were carriers of the virus, which stoked the rage and the pain that the father felt over Roberta's situation. Her illness was not inherited; she had obviously caught it from someone else.

Father Christopher describes how and why this happened in this letter, written a few days after the little girl's death, releasing his anger, his indignation, perhaps his rage.

Noemí Méndez tells us how, when she told the father about Roberta's death, the father went white. His expression froze, and, without a word, he went off toward the canefields that surrounded the miserable batey. Two tears rolled down his cheeks without a moan or a sob. It was a lonely, repressed pain.

From what Father Christopher writes in this letter, and the fact that he will write only one more, I believe Roberta's death was a turning point in the inner workings of the father in the mission. It was the stone that sealed the tomb. Before Roberta, there was still some light. After her, the darkness descended, the cold, the loneliness of an empty tomb that sealed up the heart that, with so much spirit and vigor, had arrived in the Dominican Republic barely four years before.

Dear friends of the mission:

I invite anybody who finds the title of this letter absurd to visit a batey. I'm talking about those who, by God's mysterious plan, have lived hell on earth, and it's from that hell in which they've lived that they've finally gone to heaven.

That is precisely the life of the little girl about whom I'm going to tell you in this letter. The name of this "saint" is Roberta; her "hell" is the batey of Contador. Roberta died of AIDS, of the countless accompanying diseases, and finally, according to the doctor who last attended her, she died of malnutrition, which, as you know, is a more elegant way of saying that she starved to death, plain and simple.

I met Roberta around the summer of '98. It was a few days after the first Spanish missionaries arrived for that summer. We had organized a simple summer camp for children, and two wonderful girls from Seville realized that, among the hundreds and hundreds of children who came every day—disorderly, dirty, happy, bubbling over, uncontrollable—there was a little girl who hardly played or participated with the others. She wasn't anxious, and she asked for nothing. Roberta watched the other children playing and coloring with the crayons that the missionaries brought, but she didn't run around; she wasn't like the others. She did have a very strange smile, a mixture of the most affectionate sweetness and the bitter sadness of the crucified one.

The two missionaries brought her to me one morning when I arrived at the batey in the pickup truck. She was wearing the dress she always wore, a dirty, grubby rag, and I asked her, "Roberta, why do you always wear the same dirty dress?" She looked at me and said, "Because it's stuck to my skin." I was stunned. When I could react, I went up to her, and the missionaries and I pried the clothes off her. Her body was just a big running sore. We wrapped Roberta in a sheet and took her to the little hospital in Los Llanos. When they saw us arrive with a little Haitian girl, they hurled insults at us and called Haitians all sorts of vulgar names. We understood from that response the hell that these people in the bateyes were living in.

I have no doubt at all that God permitted the awful suffering of this little girl for all those years in order to touch the hearts of all of us who had the privilege of recognizing in her the abandoned Christ, the crucified Christ.

In these three years, so many of us have had the privilege of touching, in her, the body of Christ! I think about the wonderful evangelists of the parish who would take her again and again to her medical appointments, especially Ñoña, who was like a mother to her. I think about Laura, Cira, Gonzalo, Pedro, Verónica, and so many missionaries who, one summer after another, would give her the best love of their hearts. Roberta knew the names of all the missionaries, although she didn't know very well just where Spain was.

The doctors soon discovered that Roberta was suffering from AIDS, like so many Haitians in our bateyes. That's where Roberta's personal climb to Golgotha began. She never complained about anything; she was always smiling and happy, with a delight that was contagious every time one of us would go to the hut where she lived so wretchedly.

Roberta lived all her life in the most disgusting hell. She was chronically hungry, every day of her life. When we got to her house we saw a handful of boiled rice in a filthy pot, on a miserable little flame. "What do you eat, Roberta, when you're very hungry?" I asked her once. She said, "When we're very hungry and my father hasn't brought anything home, my mother gives us hot water. It takes the hunger away for a while."

Roberta's body was deteriorating as the days went by. She had lost everything—everything except the marvelous smile with which she greeted any of us as soon as she saw us. Because we realized that her condition was deteriorating, we decided to make a last effort to take her to other doctors. My priests and one of the missionaries made several visits with her to the hospitals in San Pedro and Santo Domingo. Once, when one of her treatments was painful for her, my priests promised to buy her a toy when the visit was over. Since she had never had a toy, when she went into the shop and saw what a toy was, in an anguished voice she turned around and exclaimed, "Instead of a toy, why don't we buy some food?"

Roberta's death was as sad as her life. One afternoon she felt unwell. Her heart stopped, and she died. Except that her family didn't realize that she had died, thinking that she had fainted. Her sister Yolanda, who was fourteen, took her in her arms, went out into the road, stopped a motorist, and with her dead sister in her arms went to the hospital.

She went into the little emergency room and put her on a gurney. The doctor on duty and the nurse didn't even deign to look at her. Yolanda ran out looking for some of the missionaries, who at that moment arrived at the hospital. Yolanda told them that Roberta had fainted, and when they went in and saw Roberta's body, the missionaries questioned the doctor, who, with the most absolute disdain, said, "Here's the girl they brought. She's sick. Well, maybe she's dead." The doctor hadn't gotten up from her chair.

I don't really know why God, in his mysterious plan of love for all, wanted Roberta to be born and to live in this world in the hell of a batey. I don't know what sense it makes for her to have gone through the thousand periods of hunger and countless sufferings that she endured. I don't understand why the weight of a cross so cruel had to fall so brutally on her tiny body. I who have studied so much, a priest, confess my total ignorance and confusion. But I do know that the only beautiful thing Roberta knew in this world, besides her family, was the love and mercy of the Church. Only the Mother Church never abandoned Roberta, but fought for her, took her in her arms, gave her all the love and kindness in the world. Because the Church loved her so much—that is, because we loved her so much—Roberta had not the least doubt that God loved her.

I find it wonderfully amazing that the Church has, with no fear whatsoever, gone into the hell of the batey so that a little girl should go from that hell to heaven.

I don't understand why she suffered so, but I hope, with the unfailing faith of the Church, that God the Father has prepared the most beautiful heaven for all the Robertas of this world, whose only mission in this life seems to be to suffer. I pray to God that he hold this blessed child in his arms, through him about whom he has spoken to us so clearly, next to his fatherly heart, so that Roberta, looking into the infinite beauty that is God's face, may find the happiness that she never knew in this world.

I want to believe that the terrible words of Yolanda, Roberta's older sister, aren't true: "Roberta was actually the luckiest of us all, because she's the first one that God took from this miserable life in which my brothers and sisters and I have to go on living."

I ask all of you who are preparing so enthusiastically and wastefully for your sumptuous vacations, which you no doubt think you deserve, to remember so many girls and boys who, like Roberta, live dreadful lives. Let us not make ourselves accomplices to their misery by living as though they didn't exist, as though poverty were someone else's fault, as though we couldn't do anything about it. Don't corrupt your children by bringing them up in a fairy tale, making them believe that the important thing in life is professional success and having a great time. The "apprentice missionaries" who come here "to lend a hand" pain me so much. In so many of them we can see that they've had everything, that their parents have given them everything, and that they don't know anything about life. They're completely illiterate in religion. How can parents think that they've raised their children well when they haven't taught them anything about the horror of life for most of humanity, when they barely know anything about Christ?

When you're baking in the sun, remember Roberta. When you're water-skiing, remember Roberta. When you go out for dinner at a fashionable restaurant in Marbella or even in Outer Mongolia, remember Roberta. When you can't fit one more drink into your body and you're talking more foolishness than usual, remember Roberta. When you're bored with going to some island in So-and-so's huge boat, and you don't know what to invent to make yourself happy, remember Roberta. When you can't stuff yourself with one more sardine, remember Roberta. When you're tired of wasting your life, remember all the Robertas who are waiting for the fruits of your labors and the love in your heart! Friends, life is no joke. For many people, life is a drama, a hell. There are lives that are well lived, marvelously lived. Lives that have been worth living, that leave a mark. And there are irrelevant, superficial, empty, badly lived, wasted lives, and when we look at our hands and ask ourselves, "And these hands of mine, what have they done for others?" we see nothing.

What we need most:

Long-term missionaries

What we undeniably need most is missionaries, but not just any type of missionary. During this last period we've had several who spent a few months with us, too little time. That's not what this mission needs. The mission needs missionaries who don't have a round-trip ticket. Men and women missionaries who come to stay, who don't come for two months but to devote their lives to the Kingdom and the poor, to whom—according to the first of Jesus' Beatitudes—the Kingdom of God belongs.

We need to build chapels

It has been three years since the Blessed Sacrament was living in a little room made of boards and thatched with leaves in El Manguito, since Hurricane Georges destroyed the church. We have to build some twenty chapels for the bateyes. We have to complete the nutritional and educational center in the batey of Paloma. With our friends' help we've been able to begin work on the dining hall and educational center for women. About a hundred children, in fact, are eating there every day. But we still need to drill a well and install the accompanying equipment—a submersible pump, a tank, a generator. We need to buy sewing machines, ovens for baking classes, and so on. With this new dining hall in Paloma, in addition to the ones in Gautier and in La Palma in Los Llanos, there are now three hundred children who come to eat and, above all, to know the love of Jesus in this mission of the Catholic Church.

We need the prayers of all of you

Above all, we need the constant prayers of all of you, especially of so many women who from their cloisters and contemplative silence quietly give their lives to God as an offering for mankind, their brothers. Thank you for the prayers of so many good, humble people, who quietly pray to the good Lord for the missionaries every day. Thank you for the prayers of the adults, of the young people, of the children, of the sick. Thank you, a thousand times thank you.

Thanks to all of you

I want to thank you, in the name of all of us who work in the mission and the poor whom we serve, for your generosity to us, undeserving as we are. Thank you for the sacrifices you've made. Thank you for your very generous donations. Thank you to those who have ordered their banks to make monthly payments. Thank you to this endless list of good people who've helped us in so many ways that it would be impossible to count them, but whose generosity is there, in the sight of Jesus: "You did it to me" (Mt 25:40).

I pray to the Blessed Virgin Mary that she look upon us all with eyes of mercy so that she will take Roberta up into her maternal lap, cradle her next to her heart so that she will never again be afraid, so that she will never cry again, so that she will never again feel the pangs of hunger, so that she will regain her smile and be happy for all eternity. If I could say something to Roberta that she would hear, I would say in all our names: "Forgive us, Roberta, for the hell into which we brought you to be born, to live, and to die. Forgive us in your little girl's heart. You who see the radiant face of God, say our names to Jesus and, when our life is over, open to us—although we do not deserve it—the gates of heaven."

With my most loving blessing and the assurance of our prayer before the tabernacle of the mission,

Father Christopher

A Missionary's Meditation before the Cross

Life comes, and it leaves in the same way it arrives, and goes on its way unstoppably, inexorably, like a swirling desert wind. That is the image of life that comes to mind in reading the following letter, signed at the end of 2001. In between the previous one and this one, life was pushing on with its dawns and dusks, its births and deaths, its welcomes and farewells, unfolding in the bateyes to the endless rhythm of the cutting of the cane. The work never gives anyone a respite in these canefields. The routine does not include peaceful interludes, because when there is no food for tomorrow, the body does not rest. When that tomorrow comes, it just yields to another one, and so on forever. At this point in the book, sugar is no longer so sweet. Perhaps that is because while I drink my coffee, those people are still there, in that indescribable pit where life is death and death is awaited in hopes of life.

In this last letter, the father acknowledges that he is a poor man who has no more to give to God than hands that are empty of successes and full of failures. He is a missionary who has reached the high noon of his Good Friday and whose only hope now is that the loving hands of the good Lord will take up his mission.

This last letter, in which a man taken with love sees he has been defeated by the pain of those whom he loves in Christ, starving and crucified, may be the harshest. The father's communion with the poor attains its highest expression during this period. Christ's seeming defeat on the cross can be made out in Father Christopher's text to the point where he asks himself what he is doing there, what is the point of it. The account he gives here and from now on, of what happens between him and God, belongs to their hearts. Only they know what passed between them.

This letter is the meditation of a man before the cross. He is before not just a wooden cross, an image of something that was and is no more, but the cross that was given life in the person of a woman named Marta whose only sin was being black and Haitian. Marta's life immerses us in the deepest pain that an abused heart can suffer in this world. Marta's cross is a faithful reflection of the fact that sin has destroyed the life of men. Only love can bring happiness to a tortured, suffering heart, as we will see.

Dear friends of the mission:

In this month of November I have completed my nineteenth year in the priesthood, and that occasion suggests to me that it might be a good thing for you to know about not just the mission, but also the missionary.

I was going along the road to Los Llanos one afternoon with more sadness in my soul, and more problems, than this poor missionary could bear. On top of everything, my blue pickup truck had gotten bogged down, and I had spent hours alone, trapped in a sea of mud, in the grip of the Caribbean sun. Nobody came to help me, simply because, in this bog of cane and muck, nobody even knew I was there. When I had extricated myself and my truck, I was worn out, spent, and perhaps somewhat discouraged, I confess. The parish weighed me down; the mission overwhelmed me. It seemed to me that all these years I had been running and running from one place to another without accomplishing anything. I felt like quite a failure, saying to myself, "You don't want to dedicate yourself to Christ, give your life for him? Then choose a mission that fits your ambitions." At that moment, I arrived at the entrance to the batey of Copeyito and remembered that they had told me that there was a sick woman there, so I went into the batey and asked for her.

Marta lived in a vile hut that belonged to the Vicini Consortium, with nine members of her family: children, brothers and sisters, and her own mother. She was disabled, maybe about thirty-four years old. Her body was a skeleton covered with scabs, and she was lying on a filthy cot. In the same low spirits that I was in while I was going down the road, I went in, saying to myself, "I don't even know why I'm going in. I'm at the end of my rope. I'm dead, exhausted. I have no more to give. Life weighs me down, and even my hair hurts with the beating I've taken in my body and soul." Marta didn't know me. I approached her. The smell was dreadful, and the only room in the house was a chaos of crusted filth. I gave her my hand and offered up a grimace as a smile, saying, "Marta, I'm the father." Marta smiled a true smile, from within. She offered me a chair that had three legs and said, "Father, have you come to pray?" To tell the truth, I didn't even

know why I had come. She took me by surprise. It was she who reminded her pastor, wounded in battle, the "prayer professional", why
he had come to her bedside. Confused, I managed to mumble, "Yes,
yes, of course, that's why I came, to pray."

I instinctively opened my backpack and looked for my breviary. I
opened it without thinking, to that afternoon's Vespers, and with no
further introduction I began to pray the hymn. I'll never forget it as
long as I live. You who pray the Liturgy of the Hours know it:

> I came this evening, Christ of the Calvary,
> to pray for my ailing flesh;
> but, seeing you, my eyes come and go
> from your body to mine in shame.
>
> How can I complain about my tired feet,
> when I see yours so destroyed?
>
> How can I show my empty hands,
> when I see yours so full of wounds?
>
> How can I explain my loneliness to you,
> when I see you, so alone, raised up on the cross?
>
> How can I explain to you that I have no love,
> when I see your heart has been torn apart?
>
> I no longer recall anything,
> all my ailments have fled,
> the force of the plea I bore
> chokes me in my importunate mouth.
>
> And I ask of you only that I ask nothing of you,
> but to be here next to your dead image,
> to grow in the knowledge that sorrow is only
> the holy key to your holy gate. Amen.

Marta listened to me in absolute silence, despite the deafening noise
of the *bachata* and *merengue*[1] at the party in the brothel next door. I
couldn't see anything now except the living image of a Christ torn to

---

[1] Two types of Caribbean dance music.—TRANS.

pieces by a thousand hungers and a thousand crosses. Marta no longer had the strength to live, but she hadn't lost her smile. Her four children, three boys and a girl, arrived one by one. She introduced them all to me with true maternal pride. The girl was beautiful, with her hair in little ribboned braids, full of brightly colored plastic ornaments, all smiles and shyness. When Marta got to her, she said, "Father, this is Peter." I gaped with surprise, and I said to her, "But how can she be called Peter, if she's a girl?" Marta looked at me for a moment and said, "He's not a girl, Father. Peter's a boy."

I couldn't believe it. Seeing my surprise, Marta looked at me very earnestly. Two huge tears rolled down her cheeks as she said in a very soft voice, "Father, when a mother's in despair she'll do anything. Crazy things. I've vowed to dress my son as a girl until God saves us from the unbearable misery we live in." I didn't know what to say.

> But, seeing you, my eyes come and go
> from your body to mine in shame.

I told Marta that it wasn't necessary to require God to be good and remember the poor. I asked for some scissors and cut the "girl's" hair myself, and little by little she turned into a boy. They dressed him as a boy. Peter thanked me with a deeply grateful look. God knows what humiliations he had endured at school. He hugged me and said in my ear, "In school they say, 'Look, this girl pees like a boy . . .'" Only God knows the depth of a child's suffering.

When I asked Marta about the children's father, she said, "Each of them has a different father." I let slip some moral platitude that at that moment was surely out of place, and Marta shot back, "Father, I'm sure you've never wanted for anything, but when a woman has nothing to feed to her children, if necessary she'll go to bed with a dog." I was so ashamed of my bourgeois platitude for "respectable" people that I wanted to disappear, to be swallowed up by the earth.

When I reached home that night I went to my little chapel and in the shadowed light I looked at the cross, the cross that is the keeper of all my confidences. I looked at the crucified Christ and just repeated in my heart,

> But, seeing you, my eyes come and go
> from your body to mine in shame.

That night in the chapel, all I could do was look at the cross and repeat:

> Jesus of my life, I have known your love and goodness for so many
> years now, and yet I still go on with complaints and meanness. Good
> Shepherd, so wounded with sin and love, how can I complain when
> you have always been so good to me? I feel tonight an immense shame
> when I see the courage of a sick, disabled mother, and I, who "have
> never wanted for anything", can think only of complaining, as though
> you had to thank me for my poor favors. Look at your priest, Christ
> of Calvary, of so many calvaries where you die forgotten. Look upon
> your poor priest, your blundering apprentice missionary, who, when
> he was young, made so many promises of faithful love and friendship
> to you. Look with mercy upon my sick flesh, my sick heart. A priest
> of so many dreams and ambitions, who after years, after presuming to
> ply infinite oceans for love of you, is still thrashing about and pushing
> along in his meanness, trying to wade across the little puddles of the
> mission. I'm ashamed, because seeing you, my eyes come and go from
> your body pierced with love on the wood of a cross, to mine, so soft
> and comfortable, given a thousand beautiful things. Lord Jesus, my
> good friend and companion, in whom I have suffered and delighted
> so much, grant me that I may never complain again.

> How can I complain about my tired feet,
> when I see yours so destroyed?

From that moment on Marta was awash in great affection and care on
the part of all the missionaries. The Mother Church never wavered in
her care and attention to Marta and her children. She endured dreadful
pain throughout her body, but the greatest pain was from the wound
in her back, a running sore that never closed. Her legs, her feet, her
joints, her whole body hurt.

Marta would receive the missionaries as though Jesus himself had
come to her little hut. Yolanda, Teresa, Pedro, Juanjo all went there,
as well as an endless list of young missionaries ready to give the best
of their love. They bathed Marta, changed her clothes, washed the
sores that covered her body like the sores of a leper. Above all, they
assured her with their presence that the Mother Church welcomed her
in her arms with unlimited tenderness. We brought her food for everybody, and how often we paid what she owed the grocery store! How

often she said to us, "The grocery store doesn't give me credit anymore!"

I went to this batey many times to see her. Because it was on the way home from my rounds in the campos and bateyes, I finally reached the limit of my strength and . . . again the complaints, the inner grumbling:

> How can I complain about my tired feet,
> when I see yours so destroyed?

I learned so much from this woman! It was almost impossible to get a complaint out of her. I talked to her about God's goodness, about eternal life, until she asked me, "Father, what do you have to do to go to heaven? I'm not baptized, and my children aren't, either . . . and, tell me, do we *prietos* (black people), too, go to heaven?"

So many times, when I came back to my little chapel after seeing Marta's suffering, I had to look at the Lord on the cross: "Jesus in your Calvary, if only I could exhaust myself a little more for you. If only I could return home at dusk every day, more tired for having loved you a little more . . . if only in my love I could be more covered with dust from the road for having carried you further. If only, for loving you, my feet hurt more . . . if only, out of love for all the Martas in this world, the missionary's feet could be pierced . . . if only, out of love, I stopped fearing the stumbles on the way and my feet hurt a little more, so that yours would hurt a little less . . ."

> How can I show you my empty hands,
> when I see yours are full of wounds?

The day Marta was baptized was truly unforgettable. It was a summer afternoon in '99, the end of another day in the mission. The evangelists arrived little by little, from the various bateyes where they had been sent, and we crowded around her cot. The mood that afternoon was truly festive with the happiness of discovery. The missionaries arrived dirty and tired, but immensely happy. All of them knew Marta, and all of them loved her as a soulmate. She was so beloved that, when the summer was over, many of them wrote to her from Spain. How she enjoyed it when we read her the missionaries' letters! She cried with emotion to think that someone in Spain would have remembered her, although she didn't know very well just where that country was.

In fact, she came and asked me in her innocence how long it took the bus to get to Spain.

Marta chose her godparents, Pedro and Tere, from among the missionaries. They prepared her as best they could. We don't really know what she truly understood, but there wasn't the least doubt that something great was about to happen, that God was truly entering her life, her heart, that God was truly entering her little house. She remained convinced that God didn't care about the poverty of her hut. What's more, she was convinced that when God lived here on earth, Nazareth and Bethlehem would have been more or less like her batey.

Marta's soul was filled with happiness. A green plastic tub with a broken handle, worn out by the endless washing of clothes, by the knuckles skinned from scrubbing out the sweaty smell of the bitter cane, and a little aluminum cup were used for the baptism. We sang, and the missionaries covered Marta with kisses, hugs, and endearments. Marta was happier than she had ever been before, in all her life. The missionaries gave her a Bible that she kept as her most precious treasure. She felt like the center of the universe. She knew that God had come into her life and that from that moment on, her everyday misery would no longer be the same. Marta had received God as the only treasure of her life.

That night, all I could say was this:

> So many times I have thrown myself down on the ground before you, Jesus, with nothing to offer you, nothing more than my empty hands. So many times in this chapel, which has on so many nights heard my most intimate confidences, I have felt myself to be the poorest of the poor for having believed, in my conceit, the praise in which the world was so undeservedly dressing me. Prostrate before you, my crucified God, I humbly recognized that I've spent so many nights toiling away with my nets in the water and returning to the shore without having caught a single fish.
>
> Now, here, in the stillness of this night, I see your hands, so lacerated, so full of wounds, nailed to the blessed wood of the cross. I thought you always demanded from your poor missionary a granary that would be more and more full of the harvest, and now I know that my empty hands are enough for you. It's enough for you that my hands should slowly assume the form of yours, so that the nails should hurt mine more and yours less. I know now that it isn't applause and

worldly success that forges the missionary, but that instead his worth is measured by the wounds of nails that the world cannot see, but that leave the missionary on a cross, a little more nailed with you.

And I still complain tonight about having empty hands? Empty, yes, to extend them like a beggar to you, Jesus of all the calvaries, and so that I never again complain that the yield of the fishing or the harvest is small. It is enough for me tonight that these hands of mine should hurt a little bit more and be emptier and emptier, to bless, to caress, to heal, to love, to serve. Empty, yes, of myself, but full of your goodness and compassion. Give me the hands of a shepherd, Lord. Hands full only of your love and kindness.

> How can I explain my loneliness to you,
> when you are raised up on the cross and are so alone?

Marta's calvary worsened. The solace that the missionaries gave her vanished as quickly as the days of August. Hers was a life spent prostrate, with daily hunger, malnourished children, the unconfessable moral aberrations of a batey where everybody's fighting for survival the way the galley slaves struggled in the past. The daily monotony, as harsh and arid as a desert in which each day's landscape is identical to that of the day before. Marta's life was rotting away little by little. In the midst of all that, God sent her an angel. Her name was Marina. Only in God's heart is it recorded what this missionary did for the broken Christ called Marta.

She bathed her, dressed her, brought her food, lifted her up so many times . . . Above all, she brought her all the love in her young heart. So many hours next to her bed of pain, so much shared suffering, akin to the Passion, thanks to the love of a missionary.

Marina went with Marta to countless hospitals, in our eagerness to find the cause of her ills. We didn't understand why she couldn't walk. Her legs hurt, but she hadn't had an accident; she had become paralyzed little by little. No one knows how long the waiting times are in those terrible third-world hospitals. The lack of attention, lack of interest, indifference, disrespect . . . just for being Haitian. Only in God's heart are written the constant humiliations that Marta withstood just for being black, for being Haitian, for being poor. Finally, one day we succeeded in having her attended to in the military hospital of San Isidro. There they gave her a diagnosis of her terrible illness. Marta had syphilis, and a great many other things. The doctor said he would've liked to admit her but we had to understand that he couldn't. He was talking about her race, her color. "You must understand, Señorita, that our relatives come here, and we can't admit such people, because we'd have to disinfect the whole hospital." Jesus abandoned yet again in the ditch of life, without even a place to lay his head. Marta lived through a lot of Calvary and very little Tabor. So she went back to the batey. To its filth, its loneliness, to the den of animals that was her hut. We didn't know how to bring her help, because as soon as we turned around, her family fell upon her like piranhas and took everything. They had to survive, and hunger doesn't respect the illness of another.

> How shall I explain my loneliness to you,
> when you are raised up on the cross so alone?
>
> How can I explain to you that I have no love,
> when your heart has been torn apart?

In the stillness of the chapel, I could only say:

Loneliness, my God, loneliness.

There are so many lonelinesses in a priest's life! And they are so varied! Right here in this little chapel, how different are the lonelinesses that I've lived with you! Just looking at you, so alone, so alone and so still, naked on the holy wood, I feel that my lonelinesses can only be an icon, a mere semblance, of yours.

In your life, Jesus, you have known lonelinesses that are more beautiful and radiant than the human mind can imagine. Those nights alone with the beloved Father, nights of love and confidences, nights and lonelinesses full of giving and being given. Lonely nights when the word *Father* tastes of more love. Lonelinesses filled with intensely delightful prayer. The filial abandon in his arms, the total confidence in his plan of love.

Lonelinesses with Mary, your Mother. So many hours filled with the kindnesses and silences of lovers, when the eyes say everything and words are unnecessary! So many confidences that she will keep forever in her immaculate heart, in the depths of her soul!

Lonelinesses with your friends the apostles. Starry nights dreaming of fishing, fishing, and more fishing. Lonelinesses of friends by the fire. I wish I could be a witness of your happiness, Good Shepherd Jesus, my soul's companion!

But also, how dreadful are those other lonelinesses, steeped in gall and vinegar! When you felt nothing but betrayal from your friends in that night, when the cock crowed, you pierced Peter with the power of your gaze and the tears of blood that you wanted him to shed. My God! You walked away from those whom you called your friends and now have left you so alone. How bitter that night of dismal shouts, and no prayers. You moaned like a child and were looking in the night for the blessed face of your Father, who now was so far away, and you looked around, for if the Father didn't hear you, perhaps the humble company of those you loved with all your heart would give you some consolation that would wipe away your blood. A garden of lonelinesses, of anguish, and of tragedy. The lonelinesses of a God who sweated drops of blood out of love. Gethsemane of the soul! How harsh to love those who now love you so little!

And I, poor me, a lowly priest, so great in dreams and so poor in accomplishments. How my heart delighted in priestly lonelinesses, here in the darkness of night, with just a candle of love, of your beauty incarnate. You stole my heart in my enamored adolescence. My first love! I went with you without thinking twice, and you stamped my soul and said to me, "My grace will be enough for you." You made me so happy with that happiness that you reserve for those who, out of nothing but love, lost everything for you and left it all in the plowed land!

So many times has my heart run over with that solitude with you, when it appears that your soul is ready to burst. Oh, loneliness, accomplice of my loves! I never knew before that it would be possible to be so happy in this world. Loneliness for that deepest love that you reserve for those who, leaving everything behind for love of you, have asked for nothing more than your grace. How richly you rewarded someone who deserved nothing, who longed for you so much! How grateful I am to you for your call to me. Your voice, which when I heard it one winter evening set me running behind you, ill with love and full of grace. The loneliness of the first vocational fruits, when your gaze stole my love and you stamped my life and my breast with gratitude for you, running over.

So many lonelinesses and so many nights I have sung and whispered to you that I was suffocating with a love that I neither understood nor deserved. So many times, with my eyes streaming tears, I gave you infinite thanks for having called me by name with your power and for having entrusted to me the treasures of your Kingdom and the power of your grace. Thank you, my Lord, thank you for the undeserved gift of my calling!

But you have scattered into this priest's life, Lord, as you know, those other lonelinesses, of anguished nights, which taught me that a priest's life is pain, and that "he who knows nothing of pain knows nothing of love." When you called me, you didn't explain that all you wanted was a strong back to join with yours in carrying the cross. How bitter pain is, and how harsh the lonelinesses, for anyone who devotes himself only to you and has nothing when you leave him! How harsh it is when you hide, when you sleep, when you go away! How fearful when the wind and waves buffet the faith of a child, who is left lonely and steeped in bitterness. Who will understand that the most dreadful pain of a priest, the most enamored of men, is that of loving you so little while knowing how much you love him! How hard it is to share, like warm bread fresh from the oven, a love that men, so obtuse, don't want to know!

Loneliness, yes, and how hard it is to know that one is so faithless to one you love and have relied on so much! What sadness to love so much and yet have so small a heart.

Tonight, in the loneliness of the chapel, seeing you nailed to the cross, so still, so gentle, so alone, I come to tell you that I intend never to cease gazing at you. I now have nothing to offer you, nothing to tell you, nothing to give you. I have only the voice of my gaze. I love you, O Lord of all the crosses, even if today I do not dare to look at you. My love is poor, Lord, very poor, but please know that the one who loves you also has a riven heart. How hard it is, Lord, every morning, for someone whose soul has been torn asunder by life to smile, and to smile and smile so that others will be relieved of pain. I stare at the cross with unswerving eyes and can say only that when you called me, I did not know how much your love would demand of me. O, cross, riven loneliness!

> I no longer recall anything,
> All my ailments have fled,
> The force of the plea I carried
> Chokes me in my importunate mouth.

In its final stage, Marta's life was very cruel. As it had always been. The same hungers, the same sufferings, the same sorrows of all colors and all flavors. Her family robbed her of everything, as she lay there uncomplaining. She looked at the ceiling with her rosary of fluorescent beads in one hand and her Bible in the other. Sometimes, she held the letter of some missionary instead of the Bible. Her eyes were lifted to heaven, begging the good Lord to have some mercy upon her. She said to me, many times: "I was born to suffer, but there are so many who have nobody in this world as good as all of you to ease our suffering. Is everyone in Spain as good as you all are? If there were more like you, everybody would be happy." I left there ashamed, thinking, "Why aren't there more good people, Lord, so that the Martas of this world wouldn't have to cry anymore and would all be welcomed into your love?"

We continued to bring her food and whatever else she needed. Many more missionaries went by to see her, Pablo, Laura, Verónica, Cira, Antonio, Javier . . . too many to name them all. The good Lord knows their names, and he will reward them. I especially remember Laura, whose stay here was the longest and who lived the last chapter of Marta's life close to her.

How many nights, after returning from another visit to Marta, all I could do was look at the cross and say:

My Lord, and owner of my life,

So often does your Passion emerge before the missionary as he makes his way along the road, from so many crosses and sorrows you cry out to him your abandonment and silence. Tonight, here next to the cross, I have forgotten my sorrows, my exhaustion, my discouragement. I look at you, and the more I look at you, the more my destitution is eased and the more I understand that you did not call me to run and run, but rather to be here with you, and with my soul wrapped in silence. Your cross does not dissipate my sorrows, but I join mine with yours to allay my shivering. In all these years, O God, how many sufferings!

But it does not matter, Jesus, because when I see you, so good, gentle Lamb, so good, so good, my sorrows are forgotten, my pains, my exhaustion, my discouragements. I see you there, hanging between heaven and earth, crowned with thorns, with spittle, and with excrement. I see you naked, without beauty, without breath. Your side an open wound, your gaze upon heaven. Thieves as your companions, hanging there unsupported. The madness of a Friday and your hair afloat in the wind. The lance embedded in you, your heart open. I wonder whether I don't still lack lances, crowns, nails, and an open side, a thought that further dissipates my complaints and torments.

Jesus, what is a priest without torments? It is impossible to live so near to you without feeling the crack of the whip, the lance in the side, the hammer, the nails, the thorns as your crown and reward. What can I ask of you if you have asked that my service be to suffer before you?

> And I ask of you only that I ask nothing of you,
> To be here next to your dead image,
> To grow in the knowledge that pain is only
> The holy key to your holy gate.

Early one morning, a missionary named Mónica and I were at home. We had just come back from Lauds in the church, when there was an almost imperceptible knock at the door. It was barely dawn. We both were surprised when, upon opening the door, all we found was a boy who, trembling with fear, looked at Mónica and me and said to us, "My *mamá* is dying." Several of us ran to the batey. Yes, Marta was in agony. Her passion, her calvary, were approaching their end. That morning there was a strange silence in the batey. Even the prostitutes at the bordello had turned off the music. Death was lurking. It was nine o'clock in that hell that through love had been transformed into heaven. Marta's children pressed in and looked at their mother with a mixture of love and fear. As if by magic the disorder of clothes, garbage, and junk had disappeared. That morning, the room was empty except for a hard old bed that had already become her bier.

They all joined in tending to her sores. Her mother devoted herself to giving Marta a thousand ministrations while Mónica and I looked on, silently overcome with emotion. We prayed with her, she received absolution and the commendation of her soul, and we put her in the hands of the Virgin. The end seemed to be near, but her passion had still to deepen its bitterness for her. We'll never forget that, when we turned her over, we saw a dreadful, enormous sore in her lower back, where all her muscle mass had disappeared. She had an actual hole there. Four inches of her spinal column were clearly visible. It was an absolutely horrific sight. We were so overwhelmed that when we saw it we clung to each other a little more tightly. It was literally horrifying.

But the worst was still to come. We noticed that Marta had what seemed like long, bloody streaks on her feet and shins. We didn't understand why. We all conjectured and debated. We thought that perhaps they were part of her. Finally, one of her children, all of whom slept with Marta in the same bed, ended up confessing, "Look, Father, what happens is that during the night the rats eat my mother." Yes, brothers. It's hard to believe, hard even to write, but in the end Marta died because the house was infested with rats that climbed into bed with her in the night and gnawed at her feet, her legs, her whole body. Marta was the body of Christ, devoured by rats in their rabid hunger.

We prayed once more and left in absolute silence. Marta was in agony, and so, deep down, were we. My God! Can it be that a member of my flock, my daughter, our sister, was being eaten alive by rats? And so, each of us absorbed in our own thoughts and prayers, we returned home in sepulchral silence.

Right after we ate, Mónica and I went back to the batey of Copeyito. As if it were Good Friday afternoon on Golgotha, we were flooded by an enormous tropical storm. The thunderclaps were deafening, and the streaks of lightning illuminated the whole firmament. We went into the house. It was three in the afternoon, her Ninth Hour,[2] when Marta died. Rest in peace, daughter of God, and may the angels receive you in song as the missionaries sang on the day of your baptism.

There she was, her face covered with a sheet. We prayed. They told me there was no coffin. Marta was so poor that she didn't even have that. We went out into the rain and headed for the huge workshop where they herded together countless tractors, carts, and wagons. The cruel world of cane: hundreds of workers toiled at the labors of repair and welding. You should have seen us there, wandering up and down, asking if there was some box that would do as a coffin. They sent us from one end to the other. They finally took us to an oil-stained warehouse with hundreds of shelves filled with spare parts. Among the connecting rods, screws, axles, and hoses, a wretched coffin appeared. The scene was unforgettable! Two missionaries carried the

---

[2] The Ninth Hour (after dawn), believed to be the time of Christ's death on the cross, is a fixed time of prayer in the Catholic liturgy.—TRANS.

coffin back to the pickup truck, while the rain poured down from the sky and drummed out a lamentation for the dead! Marta's burial was as sad as her life. Rest in peace, Marta, our Christ on the cross, and be happy forever, because although so few loved you in this life, you'll see now that yes, you "*prietos*, too, go to heaven."

In the mission's chapel, I once again withdrew in prayer before the holy cross:

> Lord, Marta has died at last. We have confided her to you in your most beautiful heaven. I, who have complained so many, many times, promise tonight that I will never ask anything of you again, complain about anything again, yearn for anything again. As I did this afternoon in Golgotha, with Marta's body, I ask only to be here with the image of you in death. Grant me feet that are more and more exhausted, a heart that is more and more torn apart, a breast that is more and more pierced. That my lonely heart, pierced by the lance of love, be impassioned in more loves, in more kindnesses, in more sleepless nights. Grant that I may be with you, my wounded Shepherd, good Shepherd, gentle Shepherd, pure Shepherd. Grant me a being of un-divided heart, more-tired feet, empty hands, callused hands, fatherly hands, powerful hands. Grant me, Jesus, strong arms with which to carry everyone, sheep on my shoulders, and all the lambs of the world cradled in my arms, where next to my heart they may rest in your lap. Amen.

We pray for you every day before the tabernacle of the mission.

With my most loving blessing,
Father Christopher

P.S. I confess to you that as I finish this letter I don't have the heart to report on the brick and mortar of our construction projects, or ask you for anything. If you want to help the mission, you have the information here that you need, and if you want to help the missionary, . . . pray, pray for me again and again, that I may someday become a holy priest. May God bless you.

6

A PRIEST IN HELL

After the *passion and death* of the missionary's soul-searching, silence fell. Except for one very brief rumination about which we will say more later, not a single letter marking the path of Christopher Hartley arrived from San José de los Llanos between November 2001 and his departure from the island in October 2006. Five years of silence. That silence does say a great deal, however, about the man who arrived in 1997 suffused with the zeal and ardor of a missionary full of dreams that would not all come true. Only a few of them did, but they were perhaps the most important ones. Baptisms, celebrations, sacraments, and the simple fact of having accomplished what the Church had sent him to do: to establish her presence in places where she had never been, among a great number of men and women who needed her spiritual care as everyone does, and her social care more than the rest.

After the last letter we read, and throughout 2002, this priest began a new process in which he did not recognize himself, for which he was not prepared, and which he was not sent to the island to undertake. A process begun not for its own sake but as the upshot of his other work.

The little information we have of the father's time in the Dominican Republic between 2002 and 2006 comes from other sources. That is for the good, because some parts of the story cast a regrettable, obfuscatory cloud over it: a war in the courts and the media between the sugar industry and the missionary began with the publication of an article in the Spanish newspaper *El Mundo*. That article brought out the worst in the Vicini family, in the form of a media campaign against Father Christopher.

This cloud had a silver lining for the priest, because it overwhelmed him at times and thus gave him the chance to place himself in the hands of God as he had never done before. Father Christopher took that step, with the results that we will now see. What he understood very clearly in his mind and heart was that, having arrived at this point, he was absolutely not going to step away unless the Church sent him elsewhere. His parish was his home, and his parishioners were his family. He did not care about skin color or identity cards. He saw himself as a shepherd, a father, a friend, the village priest. And he was prepared to give his all, even his life, to defend the dignity of all his flock.

The hostilities began in January 2003, in the next follow-up meeting between the owners of the Cristóbal Colón sugar mill and the representatives of the Church, led by the bishop. The purpose of the meeting was to review the plans for ameliorating the living and working conditions of the Haitians in the bateyes, plans to which the owners of the sugar mill had committed themselves a year before. In that earlier meeting, Father Christopher and Noemí Méndez had given the bishop and the owners of the plantations, bateyes, and sugar mills a substantial file documenting the basic needs that such a plan of amelioration would have to address. Their report covered matters ranging from health and communication needs to legal conflicts between the working conditions of the cane cutters and the Dominican Constitution. In the meeting at the end of January 2003, however, one of the most important members of the Vicini family made his appearance in a rage, according to witnesses, holding in his hand the reason for his anger: an article in *El Mundo*, one of the most widely read newspapers published in Spanish.

The article, "A Priest in Hell", by the Spanish journalist Ildefonso Olmedo, was the cover story of the January 5, 2003, issue of *Crónica*, a Sunday supplement published with *El Mundo*.

With a pen that seemed to speak aloud, so detailed and photographic was its account of the facts, Olmedo related in four pages what he himself had seen and heard with his own eyes and ears during a recent trip to the Dominican Republic. This trip, and therefore the article, had its origin in Father Christopher's boldness: having met with nothing but inaction regarding improvement of the situation, he saw no option but to put himself in touch with the newspaper through a friend. And a firestorm broke out.

Olmedo's article would seem like fiction if it were not for the fact that it is accompanied by photographs as real as the father's letters and have the added credibility of their being published by *El Mundo*. Acting alone, the father could not reach many people to call their attention to what he considered to be a very evident social injustice that cried out to the heavens, so he decided that if they were not yielding to him, they would yield to the media. But that is not what happened.

In that meeting focused on Olmedo's article, what the Vicini family's representative and Father Christopher said to each other was not as important as what they did not say. The discussion ended when the father, having been accused of wanting to make himself famous at the expense of the poor, answered no less forcefully, "I don't know if I will have made myself famous at the expense of the poor, but you've made yourself rich at their expense."

Rather than diverting ourselves with details that are now unimportant, let us turn to the article of Ildefonso Olmedo: "A Priest in Hell".

∽

A Priest in Hell

by Ildefonso Olmedo,
reporting from the Dominican Republic

A trip to the Dominican Republic, where Haitians live in a hell of sugarcane: workers sold like cattle, massive deportations, armed overseers . . . The Spanish priest Christopher Hartley Sartorius exchanged a promising career in Rome to become "the father" of men who, in 2003, continue to live in slavery.

Night falls on the coconut palms to the accompaniment of the last notes of birds and fighting cocks. The hummingbird's flight has ended. On the porch of the barracks, a pot blackened by misery is heating on the coals. The dark men, devastated by yet another day of draining toil, mill about anxiously. They talk among themselves in Creole, the language of the Haitians. One of them, in English, asks the priest who is visiting them if they have delivered the mattresses for them to sleep on. This would be a time for questions, but nobody dares to break the law of silence.

Nobody saw, nobody heard. "Yes, Father, it was the field guard from the Contador batey. He hunted them down when they tried to run away. He slashed them with the machete there, in that barracks. . . . It would have been about five in the morning, before dawn. He says he can't let them escape, that the bosses pay too much per head," a peasant finally confesses, overcoming his fear. He's talking about human beings, not cattle. By the time the explanations are over, Christopher Hartley Sartorius has been driven to distraction.

The Spanish priest has been on a mission for five years in the cane-fields of the Dominican Republic, and he feels in his own body the abuses visited on the Haitians, their enslavement by the cane. "Don't ever serve someone who served," the priest mumbles when he finds out that the field guard (the police of the hamlets where the workers are confined), who that morning had arrested and beaten up a group of cane cutters, was a Haitian, like them. "Merité, the watchman of Contador," the father repeated hours later, enraged, to the manager of the sugar mill that owned all those fields. He demanded justice and an end to abuse. Behind him, in a corner of the office of Don Ricardo, the all-powerful boss whom the Vicini Consortium put in charge of the Cristóbal Colón sugar mill and who was now listening to the father's complaints, was an old, faded portrait of Abraham Lincoln, the president of the United States who abolished slavery.

The cotton was there

In Dominican lands, the sugarcane. And just a few weeks ago, at the beginning of December, the new harvest began, the harvest of 2002/2003.

Every morning, the muddy roads swarm with rusty old wagons towed by tractors, full of the new loads of undocumented men who are brought from the Haitian border, with the complicity of the army and the police and under the presumed supervision of the immigration officials. That is the sugarcane business, with its sweet riches and bitter heartaches. It is a novel of crude tragic realism, of the batey, a word that Friar Bartolomé de Las Casas heard a thousand times and that has repulsed the missionary Father Christopher Hartley Sartorius since his arrival in the Dominican Republic. Las Casas spoke out against it to the Catholic kings. Hartley Sartorius told the president of the Republic, when the latter made a visit in January 2000 to the historic batey of Gautier: "Mr. President, you are in hell's waiting room."

Batey, in the language of the Taínos, the aborigines who have been exterminated on the old island of Hispaniola, came to mean the communal space, the place of ceremonies. Today it rings more of the ghetto, of men enslaved on the plantations. The price per worker (barely forty-eight euros) in the new slave trade of the twenty-first century is as meager as the wage they are paid (around eighty euros a month if they cut somewhat more than a ton and a half per day).

Hell sometimes hides behind the face of paradise. The Dominican Republic, the Caribbean, and beautiful beaches. "The very clement mildness of the climate and the green landscape and trees are clear tokens of earthly paradise," Columbus mistakenly said when he disembarked in the islands.

You must enter the heart of the canefields yourself to hear the truth. In their songs on the plantations, the Haitians who cut the cane for the powerful sugar industry in the Dominican Republic sing in Creole the history of their sorrows. Machetes in hand, they sing about how they come and go, about how the inhuman *zafra* (the harvest of the cane) helps keep alive the family members they left behind in Haiti, about how, if they were to die in the canefields, God would welcome them in heaven. When they fall silent, the cane tells its long story of slavery.

"I came from Haiti in 1983 in a truck, because they told me they'd pay me two hundred pesos for each load of cane. They fooled me for life. I left my first wife there, and a job in a hardware store. Turns out they don't pay me more than forty pesos (about two euros) per ton of cut cane." Simon is now thirty-five years old and feels like an old man. Next to him is Juancito Chan, forty-one, who also lives in one of the bateyes owned by the Boca Chica sugar mill that until 2000 belonged to the State Sugar Council (Consejo Estatal del Azúcar: CEA). "I crossed the border to work, but I didn't earn enough to go back," he says. His words echo the novel *Over*, published in the '40s by the Dominican writer Ramón Marrero Aristy: "Every morning, before sunrise, the smelly, ragged mob lines up—with a hunger that never leaves them—on the way to the cutting of the cane, like a procession of soulless beings. . . . I see their silhouettes, and the chop of their machetes strikes fear into me. How long will men live like beasts?!"

You can hear the crunch of the cane, the shouts of the foreman waking them up to get them to their starting point at sunrise, the protests of the wagons that cart the harvest to the sugar mills to be milled, the rasping voices of the overseers on horseback with pistols in their belts, the old accusatory lament of the antislavery societies and advocates for human rights.

Ever since he became a missionary in these lands in 1997, the words of Christopher Hartley Sartorius have also wafted over these fields, in letters from the mission to his friends and former parishioners: "Looking at the cane, so tall, so silent, swaying from side to side with the wind, I've learned above all that the cane speaks. Yes, it speaks. Of the life and death of poor men bent over with pain, bent over with silence, bent over with exhaustion, bent over with blood and death. How many human lives has this merciless cane devoured? These fields are watered with the blood, tears, and sweat of countless lives of Dominicans and Haitian migrants, who have come here—been brought, even—looking for paradise on earth, only to find themselves with nothing more than a loincloth and a machete in the hell that is the cane. . . . And to think that all the cane in this part of the country—hundreds and hundreds of miles of cane—belongs to just one family!"

These are the words of the father: "the father" is what he is called by everyone, including the Vicini family, the most powerful local dynasty of the sugar industry. One member of the family was a president of the Republic, and in 1898 the signature of the patriarch was as good as currency. They are the descendants of the Italian immigrant Juan Bautista Vicini, who at the end of the nineteenth century contributed to the revival of an industry that was born shortly after Columbus arrived in Hispaniola, bearing the seeds of sugarcane that he brought from the Canary Islands. And "the father" is what the inhabitants of the little town of San José de los Llanos, in the province of San Pedro de Macorís, also call the missionary, taking comfort from his arrival because it had been ten years since a Catholic priest had sung Mass to them. "Voodoo terrorizes the people here. . . . The gospel that I bring frees them."

Four thousand baptisms

In the great eastern plain of the Dominican Republic, the largest in the Caribbean, "Father" is also what the children call out to him with devotion (he has baptized four thousand of them so far) when they crowd around him as he passes by in the visits he pays, like a penitent, to the bateyes, the remote, wretched hamlets of the workers. The father, who does not keep silence before the owners and the powers that be of the land, has become the voice of the poorest, the heir in his social work of his admired Teresa of Calcutta, with whom he shared teachings in India and whose confessor he was on more than one occasion. He still feels a deep sorrow that he was unable to attend the burial of his friend.

The day Mother Teresa died, on September 5, 1997, Christopher was on his way to the remote village in the canefields. A friend from seminary who had a parish in the area, Antonio Diufaín (from Cádiz), had finally convinced him. As Mother Teresa had convinced him years before to become a missionary to the Hispanics of New York, to leave

Rome, where he had earned a doctorate in theology and was destined to rise to the top of the curia. For thirteen years, this priest, born in his father's London forty-three years ago, who had grown up from the age of five in his mother's Madrid, immersed himself in the Bronx. On his way to the new land of his mission, Christopher kept thinking about the little woman who dared to dress her followers in the white and blue dress of India's untouchables, pariahs, outcasts, to go out among them.

Dressed in clerical black and a white collar, the nephew of the communist Nicolás Sartorius and cousin of Isabel has been able to make a place for himself in the pierced heart of the cane. This is what his uncle said to him when he went off to the seminary at the young age of fifteen: "All I ask is, when you're a priest, don't be an unthinking tool." And he certainly is not. One day, perhaps, he will dare to take on the project that seems to shadow him: to write a book about the cutters of cane, condemned forever and ever to an existence that is not life. He has already decided on the title: *Slaves in Paradise*. He would tell the story of Marta, the parishioner who was eaten by rats in a hut that never belonged to her; of people so poor that, when one of them dies, a coffin has to be made for him out of the wooden boards that wall his house. The father titled the third letter that he wrote from the mission, when he had been the parish priest of San José de los Llanos for just a short time, "It Is Always Good Friday in the Canefields."

The batey Peso Enmedio is part of the parish of Los Llanos. A demolished windmill at the edge of the hamlet, next to the rail line used by the trains that take the cane to the sugar mill, is the living remnant of the passage of Hurricane Georges through the whole island in 1998. Timalli Yac is lying on the ground, in the doorway of his wooden hut with a zinc roof. Since he stopped working as a cane cutter a year ago, he survives, half blind, thanks to the little plot of land (*conuco*) that the boss of the plantation lets him cultivate. The son of immigrants, Timalli Yac is eighty-eight years old, as old as the period that began when Haitians began cutting the cane in the Dominican Republic. The U.S. Marines were the first to bring them, during the American invasion (1916–1924) of the Spanish part of the island. Recruited since then in the hamlets and ghettos, they are cannon fodder in a land where the only law is the one that rules the planting, cultivation, and cutting of the cane. It is the law of the boss on duty, whether he is called the overseer or the foreman. The rest, including the Labor Law, is scrap paper.

The history of sugarcane on this Caribbean island is also the history of the country itself. With African manual labor supplied by the slave trade, it was one of the pillars of the Spanish colony until the middle of the seventeenth century. After that the industry withered away, only to be reborn at the end of the nineteenth century. The U.S. occupation fostered the definitive rise of the sector. From the 1920s to the 1980s, the sugar industry was the backbone of the Dominican economy and its main source of foreign currency. The structure of the sector was shaped by the dictatorship (from 1930 to 1961) of Rafael Leónidas Trujillo, who, during his last decade in power, was able to seize most of the country's sugar mills.

Only two private businesses, Central Romana (then part of the South Porto Rico Sugar Company) and the Vicini Consortium (Dominican owned), escaped his grasp. They accounted for 30 percent and 10 percent, respectively, of the country's sugar production. The situation has changed. Central Romana has taken Trujillo's place as the country's most important producer, followed by the Vicini Consortium. The situation of the bateyes, on the other hand, has not changed. Not far away from the hotel developments of La Romana and Punta Cana, from the Diente de Perro golf course and the mansions of Julio Iglesias and Oscar de la Renta, thousands of people spend every harvest in foul barracks and tinplate houses, with no electricity or potable water, mostly without latrines, and without a voice. They sweat blood in the burning sun, which sears them like a branding iron, but they are completely undocumented and have no work contracts. Some 10 percent of the population owns 90 percent of the land.

The traffic in Haitian workers was unregulated until 1952. Trujillo himself, who in 1937 masterminded the killing of twelve thousand Haitians along the border, moderated his anti-Haitianism and, by then the owner of many sugar mills, reached an agreement with the neighboring country to normalize the hiring of the cane cutters. The system survived the dictator and remained in force until the fall in Port-au-Prince (Haiti's capital) of the Duvaliers' regime, and the exile of Baby Doc, in 1986. During those years, the Dominican government bought workers from the Haitian government and then rented them in turn to the Dominican sugar mills. In the 1980s the payments for those immigrants—officially, they were accounted for as "administrative recruiting expenses"—amounted to more than two million dollars.

The private sugar producers, ostensibly on the sidelines of this buying and selling, became the employers of fifteen thousand workers. When these are added to the nineteen thousand employees of the state sugar mills that Trujillo left behind at his death, the annual flow of workers across the border was actually thirty-four thousand men. Today the figures cited by Father Christopher are somewhat smaller. He calculates that this year some twenty thousand Haitians will come to work in the harvest that has already begun and will last until June. And he maintains that the trade in human beings, which continues clandestinely but is supervised by men in uniform, will generate bribes and other payments to the authorities in the range of five million dollars.

Mass deportation

In the book published five months ago that documents, in the words of its title, *Tras las huellas de los braceros* (In the footsteps of the workers), the lawyer Esteban Sánchez, director of the legal aid office of Plataforma Vida, condemns the rise in his country of "a Mafia that operates on a national scale, dealing in huge sums of money and involving the civil, judicial, and military authorities". Everything took on the smell of secrecy, he explains, when the fall of the Duvalier regime "ended the Haitian government's practice of selling human beings so that their labor could be exploited in the sugar mills of the Dominican Republic". They bring them to work here without rights, and when the harvest is over they deport them en masse.

"It makes no sense to let them leave after the harvest, given how much it costs to get them," says the overseer in one of the plantations in Father Christopher's parish. He does not dare to talk in front of the priest about "bought bodies". With his pistol in his belt, he is his master's voice: "The Company pays between a thousand and twelve hundred pesos [something like forty-nine euros] for each man. The identity card and other immigration documents cost six hundred, and you have to pay the inspector another six hundred." Not to mention the headhunters, who are sent across the border to recruit the workers.

It is clear that the overseer wants to please the priest. "Four hundred of them arrived last night, and I immediately sent for their mattresses. This year they earn forty-three pesos [a little more than two euros] per ton of cane." Each cutter averages between one and a half and two tons for a day's work, which begins at six in the morning and does not end until dusk. They are paid every two weeks—never in cash, but in vouchers that they can use to pay the local grocery stores, which take a 20 percent commission on each voucher.

One of the many mornings on which Father Christopher makes the rounds of the bateyes of his parish, an old, nameless cutter came up to say to him: "Tell them there, in Spain, that the sugar here isn't sweet, it's bitter. And it isn't white, either, because it's red, the color of the blood spilled by so many workers." The missionary remembered then the opening words of the novel *Azúcar Amargo* (*Bitter Sugar*), by the French journalist Maurice Lemoine, that he had just finished reading: "This book is dedicated to the memory of Millien Beaubrun, a Haitian cane cutter, murdered on July 7, 1980, shot in the back with fifteen bullets of an M-1 rifle, at the Palmajero military post on the Catarey sugar factory property in the Dominican Republic. His crime was unpardonable. He had refused to continue to work without pay. He said no to slavery."[1]

It has been a little more than two years since Hartley Sartorius became the new Bartolomé de Las Casas of the cane cutters. Or the echo of the sermon by the Dominican friar Antonio de Montesinos, the first person to raise his voice in favor of the Indians back in 1511: "By what right . . . are they not human beings, after all?" Christopher, five centuries later, says he is speaking in the name of his entire diocese. As he wrote in one of his letters from the mission: "The voice of the Church was raised like a trumpet, loud and clear, before the president of the Republic and the powerful oligarchs of this island." And he was not preaching in the desert. The oldest sugar company in the country, the Vicini Consortium, agreed to negotiate with him about future improvements in the living conditions of the workers.

Although he has not been the first person in the Church to preach about the miserable living conditions of the Haitians during the harvest, his words have been heard at higher levels than any of the others. Priests such as the Spanish Julio Silla or the Belgian Pierre Ruquoy,

---

[1] Translated from the French by Andrea Johnston.

who works with Pastoral Haitiana and Plataforma Vida, spoke out before him. Noemí, the lawyer born in a batey who today works for the diocese, explains that what Christopher did was to "take the lid off the pot" at the right moment. When the state's sugar mills were privatized, the politicians stopped taking their cut from the sugar, and so there were fewer interests at stake.

The story of Noemí, the seventh of eight children, is one of personal transcendence. Her family escaped from the circle of misery in the bateyes. "Many of the girls I played with when I was little ended up dying of AIDS and in prostitution. . . . But I have fond memories of my childhood in the batey. It was when I was studying law that I discovered its dark side, in the mass repatriations of Haitians in the '80s and '90s." Now, in addition to advising the father, Noemí helps the communities that are being dispossessed of their lands by the big hotel companies. Tourism has taken the place of sugarcane as the driver of the country's economy.

Noemí sometimes fears for the physical safety of the father. She knows, because she has also worked with Pierre Ruquoy in his long fight, the threats and assassination attempts against that Belgian priest. He lives a life of poverty in batey 5 of the Barahona sugar mill, and he has been dedicating himself to the immigrants' cause for more than twenty-seven years. "In the Gautier batey, Father Hartley is salvation," said the newspaper *Listín Diario* at the beginning of 2002. By then several meetings had been held with the owners of the sugar mills that operate in the hundreds of square miles where Christopher, with words and with works, preaches the gospel. He always says that San José de los Llanos is near the spot where the first Mass was celebrated in the New World, on January 6, 1493.

He has more to say every time he sits down with the heir to the powerful company, Juan Bautista Vicini. He talks about people such as André Françoise, age sixty-nine, who has thrown away twenty-four years cutting cane in the Contador batey. Even today, a sick man alone and penniless in a decrepit bed, he does not have an identity card. The father talks about workers such as Quico, a thirty-year-old born in a batey who does have an identity card (he is Eddy Charles René, the papers say) but who all his life has been refused a contract.

Nor does the priest forget the thousands of children and men who, loaded into wagons meant for animals, arrive every morning from Haiti and receive the only papers that truly bespeak their situation: a machete, a gallon of water, and with any luck a mattress so they won't have to sleep on the floor or on the crude springs of their cots. "The Church is here with them, to shout beside them," he always says. He does not aspire to conquer paradise for them, as the Spaniards who came in their caravels did, but neither does he want these people to be transformed into a carnival display for the safaris to the bateyes that the hotels organize for tourists. The father is a tenacious man. "I live in this hell because a man who one Friday afternoon, out of love, allowed himself to be killed on a piece of hard wood, spoke my name with an unfathomable tenderness. . . . For me, these canefields are nothing but his bitter Golgotha, the cane is nothing but the cross of all his sufferings, and these poor men are icons and effigies of a broken Christ whom I would like, out of love, to bring to life." These are the father's words. The setting sun lights up the coconut palms. The men in the barracks mill uneasily about for one more night. The cane speaks.

~

Nobody in the world knew it then, but this article had touched off a war.

7

THE ENIGMATIC SIXTEENTH LETTER

Although the fifteenth letter, in which the father recounted the dramatic case of Marta, the woman who was eaten alive by rats in the bed she shared with her children, was his last, at one point the father wrote a few meditative lines that he called his sixteenth letter, which is brief but nonetheless reflects his state of mind at that time. If in the preceding fifteenth letter he recognized that he had been overwhelmed by the mission, the reflections in the following text display the palpable loneliness of a missionary who, having given his all, seems to feel little more than loneliness and abandonment.

This stage in Father Christopher's life in the Dominican Republic is a faithful mirror of the deserts that we so often find ourselves required to cross on the paths of faith. His absolute conviction, not a feeling, that God has called him to a mission, along with his iron will, bind the missionary to his post. This year was one of travail similar to what the apostles endured on the evening of Good Friday. We know nothing of that time, neither where they spent it, nor what they did, nor what they thought. The father was bewildered, alone, disillusioned, like a missionary crying in the desert unheeded by anyone, ignored and dismissed as reckless not just by those who hated him, but also by some of those who should have been closer to him. The truth is that his arrival on the island unleashed the fury of a hurricane in a place where the situation as it stood was so deeply rooted in history and context that very possibly the people who might have been able to set things right from within would not even have realized it but for the arrival of someone new to the scene, like the father.

The fragmentary letter we have, no more than a simple reflection of a state of chaos, very clearly shows Father Christopher's state of mind at the time. The question that gnaws at me is how a missionary who seems to have fallen with his mission into a tenacious spider's web escapes from it. His options were to throw in the towel, turn a deaf ear to what he had lived through during those years, or press on. Here we see him as he was in 2002, freeing himself from the threads that clung to him and finding his way forward.

~

"In the evening of life"

As I had done so many times in my life as a missionary, I was traveling this afternoon down a muddy, mired road. I was alone in my old blue pickup truck, one of the rare occasions when no one was with me, and I stopped for a long time. I didn't stop because I had gotten stuck, as on so many other occasions. I didn't need to wait anxiously for someone to come and rescue me with a tractor or a team of oxen. I stopped simply because I had a deep need to stop, to come to a halt along the road. Here in the inviolate silence of the canefields, far from intrusive noise.

Ideas to be developed

There are other roads, paved roads, with neon lights, rows upon rows of offices and fine restaurants. Some with muddy clothes, others with mud in the soul or heart—all choose the road they want to take in life. Sometimes, for a fleeting moment, the ones who travel calmly along the paved road visit the muddy one, and vice versa. I, too, had visited the paved road . . . and I aspired to find companions for that fleeting journey. Where does each road lead? There are those who have known only one of the two.

8

MARIASELA TONIGHT

We are in a house like any other in the Dominican Republic, in October 2003, sitting in front of the television set. It is prime time on Sunday night, and the program is a show that has been on the air for more than six years. The images it presents, to the amazement of the whole Dominican Republic, reflect the misery of a people whose faces look out from the television screen and into the houses of all those who, until then, did not even know they existed—and there they were, right in front of them, in the canefields. Suddenly, the sweet voice of a woman reaches out to her audience, sitting comfortably on their cushioned sofas, to describe a hell on earth:

> They travel at harvest time. They cross the border with the consent of the army and under the supervision of the immigration authorities. They arrive late at night so they won't know where they are and can't flee, because behind the beautiful landscape of the canefields that greet us in our eastward journey, men, women, and children live like beasts. This is the story of the Haitian workers and their families, who live in the bateyes and sugar mills. It's a story that has been enacted over and over again, for more than a century, before the indifferent gaze of the society that harbors them.

The voice that so rudely shook the audience was that of Mariasela Álvarez, one of the most popular figures of the Dominican Republic's recent history. The winner of the Miss World contest in 1981, Mariasela became an architect following her tour of the world in her beauty queen's crown. After opening her own architecture practice, she made the move to commercial television as a presenter of variety shows. When Father Christopher arrived on the island, she reached her peak in this role on the popular Sunday program *Mariasela Tonight*. For more than two hours each week, Dominicans enjoyed a varied program that ranged from musical shows to live interviews with celebrities. Among those who appeared and sang on the program over the years were international figures such as Juan Luis Guerra, Alejandro Sanz, and Ricky Martin. Mixing these entertaining segments with investigative reporting and social content, the program made room for a small segment called "Touched by God", in which various people, whether famous or not, described their conversion and thus gave the public the chance to know God. Mariasela had experienced her own conversion not long before, after a series of spiritual exercises with Father Emiliano Tardif,[1] a Canadian missionary in the Dominican Republic who was known around the world for his gift of healing, among other things.

In one of her segments Mariasela wanted to report on Father Christopher and the situation in the bateyes of San José de los Llanos, a situation that she had known absolutely nothing about, even though she was a well-informed, cultivated woman who was born in the Dominican Republic and had access to the media. In fact, until her forty-minute presentation, almost no one in the Dominican Republic knew anything about the conditions in which thousands of Haitians were living on the sugarcane plantations—in their own backyard, as the saying goes.

The cat was let out of the bag when the *El Mundo* article, included in chapter 6, came to the attention of this restless and daring woman, who is as comfortable visiting the Haitian bateyes with camera in hand, up to her ears in mud, as she is modeling on the runway.

Just as the article by Ildefonso Olmedo opened the eyes of Spaniards to the very distant reality that was being lived out in the bateyes of the Dominican Republic, so Mariasela's program, which was the most popular in the country and hosted by a more internationally known personality, opened the eyes of the Dominicans themselves.

Mariasela is seated on a terrace in Santo Domingo, in January 2012, recounting how her venture, as she tells it, had such a resounding impact on her life. Here, then, is Mariasela Álvarez.

---

[1] Emiliano Tardif (1928–1999), a missionary of the Sacred Heart of Jesus and pioneering priest of the Charismatic Renewal.

Mariasela, you've played an important role in making Father Christopher Hartley's work known in the Dominican Republic. Knowing what he's doing, and given the adverse effects it could have on you personally, why do you do it?

When I read that article in *El Mundo*, I was puzzled by many things. On the one hand, the thought that those people should be living in such bad conditions in my own country outraged me. I don't care whether they're Haitians or Dominicans, because they're people. On the other hand, I was moved by compassion, by the fact that I could help. I had lived my own conversion not long before, and I had opened a home here in Santo Domingo, operated by the Daughters of Charity, for children with AIDS. Third, the strong personality that this Spanish priest projected caught my attention. So I got in touch with him and threw myself wholeheartedly into the project of reporting on it. I wanted to visit the bateyes. I went during the filming, and I supervised the script and the final cut. It was one of the reports that I've been most involved in. As a reporter, I think the subject called for it.

What did the report consist of?

First of all, the images themselves of some bateyes with the accounts of some of the cane workers and the women who lived there. Also, we looked into the statement that the industry had published denying the content of the article in *El Mundo*, and we investigated whether it was true that *El Mundo* had lied or whether what they had said was true.

What was the result?

We made it clear that *El Mundo* hadn't lied. I wanted, in any case, to get in touch with the Vicini family, to be objective and give them the chance to speak, but there was no way. All I did was report reality.

And the media reaction?

Tremendous. This was a bomb, my dear. Because until then the reality of what was happening in the bateyes was very little known in the Dominican Republic. The program made the father famous and made the Dominican people aware of the situation that existed in the bateyes of Los Llanos.

How could this reality have been unknown?

Because nobody had bothered to tell it. I assure you that that's so. I'm from here and have lived here all my life. This forty-minute segment opened the eyes of the Dominican Republic to a situation that was very problematic and unjust for the Haitians. But don't be surprised. I'm sure you also have complicated situations in Spain, right on your doorstep, and nobody says anything.

You said something. Why?

Yes, I couldn't not say something. I had to tell it.

Have you paid a price, as a media personality, either personally or professionally, for bringing the situation in the bateyes into the homes of Dominicans?

Well, nobody dared to say anything to me directly. I was a very well-known personality in my country, a very beloved woman with a big following. But it's true that there was a certain part of the population that accused me of being pro-Haitian. Me, when I've taken the name of the Dominican Republic around the world with so much pride and effort, they called me an enemy of my country! This was unfair. This wasn't a question of Haitians or Dominicans, but of human beings. What's more, the Dominican people are a great people, caring, friendly, and welcoming. That was clear from the fact that, for months after the program was aired, my office was inundated with boxes full of clothes, food, and all sorts of other things, which Dominicans sent us and asked us to distribute to the Haitians in the bateyes. It was a revolution. The same thing happened with the earthquake in Port-au-Prince in 2010. My country reached out to Haiti, because we're a great people, generous and admirable.

We're trying in this book to follow the footsteps of a missionary from whom we have only a handful of letters. I'm going to ask you, because you've met him, to tell us about him, to tell us how he was, to give us some insights that can't be reflected in what he has written.

Father Christopher was a missionary who loved his vocation. If he hadn't been so devoted to his calling, he wouldn't have done what he did. What he did wasn't easy, and it cost him a good deal of pain, of suffering. He suffered for those people, with those people. The pain he suffered sometimes caused him to argue with people. He argued with me more than once, for example. That happened very often, because the father also had a very strong character, but we should say that it was a character that was up to the challenge of the situation. I think only somebody like him could have done what he did here. He's a brilliant person, a tireless fighter, a man who opened a way forward through evangelization. I learned to love him. I think we all did. When we realized that he came to help the poorest people and that a character like his was necessary, we all learned to love him. Sometimes somebody has to shout and pound the table. But I'll tell you straight out that I'm glad such a person is working on the side of the good, because I don't even want to imagine him being on the other side. You understand.

You say that what he did, he did out of evangelization. What do you mean?

That's for sure. The father celebrated Mass here in a different batey every day. He baptized thousands of children, educated Christians. He went back and forth every day with his pickup truck to visit the poor and the sick, to take them Communion, to give them company, to console them. He was a man with an outsize temperament, who incarnated his faith.

Can you remember any part of your segment that should get particular attention?

Yes. There's a moment in it when the father's in a miserable little hut, where a sick woman's lying on the bed and can't get up. Seven children, her children, are milling around next to her. They're naked, some of them are sick, they're all hungry. The father picked up one of the girls in his arms and said, "This girl here's an inhuman misery, but it's the only way that this business can make money, at the expense of the human lives that have been destroyed along the way. The problem isn't that there's no compassion; it's that there's no justice. These children are being deprived of their rights. There are laws in this country, in the world, that protect the rights of children and workers. The situation as it stands exists only because nobody here has done anything about it. Nobody's denounced it, nobody's protested against it. Nobody's come to see it. What's more, anybody who does come to see it puts himself at risk. Not just at risk of physical danger, but at risk of dishonor. Starting tomorrow, you'll be able to see how your name is smeared, how they defame you. Starting tomorrow, you'll be able to see how they assassinate your character, your good name, the way they can that of a priest or of the Church. It's not possible to defend the rights of the poor unless you're ready to run the risks that implies. I want every person who sees this to think that he's reading a page from the Passion of Christ. It's terrible to see this and remember these words of the Lord: 'You did it to me.' These people aren't even treated as if they were people."

Just then, the little girl began to caress the father's beard with a tiny finger, and the father went on: "I can come and give them a bag of rice out of charity, but if I do, I'm insulting them, because these people have worked. It's just that they haven't been fairly compensated for their work. It's an insult to give them a bag of rice. They thank you, because if they don't they'll end up hungry, but can't a man feed his children, buy them a school uniform, or a Christmas present? Why can't he, if he's earned it and worked for it, and deserves it?"

What effect did Father Christopher's presence have on the island?

He opened a way forward. He confronted the powers that be and put a face on the poorest of the poor. He didn't ask for gifts or favors for them, just fairness. But he also didn't do that out of social justice, or for revolution, but rather out of evangelization, as we've said. Christopher was a first-rate missionary. Remember that he came of age in the shadow of Teresa of Calcutta, and as I've said, he loved his vocation.

What do you think moved him to do what he did?

It's hard to understand why he took on the industry if he didn't do it out of love. Christopher was attacked, slandered, insulted. Both he and his helpers were threatened, and nobody will go through that except out of love, not for money or out of selfishness. His cause wasn't revolution. His cause was the poorest of the poor. He was the only person on the island who really gave his life for these people. Others have helped them, but he gave them his life. He became one of them, and thus they lived in him. For them, he was the answer to so many of their prayers. God sent him to tell them that he was by their side. It's true that Christopher has his faults, but I also believe that he was sent by God. That's what the poor people whom he took care of and looked after say. Remember, for these people who were born into misery, that was simply how life was. They were poor just as cane is green. The Church, in the person of Christopher, taught them the dignity that is theirs as the children of God. They made Christopher theirs because they felt he was one of them. They're waiting for him even today, and it's now more than eight years since he left.

You told me he left without saying good-bye to anybody. Why do you think he did that?

You'll have to ask him. What I can tell you is that he was very sorry to leave. He loved this place, these people. I don't think he has ever gone away completely. I think he's somehow still here among these people. But maybe, in another part of the world, there are other poor people who need the presence of the Church in the form of an earthquake. That's his vocation, and for him, his vocation and his service to the Church come first, before anything else.

~

At the end of the documentary we can see Father Christopher explaining what he hopes for from a test as challenging as the one he endured during that time. "I hope that when I die, some of these people will be able to say to the Lord, when I'm at the gate, 'Let him come in; he was good to me.'"

That is how Mariasela's documentary ends, a program dotted with short quotations from the father, so we now have his voice and his gaze in addition to his letters. Little by little, we are getting closer and closer to this person who left a public and notorious witness to the mission of the Church in a more-than-problematic situation. It is with that gaze that the documentary ends, a fiery gaze born of the conviction of somebody who somehow knows he is in the right, looking at the camera and saying: "I've been warned many times and urged to be prudent. I know that these people hate me and that there's a visceral hostility toward me personally. People have been sent to tell me, with the most absolute possible disdain, 'Tell that reverend that any day now he'll wake up in a muddy ditch with his mouth full of flies.' I know my telephone is bugged. I live under a lot of pressure. But it's clear that this priest doesn't have a reverse gear. That the Church doesn't have a reverse gear. Change is coming."

THE END OF THE MISSION, THE BEGINNING OF SOMETHING NEW

After the article in *El Mundo* and Mariasela's program, there was no turning back from the fight to the finish that had taken shape between the two sides in San José de los Llanos. On the one hand, the sugar industry, personified by the family that owned the lands and the bateyes that belonged to the Cristóbal Colón sugar mill, of San Pedro de Macorís, resolved to continue, not only in its own plantations but in the entire island, the production of sugar as it had been established more than a hundred years before. On the other side was the Catholic Church, personified by the parish priest of San José de los Llanos, Father Christopher Hartley, who invoked and clothed himself in the Church's teachings and doctrine of social justice and human rights and argued for a radical change in the policy regarding the living and working conditions of the workers in the commercial exploitation of the canefields.

The exposure of the subject to public opinion and the complete rupture of relations between the two sides set off an endless series of maneuvers in opposite directions that marked the last three years of Father Christopher's service as a missionary in the Dominican Republic. The father and the lawyer Noemí Méndez came to realize that more than three years of fruitless negotiations not only had not at all advanced the recognition of the dignity of the workers, but rather had widened the gulf between the positions of the two sides. So, given that the higher-ups were paying no attention to them, they decided to concentrate on those below, and Noemí had the idea of launching an effort to train small groups of the residents of the bateyes and the little campos. They chose a leader for each group, who would teach the rest of its members about such basic ideas as human rights and the Dominican Constitution, which protected their rights and set forth the obligations of the employers.

César Vallenilla works for CEDAIL and at the time was working very closely with Noemí Méndez, the father's right arm in legal matters. César's knowledge of the bateyes comes from his personal experience as a Jesuit novice, when a part of his education and work included cutting cane side by side with the Haitian migrants and with the Dominican workers. So from very early on, almost from his childhood, César has shared their sweat, their talk, and their pain, looking into their eyes, listening to their complaints, and drying their tears. This onetime aspirant to the Jesuit order, who finally hung up his habit and married to found a family, tells us that the conditions in the bateyes were "very dehumanizing, very harsh, with no hope or happiness. That way of life turns people into animals, or worse, because some animals are better cared for than the workers."

César witnessed firsthand the process of the father's transformation, a process in which César emphasizes the importance of little Roberta, the girl who died of AIDS and for whom the father had conceived so much affection: "When Roberta died, the father experienced a mystical transformation, a manifestation of God in him, which turned him into one of them, a dispossessed and uprooted Haitian. That very painful experience made him stronger, even changed his looks. His love never stopped being love, but he matured very much; he became whole, firm, a rock, and it was impossible to turn him back in the face of no matter what difficulty. Roberta's death strengthened his vocation and turned the father, by the grace of God, into the nemesis of the devil."

And we ourselves have seen, in the fourteenth letter from the mission, that Roberta's death was an inflection point. Our confidant remembers how "with that transformation of the father other people also were transformed, in the sense that they wanted more, they armed themselves with courage and clothed themselves in dignity, the dignity that the father reminded them they had."

How did the father convince them? "It was very simple," César recalls, "he had no fear, he wasn't afraid, and courage is contagious. The father embodied the truth of the gospel that every man is a son of God, and when that truth is incarnate, it's contagious, it's passed on."

For César, it wasn't just passionate gestures against injustice that gave the people courage; "it was evangelical ardor, the eagerness that the father showed when he arrived at a batey in loving the people, consoling them, embracing them, celebrating Mass and the sacraments. He was a messiah, a savior, and that can't be except out of love."

To spread that transformation among the poor inhabitants of the bateyes, the father's team established courses to teach the workers that they had rights. After distributing copies of the Dominican Constitution and the labor laws, they formed teaching teams that met periodically to teach workers how to defend their rights. It was not easy at the beginning, as César recalls for us: "First we had to teach them that they were persons. They didn't have any conception of themselves. Keep in mind that many bateyes didn't have even a single mirror. When we told them to draw an animal, a horse or an ox, they drew it, but when we told them to draw a family, or themselves, they didn't know what to do; they were blocked. And if they had no concept of a person, there was no way they could have a concept of the rights of a person!"

As an example of the difficult and arduous educational campaign that this team set in motion, there was a workshop titled "Who Am I?" that was supposed to involve no more than three sessions, but there were bateyes where men and women needed as many as nine.

After the team had explained to them who they were, the next step was to teach them that they had rights. They taught them to learn for themselves what those rights were, more in their breach than in their observance. Noemí Méndez tells us that they would gather together the people of the bateyes and ask them how things were going and what their problems were, but nobody said anything, not so much because they feared reprisal as because they did not identify injustices as problems but rather as normal parts of life.

All of this changed the day one of them decided to speak up, "with the courage that a few too many drinks had given him," Noemí recalls, "in a batey where everybody said everything was fine. And this man, whom I'd rather not name, asked in a very loud voice how the others could say everything was fine when their life was misery. From then on, some of them began to stand out as leaders, the ones who spoke up in the meetings."

So they named a group of five teachers from those who worked at CEDAIL, among whom were César Vallenilla and Noemí Méndez.

"This group took charge of selecting and training the coordinators in each batey," César says. "It was an impressive accomplishment because we saw with our own eyes how, for the first time in these campos and bateyes, something got done without being organized by the Company. Little by little they lost their fear and moved forward, motivated by their awareness that they had rights, that they had dignity, that they were workers, not beasts of burden." That was how, even though it seemed nothing had changed, change was stirring in the bateyes and campos, and not from the outside, which is where the father had set his sights when the conflict began. No, the change came from within, from the heart of the plantations, from the conscience of men and women who had heard for the first time in their lives that God had given every man dignity. No more, no less. In César Vallenilla's words, "They lost their fear, and fear was the cornerstone that supported this business. Their life is what it is, and they're afraid of the overseer, the field guard, because if they don't do what those people say, they can slap them or beat them or fire them and leave them in the most absolute misery. The business is organized in such a way that once you go into a batey, you can't get out again."

This might seem absurd to somebody who does not know the context, but, according to César, the reality is that "all the bateyes are built in such a way that you can't leave, because they're very isolated and you don't have any money. They're prisons made of sugarcane in which the worker enters alive, young, energetic, and hoping for a better life, and then leaves only when he's dead, when all the juice of his life has been extracted, when all that's left is the bagasse."[1]

As we sit in the doorway of a cement hut that has no running water or electricity, which serves as home for an old, sick man, ground up like the cane, empty-handed after a lifetime of working, the question knocks again and again at the door of the mind, and it is César who answers: "You mean, why don't they commit suicide? Because, among other things, they're promised that the next harvest will be better, because somehow they hope that tomorrow will be different, that it can't keep on being so bad. Sometimes they distance themselves so much

---

[1] Bagasse is the husk or residue of a material after the juice has been extracted from it. It is what is left of the sugarcane, for example, after it has been milled and pressed, and it is used as fuel.

244 *Slaves in Paradise*

from their poverty, they're so unaware of the injustice they endure, that they don't suffer from it. They just assume it. They live and die that way, that's all."

When we ask him about the seeming revolution that appears in this story of Father Christopher in the canefields, César furrows his brow and, smiling, blurts out emphatically, "The revolution in the bateyes was prayer! These people were taught to defend their rights, but before they could be taught that they had rights, they had to be taught that they were children of God and not animals. Every training session began with prayer, and every one ended with it. When we went home, they stayed, and it was prayer that sustained them. They held tight to God the way a root does to the soil, and they began to drink from the life that the father brought them, which was prayer and the sacraments."

The help that this group of volunteers gave the father took its toll. "We were stigmatized, because a good part of the population took a position against the father. I decided, in fact, to leave the bateyes," César acknowledges. "It was hard, but I had to step aside. It's not easy to have to tell your daughters to look both ways when they go out into the street."

The opposition to the father's movement, which the owners of the plantations and bateyes instigated against everything he did, as described by witnesses, took the form of a media campaign accusing him of wanting to Haitianize the country, of being an enemy of the Dominican fatherland, of wanting to take away jobs and housing from Dominicans to give them to Haitians. These accusations and stigmas did not stop with the father but extended to all his associates, to the point of putting life at risk.

Álex Castro, a Dominican from San José de los Llanos, recalls having been persecuted for his attachment to the father and his work. Having met him when he was quite young, he saw in him something that was intensely magnetic: "I think it was his authenticity, his courage, his way of looking you in the eye and of doing and saying things." Álex's worst sin was not that he became a friend of the father and helped him in what he did; it was falling in love with a Haitian woman from a batey and marrying her. From then on, Álex himself acknowledges, he felt "more afraid" in his town of Los Llanos than in the bateyes: "I'm safer with the Haitians."

The media campaign was far-reaching, compromising even the Church and putting her in a difficult and controversial position. As time went by and the wind shifted, the father saw how his time in the mission was gradually coming to an end. It had changed him forever, as it had those whom he and the gospel had transformed. In the end, his house was stoned, the streets leading to the parish church were cut off by trenches filled with burning tires and garbage containers. Dominican society was split, and the father felt obliged to celebrate Mass surrounded and escorted by the Black Helmets, a special corps of police. Anonymous death threats became daily fare for a man who saw himself trapped between obedience to the Church, in the form of persisting in the mission, and the tension that had been stirred up around him. Someone who wishes out of fear to remain nameless says that "they didn't kill the father because it would have set off an international conflict. They just hoped he'd leave, and they achieved that by putting pressure on the Church."

In the autumn of 2006, Father Antonio Diufaín was asked by the bishop of the diocese to leave his parish and mission. As some saw it, the request was made in the hope that once Father Christopher saw that his great friend and confidant, his confessor, was leaving, he would give in and pack his bags. But that did not happen. In his homily following Father Antonio's departure, with unprecedented anticipation and the Black Helmets almost serving as altar boys in the church, the father swore before a fervent congregation that he could be made to leave the country only "in a pine box, or at the order of the bishop", and that whatever happened, whether he stayed or went, he would be there with them forever, that he would never abandon what he called "my people".

But, at the express request of the bishop, a week after Father Antonio Diufaín's departure from the Santo Domingo airport with Madrid as his destination, Father Christopher followed him. He left without saying good-bye to anybody and without leaving anything behind in writing. Noemí testifies that he packed his suitcase without saying a word, good or bad. No comment. No explanation. No reproach or regret.

When his Iberia flight took off toward the Caribbean sun rising on the new horizon, no one in San José de los Llanos realized that Father Christopher was leaving, never to return to his campos and bateyes.

Before he left, as he crossed the canefields on his way to the airport, he swore to God and to those poor people that he would fight for them for the rest of his life. Perhaps he did not say good-bye to anybody because, in his heart, he was not leaving.

This priest of the Church left behind him the six thousand men, women, and children he had baptized with his own hands; the more than a hundred elderly people who had been taken in at the house that, with his contacts and work and the help of a group of women as brave as lionesses, they built so that love could be given at the end of their lives to people who had never received anything but blows; the five dining halls where five hundred children ate a dish of hot rice every day, with chicken, beef, or fish; the patients admitted to the hospital that the father restored in San Pedro for the Catholic Church; the seven chapels built as places of prayer in open spaces and villages where Mass had never been celebrated; the eyes filled with a thousand tears; the ear-to-ear smiles that appeared at the mere sight of the dusty blue truck approaching with just a pastor as its passenger; the Masses celebrated in the pouring rain, the burning sun, the shade of a mango tree, or the sweet caress of the Caribbean breeze, in the evening, in the miserable batey where so many were born into desperation but died as Christians, clothed in rights, dignity, and hope.

Behind him, too, were the sorrows, pains, and miseries of a missionary who had arrived in the Dominican Republic with the sole purpose of evangelizing, who had become famous only reluctantly, and who had given his life for his flock not for the sake of fame or riches or praise, but rather because he saw in them the image of Christ humiliated, trampled, and dragged, whom he loved.

After he left, and this reporter has heard this himself, the hearts of hundreds, of thousands of Haitians and Dominicans who had known Father Hartley were flooded with sorrow. But it is just as clear that once he had gone, they realized they could live without him, and without fear. They realized that even though their living conditions continued to be horrendous, they were free men, authentic children of God who owed nothing to anybody on account of the fact that they were black or Haitian or cutters of cane. They realized when the father left that they were sheep in the flock not of a missionary priest but rather of God, that they were loved and worthy of respect. The restless character of the priest had brought change. The seed of the gospel that this passionate, controversial man had sown, more with sorrow and suffering than with joy and consolation, bore fruit, though he would not be there to watch it grow.

Thus ended the father's sojourn. Thus ended the work of this man, who was sent from heaven like a cyclone, like an earthquake, like a hurricane that left nothing as it had been before, who sowed new sugar in the canefields of the Dominican Republic.

IO

SOCIAL JUSTICE AND THE CHURCH

Following in Father Christopher Hartley's footsteps has brought us very close to him, through the handful of letters he wrote and through the witness given, years later, by those who knew him. Yet the tracks we have followed would be swept away if we were to omit from this book the texts of the Second Vatican Council, on the motivations of the Church and social justice as seen from the Christian perspective, which the father himself cited. In his reports, homilies, and speeches, the father often supported his points and arguments with quotations from the social teachings of the Church.

Judging from the most detailed accounts of what happened in the bateyes and plantations of San José de los Llanos, including the private conversations between him and the workers, the father armed himself with pastoral reasons for carrying on his fight. For example, in his report for the meeting between the Diocese of San Pedro de Macorís and the Vicini Consortium on June 20, 2002, the father recalled how the Second Vatican Council, in its Pastoral Constitution on the Church in the Modern World, *Gaudium et spes* (Joy and Hope), states:

63. In the economic and social realms, too, the dignity and complete vocation of the human person and the welfare of society as a whole are to be respected and promoted. For man is the source, the center, and the purpose of all economic and social life. . . .

Reasons for anxiety, however, are not lacking. Many people, especially in economically advanced areas, seem, as it were, to be ruled by economics, so that almost their entire personal and social life is permeated with a certain economic way of thinking. Such is true both of nations that favor a collective economy and of others. At the very time when the development of economic life could mitigate social inequalities (provided that it be guided and coordinated in a reasonable and human way), it is often made to embitter them; or, in some places, it even results in a decline of the social status of the underprivileged and in contempt for the poor. While an immense number of people still lack the absolute necessities of life, some, even in less advanced areas, live in luxury or squander wealth. Extravagance and wretchedness exist side by side. While a few enjoy very great power of choice, the majority are deprived of almost all possibility of acting on their own initiative and responsibility, and often subsist in living and working conditions unworthy of the human person.

A similar lack of economic and social balance is to be noticed between agriculture, industry, and the services, and also between different parts of one and the same country. The contrast between the economically more advanced countries and other countries is becoming more serious day by day, and the very peace of the world can be jeopardized thereby.

Our contemporaries are coming to feel these inequalities with an ever sharper awareness, since they are thoroughly convinced that the ampler technical and economic possibilities which the world of today enjoys can and should correct this unhappy state of affairs. Hence, many reforms in the socioeconomic realm and a change of mentality and attitude are required of all. For this reason the Church down through the centuries and in the light of the gospel has worked out the principles of justice and equity demanded by right reason both for individual and social life and for international life.

The report did not leave it at that. Father Christopher knew the texts of the Council intimately, and in the environment in which he lived they came fully alive for him in ways beyond the intellectual. Therefore, the father went on to recall that "the Holy Church is extremely concerned about the current working conditions in which we are living in the Dominican Republic and particularly in the sugarcane sector. For innumerable people, life is full of shortages and hardships. Therefore, the teachings that the Church gleans from the Gospels urge us today more than ever to act, and the reason is that we live in conditions of flagrant social injustice." He went on to quote *Gaudium et spes*:

65. Economic development must remain under man's determination and must not be left to the judgment of a few men or groups possessing too much economic power or of the political community alone

or of certain more powerful nations. It is necessary, on the contrary, that at every level the largest possible number of people and, when it is a question of international relations, all nations have an active share in directing that development. . . .

Growth is not to be left solely to a kind of mechanical course of the economic activity of individuals, nor to the authority of government. For this reason, doctrines which obstruct the necessary reforms under the guise of a false liberty, and those which subordinate the basic rights of individual persons and groups to the collective organization of production must be shown to be erroneous.

Citizens, on the other hand, should remember that it is their right and duty, which is also to be recognized by the civil authority, to contribute to the true progress of their own community according to their ability. Especially in underdeveloped areas, where all resources must urgently be employed, those who hold back their unproductive resources or who deprive their community of the material or spiritual aid that it needs—saving the personal right of migration—gravely endanger the common good.

The next section is replete with the same teaching, as Father Christopher recalled.

66. To satisfy the demands of justice and equity, strenuous efforts must be made, without disregarding the rights of persons or the natural qualities of each country, to remove as quickly as possible the immense economic inequalities, which now exist and in many cases are growing and which are connected with individual and social discrimination. . . .

Justice and equity likewise require that the mobility, which is necessary in a developing economy, be regulated in such a way as to keep the life of individuals and their families from becoming insecure and precarious. When workers come from another country or district and contribute to the economic advancement of a nation or region by their labor, all discrimination as regards wages and working conditions must be carefully avoided. All the people, moreover, above all the public authorities, must treat them not as mere tools of production but as persons, and must help them to bring their families to live with them and to provide themselves with a decent dwelling; they must also see to it that these workers are incorporated into the social life of the country or region that receives them. Employment opportunities, however, should be created in their own areas as far as possible.

In economic affairs which today are subject to change, as in the new forms of industrial society in which automation, for example, is advancing, care must be taken that sufficient and suitable work and the possibility of the appropriate technical and professional formation are furnished. The livelihood and the human dignity especially of those who are in very difficult conditions because of illness or old age must be guaranteed.

The father also had arguments, emanating from the Catholic Church in Rome, on the working conditions that every businessman and employer must offer his workers and employees, showing the strength of the Church's position in forceful terms:

67. Human labor which is expended in the production and exchange of goods or in the performance of economic services is superior to the other elements of economic life, for the latter have only the nature of tools.

This labor, whether it is engaged in independently or hired by someone else, comes immediately from the person, who as it were stamps the things of nature with his seal and subdues them to his will. By his labor a man ordinarily supports himself and his family, is joined to his fellow men and serves them, and can exercise genuine charity and be a partner in the work of bringing divine creation to perfection. . . .

Since economic activity for the most part implies the associated work of human beings, any way of organizing and directing it which may be detrimental to any working men and women would be wrong and inhuman. It happens too often, however, even in our days, that workers are reduced to the level of being slaves to their own work. This is by no means justified by the so-called economic laws. The entire process of productive work, therefore, must be adapted to the needs of the person and to his way of life. . . .

68. In economic enterprises it is persons who are joined together, that is, free and independent human beings created to the image of God. Therefore, with attention to the functions of each—owners or employers, management or labor—and without doing harm to

the necessary unity of management, the active sharing of all in the administration and profits of these enterprises in ways to be properly determined is to be promoted. . . .

Among the basic rights of the human person is to be numbered the right of freely founding unions for working people. These should be able truly to represent them and to contribute to the organizing of economic life in the right way. Included is the right of freely taking part in the activity of these unions without risk of reprisal. . . .

When, however, socio-economic disputes arise, efforts must be made to come to a peaceful settlement. Although recourse must always be had first to a sincere dialogue between the parties, a strike, nevertheless, can remain even in present-day circumstances a necessary, though ultimate, aid for the defense of the workers' own rights and the fulfillment of their just desires.

In short, Father Christopher, envoy of the Church, was not asserting his personal conclusions in the reports he presented to the Vicini family, but rather those of *Gaudium et spes*.

THE GOODS OF THE EARTH AT THE SERVICE OF ALL

69. God intended the earth with everything contained in it for the use of all human beings and peoples. Thus, under the leadership of justice and in the company of charity, created goods should be in abundance for all in like manner. Whatever the forms of property may be, as adapted to the legitimate institutions of peoples, according to diverse and changeable circumstances, attention must always be paid to this universal destination of earthly goods. In using them, therefore, man should regard the external things that he legitimately possesses not only as his own but also as common in the sense that they should be able to benefit not only him but also others. On the other hand, the right of having a share of earthly goods sufficient for oneself and one's family belongs to everyone. The Fathers and Doctors of the Church held this opinion, teaching that men are obliged to come to the relief of the poor and to do so not merely out of their superfluous goods. If one is in extreme necessity, he has the right to procure for himself what he needs out of the riches of others. Since there are so many people prostrate with hunger in the world, this sacred council urges all, both individuals and governments, to remember the aphorism of

the Fathers, "Feed the man dying of hunger, because if you have not fed him, you have killed him," and really to share and employ their earthly goods, according to the ability of each, especially by supporting individuals or peoples with the aid by which they may be able to help and develop themselves.

This encyclical therefore affirms that Father Christopher did not go to war on his own account, but rather in support of the rich and powerful authority of the conciliar fathers and the Catholic Church, an institution rooted in the defense of the weakest, the poorest of those who suffer, not only in her texts, doctrines, and intentions but in her works and acts. Father Christopher Hartley, whose footsteps we are following in this story of drama and sweat among the canefields of the Dominican Republic, is thus not a lone hero, a standard bearer for the poor, or an independent revolutionary, but rather a simple exemplar of so many other missionaries, priests, clerics, and laypersons, all of them members of the Church, who defend social justice as an inherent element of charity.

II

FACE-TO-FACE WITH
FATHER CHRISTOPHER

After several months of work, tracing his trajectory, we finally sit down with this missionary priest about whom we have heard and learned so much but with whom we have had no more than a couple of interviews, long ago and under different circumstances.

The freshly brewed coffee we share is from the Dominican Republic. We serve it to him hoping its aroma will stir old memories, slumbering somewhere that perhaps he would prefer not to revisit. Yet we realize Father Christopher is still living in the Dominican Republic, regardless of the space and the time that separate them, when we notice that he does not put even a grain of sugar in his bitter black coffee.

A graying beard encloses his face, with a gaze as intense as fire and eyebrows shaped by experiences with which no one but a missionary, whose only treasures are stored up in heaven, can enrich himself. His face is that of a man who has crossed the equator of his life with his head held high, who has always attributed his wise decisions to the good Lord, to whom he offered himself when he was just a boy, and who, when he has erred, has acknowledged it in the secrecy of the confessional. He knows he has given offense, that he has sometimes been brusque, but he knows also that at other times it is precisely because he has acted with such surgically precise purpose that he has provoked attacks. Neither of these are of any concern to him; he simply opens his heart to the recipients of his letters, written some time ago, to answer the first question like a volcano, launching words nonstop like bombs of lava that come and go in a frenetic dialogue between one who wants to know and one who wants to tell. This is, all in all, the same Father Christopher, the author of the letters that were written

254

some time ago and have revealed to us, from a missionary's heart, one of so many realities in which the Catholic Church has a presence.

~

Father Christopher, the first question I want to ask is why a person reaches the extreme point that you reached in the Dominican Republic, risking your neck, your good name, and your reputation, for people who aren't your family, who don't live in your country, who aren't going to pay you, when you could have instead gone home and left it at that.

Between the two options, risking your life for them or leaving them and going home, there's another one, which for me is the saddest one of all: being there, face-to-face with them, and doing nothing. Once I arrived in the Dominican Republic, I could have limited myself to religious activities that would have neither complicated my life nor changed the status quo. As you can see, that's not an invisible, microscopic reality. If you want to do something to change that reality, there it is; you don't need to invent it. I have to say, although it pains me, that I wasn't the only priest in the bateyes and campos. I'll just say that there were people who went into the bateyes on tiptoe or simply didn't go into them, as though there were no one there. Some of them took cover behind what the Dominican bishops supposedly said, that they couldn't baptize people who hadn't been legally registered in the country.

Was that so?

I consulted the *Code of Canon Law* and saw that that statement was totally absurd. When two people say to you, "This is our child, and we want him to be baptized", you not only can baptize him, but you should. I came to understand over time that the statement was a clever argument dreamed up by somebody to avoid complicating his life.

How much did you know about the reality of the parish of San José de los Llanos when they assigned you there?

Absolutely nothing. I already did know the reality of poverty, which was what I was expecting to find in the Dominican Republic. I had known poverty in India and in the homes of the Missionaries of Charity that I had visited. But I was completely unaware of the reality of social injustice.

Aren't they the same thing?

Not so much so as they might seem. Poverty is the lack of resources. You're born in a desert where there's nothing, and you're poor. But the social injustice that I saw was poverty without lack of resources. Those people earned a decent life by the sweat of their brow, but they were denied it.

What did you think once you had distinguished between those two realities?

I realized that I had a responsibility.

Why? You were just a parish priest, a missionary and a foreigner who could have limited himself to celebrating Mass and catechizing in the parish. Yet you ended up coming across as a zealot.

In the first place, I'll tell you that, in everything I did, I stayed within the territorial limits of my parish. I went from one place to another in my parish, where I saw the face of social injustice up close. A priest has eyes and ears; he's not an automaton. When I saw those people and took into account that I was their parish priest, I understood that I had to serve them in all their needs. That was my only qualification for serving them in their needs: that I was their parish priest.

But if I'm not mistaken, you went into private property, into the plantations and bateyes where they lived. Is that within the ambit of the parish?

I availed myself of the articles in the Dominican Constitution that protected me in going into the plantations by virtue of being the parish priest: the right to freedom of movement, the right of assembly, and freedom of worship. If these people have the right to worship, the right of assembly, and the right to have their parish priest celebrate Mass wherever they are, within the geographical limits of the parish, why wouldn't I be able to go see them?

Many people accuse you of being a social revolutionary, a liberator, or a pro-gressive priest. Do you see any of these labels as being appropriate?

Anybody who knows me knows that I'm more old-fashioned than the Council of Trent, that I was educated at the Toledo Seminary under Don Marcelo, and that I came of age at the feet of the Blessed Mother Teresa of Calcutta. The problem is that many people see a pastor's job as just a series of religious services. But a pastor's job goes far beyond that.

How far beyond?

Well, wherever there's even just one person, my ministry is there. Re-member that when I became a priest I was given responsibility not just for souls but for persons. A soul floating out there is a ghost, just as a body without a soul is a cadaver. I became a priest not to look after ghosts or cadavers, but rather to look after whole persons. It's the person, not the soul, that's made in God's image. This is very important, because that realization is the realization that the creed of your faith is what determines how you're going to make the individual decisions that you have to make in your sacerdotal or Christian life. So I realized that I was responsible for these people as whole people —for their souls, yes, but for their bodies, too. When I realized that, the gospel began to bloom, to be renewed, in my life.

Was there one particular fact that caused this renewal?

Not one, no; all of them. Have you been to the bateyes?

Yes.

Have you seen what it's like there?

With my own eyes.

Look at Matthew 25, verses 35–45, and tell me what it says.

> "For I was hungry and you gave me food, I was thirsty and you gave me drink, I was a stranger and you welcomed me, I was naked and you clothed me, I was sick and you visited me, I was in prison and you came to me." Then the righteous will answer him, "Lord, when

did we see you hungry and feed you, or thirsty and give you drink?
And when did we see you a stranger and welcome you, or naked and
clothe you? And when did we see you sick or in prison and visit you?"
And the King will answer them, "Truly, I say to you, as you did it to
one of the least of these my brethren, you did it to me." Then he will
say to those at his left hand, "Depart from me, you cursed, into the
eternal fire prepared for the devil and his angels; for I was hungry
and you gave me no food, I was thirsty and you gave me no drink, I
was a stranger and you did not welcome me, naked and you did not
clothe me, sick and in prison and you did not visit me." Then they
also will answer, "Lord, when did we see you hungry or thirsty or a
stranger or naked or sick or in prison, and did not minister to you?"
Then he will answer them, "Truly, I say to you, as you did it not to
one of the least of these, you did it not to me."

That's why I did it. Because it describes something there that's as concrete as feeding someone, giving him drink, clothing him. Some people interpret this passage as allegory or as a frill. But I, when I read it,
see water, food, and clothing. It couldn't be more tangible or material.

*Some people might find this part of the Gospels only remotely applicable to
them.*

It's true that if you live in the West you have to read it as something
imaginary or spiritual, but not so much so, because to be of help you
don't have to go very far. You don't run across naked people in the
street every day, dehydrated, malnourished, and sick, or in jail. I didn't
run across them, either, until one day I found them, and I realized
that what you read out is what the Gospel says.

*What impact does this new reality of social injustice have on your vocation?
Doesn't it diminish it, because you have to take time away from prayer to attend to needs that are, let's say, less religious?*

Not at all! None of this diminishes my vocation. Quite the contrary.
I discovered a beautiful synthesis among administration of the sacraments, social work, and fighting for the rights of those to whom I
administer the sacraments.

But from reading your story one can think that you left off evangelizing in order to inculcate a social awareness.

Well, that's because the story has not been told well. What I most dedicated myself to in the Dominican Republic was evangelization. I know very well, though, that I didn't become famous or controversial on that account. But everybody in my parish knew the batey where I'd be celebrating Mass every day of the month. Every afternoon, in a different batey, I'd be celebrating the Eucharist. That was my mission; the rest followed after. Nobody every confused me with a fighter for human rights. I was the father, to the full extent of that word's meaning.

Which is . . .

Well, that I wouldn't concern myself with just their souls, but rather with the whole person. What father of a family concerns himself only with whether his children know the Creed, but not with whether they do their homework, what games they play when it's time to play, or what they eat? A father makes sure his child knows the truths of his faith, goes to school, gets time to rest, and eats well. A father concerns himself with everything about this person who is a child. I discovered that fatherhood in the needs of my children. I realized that they were the living image of a flock without a shepherd, and the first thing that a shepherd does is gather his flock together. The wonder is that where these people gathered together wasn't around a book of human rights or a lawyer. These people gathered together around an altar. What united these people was prayer, song, celebration, and the liturgy. These people were convinced that, in the middle of their misery, God was with them, that he hadn't abandoned them. They were convinced that God walked along with his people, and that the God in whom they believed—a God whom I was discovering along with them—was a God who trod the same mud as they trod.

What God did you discover with them?

With them I discovered all the depth of what the great mystery of the Incarnation means: that God has trod this mud. I discovered the

God of the barracks, the God who walks with them, barefoot and in rags. In the Dominican Republic I began to think that when Christ became the son of a carpenter, it presumably wasn't because that was a particularly appealing profession. Being a carpenter meant leading a life that was pretty irrelevant, common, dark, gray, and modest. So it was very easy for me to think about how, if Christ had been born in a batey, he would have been a cutter of cane, like them.

When I saw a barracks in a batey, what it meant to me was that it could have been the little home of Mary, Joseph, and the Child. I gradually discovered all this to the rhythm of the liturgical year, celebrating with them the mystery of the Nativity, having seen women give birth in conditions that weren't that different from giving birth in a stable; celebrating with them their most important religious festivals, like that of Our Lady of Perpetual Help, the patron saint of Haiti. Now that I look back on it, . . . I still don't know from where they brought out those impeccable clothes, so white and clean, as though they were going to a wedding. They took the things of God very seriously! Look at how the day that the father came to celebrate Mass in the batey was the day that everybody bathed. They got all dressed up even though Mass was celebrated in the shade of a mango tree, in an open space in the batey.

Little by little I came to the realization that, for them, the priest wasn't the protagonist of my visit; he was the one who brought someone who was greater than he was. So I'll never have the slightest doubt that the protagonist of everything I've lived through has been Christ. It's just that by the mystery of the Incarnation and the sacramental nature of the Church, without a visible and perceptible sign, Christ won't be present.

Is that the importance of the missionary priest, more than drilling a well for water or building a dwelling?

Exactly, because just as there's no Eucharist without bread and wine, so the Shepherd won't be there without a priest. How will Christ, the Good Shepherd, walk among his flock?

Christ is God; he can come in any way he wants.

Yes, but he has wanted to come, and he has wanted to come in this way. He has made the choice. I didn't invent the gospel, or the story of salvation, or the sacraments. Christ has chosen the form, and also the one whom he calls. We just say yes. Just as you must have water for baptism, you must have a perceptible sign of the Good Shepherd, and in this case it's the priest. And no one need worry. If a well is needed, the missionary will also drill that.

Is that the difference between a missionary and a volunteer aid worker?

Of course. I would never have given my life if Christ hadn't called me. I very much admire those volunteers who leave everything behind and go to Africa to drill a well just because there's no water. I went because I felt the calling. I don't know what the motivation of a volunteer might be, and they deserve my complete respect, but my motivation, beyond doubt, is Christ and the proclamation of the gospel. What if I go there to preach and see that there's no water? Well, obviously I'll drill a well, but for Christ, not for the well.

Would that be the charitable work of the missionary, then?

No. Charity is everything. That would specifically be another beautiful aspect of the gospel, an example of something that theology calls signs of credibility.

For those of us who haven't studied theology: what are signs of credibility?

When John the Baptist's disciples come to ask Jesus whether he's the Messiah, or whether they must wait for another, Jesus doesn't tell them to read the catechism, or to read the Nicene-Constantinopolitan Creed. He tells them: "Go and tell John what you hear and see: the blind receive their sight and the lame walk, lepers are cleansed and the deaf hear, and the dead are raised up, and the poor have good news preached to them" (Mt 11:4–5). That's the gospel! Jesus doesn't say who he is in any way other than through signs of his credibility. So, in the light of this Gospel, I asked myself in my mission in the Dominican Republic: Why are these people going to believe me? Why are they going to believe what I tell them? Why are they going to believe in the Eucharist? What signs of my credibility can I offer them? Because the first thing Jesus did wasn't to establish the Eucharist. Jesus first offered signs of his credibility so people could begin to understand who he was—his identity—and why he had come—his mission.

Remember that since Christopher Columbus set foot on Hispaniola, more than five hundred years ago, there were many places in my parish where Mass had never been celebrated, and many where, until I arrived, they had never seen a priest. Why were they going to believe me or pay any attention to me? To them, I was like a Martian who had just landed.

What signs of credibility did you offer them?

My sign of credibility was just love. When I found myself with a person who was sick, I looked after him to the best of my ability, or I put him in the car and took him to the clinic. Or when Christmas came, I distributed baskets of food door-to-door, so they'd understand that that day was a great day. How am I going to catechize them about God's birth? Do I just go into their house and say, "Today's December 25. The Word has been made flesh. It is Emmanuel"? I had to give them signs of one sort or another! I know that that basket I brought them wasn't the solution to their hunger but a sign, a testament to the love that the Lord bore them.

Father, once you began to offer those signs of credibility in the bateyes, things got complicated. Were you afraid?

Yes, I was afraid. One of the things I learned in the mission is that I had never been afraid before, so I didn't know what fear was, and that one of the most sordid aspects of fear is precisely that it's indefinable, that it can't be dissected, or weighed, or surgically removed. In fact, it couldn't even be explained. Now I know that fear is simply having the feeling that something bad might happen to you, without being able to go into the details of how it might happen. But yes, I was afraid, many times. It was a fear that often seized me and justified my not going into the bateyes for three months at a time. I knew that there were people there, but I didn't want anything to happen to me. My fear could be seen in the fact that I had a fever, or that I was trembling.

When did that happen?

I felt genuine terror when I read my speech before President Leonel Fernández—a speech that I would have read five years later without batting an eye.

You changed that much?

Yes. As much as they did. As much as the poor. After five years with them I was no longer the same person, and they weren't either. The transformation in their lives was inextricably linked to the transformation that I lived in mine. If I hadn't changed, they wouldn't have changed.

Did you influence them more, or did they influence you more?

I think it was the same on both sides, with Christ in the middle. Because it's true that, until I came, nothing had changed, but my own change was also essential to their change. I know that I couldn't have helped them if I hadn't been ready to change from a lizard to a crocodile. They look a lot alike, and the danger was that I thought of myself as a crocodile when I was nothing more than a lizard. But they turned me into a crocodile.

How did the poor influence you?

Thanks to them, my heart grew. I realized how small I was and how much bigger the poor made me. I realized that, at the end of my time in the Dominican Republic, I was ready for anything. Before I went there, that readiness existed only in the poetic and absurd phrases that I had learned in my schooling. It's easy to say it when you know it's never going to happen.

They changed me because, as I came into their lives, their homes, sitting down at their tables, and as I let them come into mine by talking about my priesthood and ministry, they stopped being an ethnic group or social mass and began to be my friends, my children, my companions, my brothers. I gradually realized that their fate and mine are inseparably linked, the way Christ is linked to the fate of mankind, through the Incarnation. I stopped being a kind of pious functionary and became one with them and, in the midst of them all, one with Christ.

I realized that, just as things would never be the same on these plantations, my life wouldn't either. They transformed me, as a Christian and as a priest. I can no longer conceive of my life as it was before I lived with them. It was an honor for me. I discovered in them the true greatness of those who have nothing. Those poor people evangelized me. I discovered how the great values of the gospel were not, for me, more than pure theoretical speculation. I'm saying the values, not the truths. I was evangelized by the poor.

How could it be that the poor evangelized a doctor in theology from an aristocratic family?

I can remember many very beautiful anecdotes that are full of meaning. For example, when they said, "Don't worry, Father, nothin's gonna happen to you because we're praying for you. . . . We put all our trust in God, don't be afraid. . . . God will take care of you", I would say to myself, "But how can they be so sure? They've spent their whole lives tightrope walking without a net!" I spent my whole life tightrope walking, but I had Social Security and private insurance. I had the Spanish embassy and a great family that would have put a regiment at my disposal to deal with any problem. But my parishioners trusted in God without ever having had anything.

Having a safety net distances you from God?

I don't think so. Maybe it's that, when we distance ourselves from God, we look to our safety net. I had lived that way. In the end, it's a matter of trust. A matter of taking out medical insurance in case the gospel fails me, in case God doesn't take care of me in the end or forgets that he's my Father. In contrast, the only security the poor have ever had was God. So they evangelized me.

Going back to fear, how do you conquer it?

Love makes it possible for you to conquer it. It was my love of them, with all its consequences, that made me forget my fear. What's more, I loved them effortlessly; don't mistake me for a hero. It was so easy and so beautiful to love them! Loving them was simply like putting snow in the sun and letting time go by. I melted. The love for Christ in these people gave me strength and made me forget my fear. Something similar happened with responsibility. When I came to the mission, responsibility weighed on me; I wanted to go everywhere and do everything. And with love, not only did that responsibility stop weighing on me, but I got more efficient in my work; everything was easier. But the best thing about love isn't that you overcome fear; it's that love is contagious.

How?

The more I changed—the more they changed me through my love for them—the more many other lives around me changed, and not just mine and those of the people in the bateyes. The volunteers who came also began to change through their love for them. Everything that happened followed from the fact that, little by little, I overcame my fear through love and my love inspired trust in the people. The more I was filled with happiness and enthusiasm, the braver people became. Look, it's love that conquers fear. In this case, love came to them through a visible sign. Just seeing the dust of my ATV in the distance made them happy that the Church was with them. They knew that the Church, the father, the pastor was going up and down through the campos and bateyes. So, to answer your question, I'll say that what conquers fear is love, because the more aware I was of the fatherhood that didn't come from flesh and blood, but from the Spirit and grace, the more I realized that that gave me the confidence to conquer fear. Love made me conquer fear.

Father, in the middle of this whole story, the visits to the bateyes, fear, public statements, problems . . . did you have time for prayer?

For me, thank God, ever since I was a young seminarian, they taught me to pray, and they helped me discover how easy prayer has always been for me, what a small effort it is, and how much I enjoy it. I was taught by great masters of prayer. In the Dominican Republic it was the same as ever. When I got there, I didn't come out of a bottle of formaldehyde. I was formed by great teachers of prayer such as Don José Rivera—whose canonization proceeding is now going on in Rome —and Mother Teresa of Calcutta; and great teachers who were priests, such as Father Mendizábal, Don Baldomero Jiménez Duque, and other great names. All these people left an indelible imprint about prayer on a young man, a seminarian, and that had its effect—so much so that the Lord has never given me days on which there wasn't time for the Liturgy of the Hours, the celebration of the Eucharist, or personal prayer, because I'm telling you truly that, without that, everything comes undone.

Father, many ordinary mortals find prayer very difficult. What did these great teachers teach you, some of which we might learn?

As I said, they didn't get me out of a laboratory. What those teachers taught me and gave me can be summarized in very simple terms, that to pray is to love. Deep down, "the only true prayer is that of a soul taken with love", as Saint John of the Cross said. Where there's no love, there's no prayer. Yes, we have *prayers*, words to be recited, but true *prayer* is what the soul taken with love does.

From what you say, then, you never stopped praying in the middle of your work and the afflictions that come through in the letters you wrote.

I arrived in the Dominican Republic with my misery and my sin, with all my history of conversion, and at the same time I arrived taken with love of Christ. Love of my vocation. One very important aspect of all this is in my doctoral thesis, which I titled, quoting Saint Augustine, "If You Love, Shepherd".[1]

What is it about?

About the priesthood. It's odd, but when you think about it, I spent three years in Rome studying the subject of the priesthood, and a year and a half later, I find myself in a situation in which I have to put into practice all the wonderful things that John Paul II talks about in his apostolic exhortation *Pastores dabo vobis* (I Will Give You Shepherds, 1992). Just choosing this subject, "If you love, shepherd", was already an expression of what I had in my heart and of the idea that a pastor's prayer is the prayer of one who is taken with the love of Christ. That's what sent me to the plantations! I realized through my prayer that the shepherd is he who gives his life for the sheep, who leads them into green pastures, who doesn't flee when the wolf comes. When this

---

[1] The phrase from Saint Augustine (in Latin) that the author refers to is "Si diligis, pasce." This phrase may arguably best be rendered into English as it has been in this book: "If you love, shepherd" (with "shepherd" used as an active, imperative verb). —Ed.

subject is linked to the subject of fear, it becomes clear that courage isn't the absence of fear. No, courage is the fruit of love even in the presence of fear. "Love is strong as death" (Song 8:6). And a soul that prays is a soul taken with love.

How does one know that he's taken with love? I'm not talking about romantic love, but about the love you're talking about.

The question that has to be asked in specific situations in life is, What am I feeling more, love or fear? A person who feels fear more than love will run away. One who feels more love will stay. In fear, yes, but in love more than in fear. In the end, love will alleviate fear. What happened to me is that, when things were at their worst, at the end of my time in the Dominican Republic, I was the least afraid. I no longer cared about the anonymous death threats and all the rest. They stoned my house with me in it, and I didn't care. My fear never prevented me from doing the things I had to do. I say that not because I think I'm perfect, but as an example of the fact that love can conquer fear. If I've failed to do this or that thing, it has been out of laziness, or by mistake, because I was angry, or whatever, but not out of fear.

Given your explanation that neither work nor other circumstances took you away from prayer, what role did prayer play in the middle of your mission?

Prayer gave me an indissoluble bond with Christ and with these people, so I wouldn't later have had the right to look the Lord in the eye if I hadn't honored him in the people to whom I had been sent.

It isn't that prayer became a personal matter between Christ and me, which it was, but it became rather a matter of somehow expressing through my prayer the cry of all those people.

What's the cry of those people?

The same cry that can be heard from the cross, when Jesus says, "I thirst" (Jn 19:28). In that "I thirst" of Christ, I heard all the thirsts of all those people: a thirst for a better life, a thirst for respect, a thirst for human dignity, for giving a crust of bread to their children after having worked all day. All the thirst of a man's heart was condensed in the poverty of my prayer, and all the thirst of a man's heart can be condensed in his prayer.

Prayer also led me to discover myself as a son and helped me to discover others as sons. I prayed, "I am here; I am your son." That way, I found that I, too, was poor, needy. For that reason, I, Christopher, wasn't the one who had the solutions to all the problems of the people in my parish, nor was I the one who was going to resolve the labor conflicts between the workers and the Company. I was simply the medium of a cry, of pain, of sorrow. The voice of the suffering of all these people that I took to my heart in the clamor of everyday life. That's why it was so easy to pray. I had so much to share with the Lord, in the solitude of the chapel, every day!

In prayer I gave voice to the cry of the poor before God, just as prayer also made me the voice of a reply to them that didn't come from me, that I heard in my prayer: "Do not be afraid. . . . I have conquered the world." I heard that reply in prayer and made myself the voice of that reply. I made myself its voice by repeating it in words, but also with the witness of my life. When in prayer I could hear Christ saying, "I am the Good Shepherd; I am the life", I realized that I was the voice of those words, because it is I, the priest, who has to go from the chapel to the batey to give them priestly life, sacramental life, like the brothers, friends, and children of mine that they are. I therefore believe that the key to my time with them, and the key to any mission, was and is love. The battle is and was won in prayer. Not only was prayer no hindrance in what I had to do: Christ spurred me on in prayer.

What can you tell me about communal prayer? After all, you weren't a free-lance hired gun; you were a parish priest.

If there was a transformation in my parish, it was because it was a parish in which we prayed a great deal. Every day we prayed Vespers and Lauds, and the Blessed Sacrament was exposed every Friday afternoon. We had retreats for Advent and Lent, and also feast days for youth, and vigils. That's what we did in my parish. Now that I think about it, people would have been very surprised if I hadn't given them the opportunity to pray communally, as a parish. They expected no less from me.

I'll tell you a story about this that didn't happen to me, but to Father Antonio Diufaín. It was shortly after Hurricane Georges, in 1998.

Father Antonio's a very well-organized man, and he has an impressive capacity to deploy resources in complicated situations. He and some volunteers in his parish organized a distribution of building materials for the reconstruction of the houses of people who had lost them in the hurricane, and he went to a batey. An elderly woman was leaving from the father's truck loaded with boards, nails, wires, and such when she suddenly turned around and said, "Father, you've forgotten us." Poor Antonio, who was exhausted and mystified, asked her how she could say such a thing, when he had just given her a pile of supplies with which to rebuild her hut, and the elderly woman told him, "It's been a month now since you came to celebrate Mass." That's what this lady expected from Antonio, and it's what my people expected from me. It's what people expected from their priest. They were hungry for the Eucharist! For bread, too, yes, but also for the Eucharist.

All in all, I have to say that the life of prayer played a fundamental part in my maintaining an awareness of my identity. Because I never stopped praying, I never stopped being who I was. I know that the result of failing to pray would have been to believe that I was the cause of everything that happened there. That would have meant the collapse of everything.

Prayer reminded me that somebody else was writing this marvelous story. Somebody else was the composer of the symphony of the parish. It wasn't my music. Prayer gave me the ability to read my sheet music, the clear eyes I needed to play the note D where there was a D. There were many times when I got in my head that it was a C, and when I played C it didn't sound good at all. When I set myself to composing rather than interpreting, the parish didn't work. Saints are people who don't sound false notes, who are faithful to the part they are given to play.

To carry the musical analogy further, did you play a C where there was a D very often?

Yes, more than I would have liked. So I had to confess, repent, and reform. Those mistakes helped me, because although they made me and others suffer, they humbled me, brought home to me my own fragility. I played many false notes, and I'm still playing them. Sometimes I realized it right away, sometimes later, and there are no doubt other notes that I'm still playing wrong without knowing it, because of my own deafness. But I do believe I learned a lot of music. I learned to be obedient, to listen. The music of prayer tunes the ear of the heart, and prayer tuned mine. Making mistakes and begging forgiveness taught me something that applies not just to a missionary but to everybody, and I would have been much, much the poorer if I hadn't even opened the sheet music.

How can priests and missionaries apply what they've learned from their own mistakes for the benefit of others?

By recognizing that in reality we form a part of a symphony that was written for all men. I'm not an extraterrestrial who has just fallen from the sky. God has written a part for every one of us, accompanied by various others from time to time, and the problem isn't if we play our part badly and learn as we go, but if we don't even begin to play our part. God's symphony is always an unfinished one, which doesn't end with the part that's written for us to play in it. The history of San José de los Llanos doesn't end with me; I don't have to direct it to the last note. The players will come and go, and together we'll go on learning.

What does a doctor in theology have to learn from the poor?

I remember very well a lady in a little campo called El Coco. Her name was Doña Elupina, and she was a catechist in the little campo of Paña Paña. One fine day, when I was celebrating Mass there, I asked the congregation what a wise man is. I expected a long, canned reply, full of resounding adjectives and paeans to the character of a wise man, when Doña Elupina answered: "He who knows God." She thereby showed me how wise she was without knowing it.

You see, in the seminary as well as in my doctoral studies, I was provided with a lot of information and learned a lot, but among the poor I discovered the truth that's contained in the words of Saint John of Ávila, the patron saint of Spanish priests: "A priest is a man who knows what tastes of God" (que sabe lo que sabe a Dios). It's a pun in Latin and Spanish, with the first *sabe* referring to knowledge and the second to taste. I discovered that the poor tasted God very keenly. They know what does and doesn't taste of God. I learned that from

Doña Elupina, because knowledge isn't just conceptual knowledge. I could be given an entire encyclopedia about the mystery of the taste of an orange, but there is no substitute for biting into an orange and tasting it. They had tasted God, and therefore they truly knew him, without ever having studied.

How did they know him?

By putting all their faith and trust in him. That's how God manifests himself. When we don't place our hope in him, when we reject him, when we replace him with something else, we don't see him passing by next to us. But when you put your trust in him, when you devote your attention to God, it's impossible not to see him.

There's a phrase that the Dominicans use a lot and that I love. Whenever something incomprehensible happens, they say, "God is the one who knows." A poor man is humble enough not to pretend to understand, while we, in our sophistication and material abundance, think we have the right to know everything, to ask God for an explanation of everything. The poor don't need any explanations to keep on living. The poor are humble enough to accept life as it is.

How do the poor pray? How do they address God?

The prayer of the poor is that of those who've submitted to the will of him who is an incomprehensible infinitude to us. What's more, they're people who pray by fighting for their faith. They've fought for their faith, and they know how to suffer for it. I didn't know what it was to walk through the mud with shoes in hand, to go to a Mass without dirtying them, because I owed it to the Lord to celebrate Mass in clean shoes, and they showed me the way. When I saw them walking to Mass barefoot through those quagmires and roads, holding their shoes in their hands, they taught me how great the Liturgy and the worship of God are. I had never seen anyone leaving their house at dawn, three hours before the Eucharist, so as not to be late. I did see them do that.

Because they never had a right to anything, they didn't feel they had any rights before God, and they therefore were able to experience anything God gave them as a gratuitous gift, not as a right that they could claim of God. There's no negotiating with God. How often does prayer turn into that! Doing a series of things to get other things from God. They weren't like that, and their prayer was that of people who live that way.

What did they teach you, not as a theologian or priest, but as a Christian in daily life?

They taught me to express my faith in the simplicity of the everyday. That there wasn't a time for God, such as eleven o'clock on Sunday, while living like an honest pagan the rest of the week. Their life was suffused with the presence of God, with respect for God. I discovered in them a quality of which I didn't know the meaning because I had never seen it before: the fear of God, the reverence for God. The reverence for all that's sacred.

I discovered that the society in which the world of the poor moves is a society that fears God, and that the poor respect God. We, those who aren't poor, sometimes address him with familiarity and too much presumption and overconfidence. They don't. They have a sense of the religious, a profound sense of mystery.

I especially discovered in the Dominican people their extraordinary faith in the Virgin of Altagracia, the Mother of God, and how in the depths of such a fragmented society, the sanctuary of the Virgin of Higüey[2] is what holds together and expresses the national identity. I thought it was wonderful to live in the midst of a people whose identity could be defined only as being united by a religious character, because the rich didn't have anything to do with the poor, and neither did the whites with the blacks, and yet everybody sat together at the feet of the Virgin of Altagracia. The whole people came together around her.

I saw in them the enormous faith that the poor had in God, in the Virgin Mary, but not as a last resort. How many times does it happen in our lives that at the door of a hospital operating room, the surgeon you've paid through public or private health insurance comes out and says, "All you can do now is pray." What for us is the last resort is for them the only resort.

As a Christian, I also learned from the poor how to share everything. I was very struck by their beautiful expressions, like "You can't refuse anyone a plate of rice." And it wasn't an empty expression. If

[2] The Basilica of Higüey, or the Sanctuary of Our Lady of Altagracia, the patron saint of the Dominican Republic.

somebody turned up at their house at noon, he had a right to a plate of rice, and they gave it to him.

We who don't live in poor countries talk a lot about sharing, but I say, "Sharing what?" Giving some Romanian who's selling Kleenex at a stoplight the small change that's cluttering up your pocket isn't sharing. I learned there that sharing isn't giving of what you have left over, because the poor have nothing left over. When they give, they give out of the little they have, and that taught me the true measure of generosity, which isn't the excess but the necessary. For me, those were simple examples of what a Christian is, which were transforming me without my realizing it.

I also learned that nobody's so rich that he doesn't need anybody, and nobody's so poor that he has nothing to give. There were rich people who gave nothing, and poor people who gave their all. And it was fine to ask. In my case, it was out of pride and self-sufficiency that I tried to deal with everything without asking for help. But I realized that they asked for help very easily because, being poor, they were used to doing so. I learned to ask on behalf of the people I was serving, and I turned into a beggar. For years I begged nonstop from offices, people, businesses, friends, family, businessmen, asking for food, land, other resources, whatever.

From the point of view of the daily life of a Christian, I think there are many pages in the Gospels that are impossible to understand from any perspective other than that of the poor. If we don't put ourselves in their shoes, it's all pure theoretical speculation.

Father, you saw many of them die, and you accompanied them to their death. How does it feel to be so close to death?

That's another thing I learned from the poor: accepting death as natural. I think one of the most absurd things in our highly refined world is man's helplessness in the face of the mystery of death. The poor lived, and confronted death, with faith. A faith that has nothing to say to you in the hour of your death is completely irrelevant, however many books on theology you may have piled up on your bookshelves. If those books don't have anything to tell you when your father or mother dies, they're nothing more than a pile of scrap paper.

They cried their hearts out over the death of a person. They cried over it, but they also celebrated it. They taught me, in the face of the mystery of death, that only faith can illuminate it, because they never questioned God in the face of death. They just said, "God is the one who knows." They taught me to live that way, and I didn't know.

Father, we're nearing the end of our journey through your memories of your stay in the Dominican Republic. We've followed your path through those letters that haven't yellowed with age, but rather, I believe, have whitened. I can say today that I think what you wrote in the midst of your hopes, dedication, controversy, and fear, is going to illuminate an important part of the life and the story of anyone who looks into them. The only question I have, of the many that are posed by a heart as anxious as yours, the heart of a missionary, is why, when you left the Dominican Republic, you didn't say good-bye to them, to your people, to the poor, to those who lived with you through an adventure that, from what they've told us, changed their lives forever.

I didn't say good-bye to anybody for several reasons, some of them spiritual and others, let's say, more practical.

First among them is that I didn't feel as if I was saying good-bye. I had given them my word that I'd never abandon them. Wherever I went and until my last breath, I would work for the full liberty and the full dignity that was their right. So I felt as though I was changing where I lived, but not that I was abandoning a task that has an end.

The second reason is that, for me, "always" has been "I'll see you later." We'll see each other again, on earth or in heaven.

Another reason was that I had seen, just a week before I left, how hard it was when Father Antonio Diufaín said good-bye. It was very hard to see the pain they felt when their pastor was wrested from them, in a good-bye that he endured very nobly and without giving any explanation.

I also didn't want to give the enemies of our cause the chance to turn my good-bye into an occasion for celebration, not so much for my sake as for the sake of those I was leaving behind. If I had said I was leaving, they would have celebrated my departure as a victory, on the doorstep of those who loved me.

I should say that I don't know if I did the right thing in not saying good-bye to anybody. I don't know if I made a mistake. I'm just telling you why I did what I did.

Although at the time it was possible to see your departure from the island as a defeat, and in fact it was in many respects, I don't see you interpreting it that way.

Because it wasn't. I had said, a whole year before I left, that I felt my task there had come to an end. I had already contributed everything that could be expected of me. I know that in this life some people reap the harvest that others have sown. I reap what others have sown, and I sow what others will reap. One person sows, another one waters, another one reaps, and it is Christ who gives the fruit and makes it grow. My eagerness to stay, to cling to that reality, could perhaps have ended in vanity. But it wasn't a defeat; it was a victory. Not for Father Christopher or the poor, but for Christ, the light that has defeated the darkness, the good that has defeated the evil. The victory is his.

What shape has that victory taken? I've been there recently and the living conditions of those people are still very harsh, despite the fact that conditions have improved noticeably over what they were when you arrived in 1997.

Christ's victory in the parish of San José de los Llanos is manifested in the spiritual progress, the holiness, of the town, but that can't be measured or depicted in a graph on Excel. That victory consists in the fact that Christ has been proclaimed, that the town has received the Word and celebrated the sacraments. In the fact that his Kingdom has come, in the middle of that hell.

That victory consists, too, in an obvious social transformation, which is also the result of the presence of the Kingdom, because I believe that if there was a change that was worth the effort, it's that it was the result not of human forces but of the strength of the gospel.

The gospel, the proclamation that God has been made man like them, infused those plantations where it had never before been preached, where the sacraments had never been celebrated, where they had never had the opportunity or the right to be brought to the baptismal font. Christ's victory there has been manifested in the change in their way of life, from that of animals, of beings without souls, to that of persons, of men and women aware of their worth, and those changes are totally irreversible. The reign of terror cannot possibly return to those plantations, because they now are aware that they are children of God, which they didn't know before.

Was it hard for you to leave?

I've said and written that if anything happened to me during my time there, it was my dream to be buried in the secret makeshift cemetery at the entrance to the batey of Dos Hermanas, in the place where so many people were laid to rest without a tombstone, with no memorial, in an anonymous spot. I was so much a part of them that even in death I wanted to be with them in the mud of the canefields. That for me would have been the ideal thing, and that's how I left it, in writing.

As I've said, it had been a year since I saw, in prayer and in the events of daily life, that I had done what I had to do. Emotionally, I wanted to be with them, I would have stayed there for life, but what's beautiful about it is that I realize that the only one who was going to stay there forever was Christ, and that my leaving would precisely be a testament to the fact that I was no more than a laborer, a worker in the vineyard, and not the owner of the sown field.

In the book of Exodus, God always tells Moses, "I have seen the affliction of my people" (Ex 3:7), not "your people"; and those people didn't belong to me. They belong to him. I was just a sign of the Lord among them. The reality that I represented, the invisible reality, is one that doesn't change. It doesn't matter whether I want to go or stay, because whatever I do, it's Christ who has never left the bateyes and never will.

You left on October 2, 2006, took a sabbatical year, and then went on to another mission. Where is it, and since when have you been there?

In Ethiopia, in an area bordering Somalia, where there are no Christians.

None?

I celebrate the Eucharist alone every day, and on Sunday and special days six of us come together.

Why did you go there?

By vocation, I feel myself to be called to be a missionary proclaiming the gospel where it has never been proclaimed. Just as others feel themselves to be called to any other kind of life or service in the Church,

I feel myself called to the first evangelization. To plow the earth that has never been farmed, to plant the first seed. That's what I do there, in Ethiopia, in an area where Christ has never been proclaimed and that has never seen his presence.

What sense does it make, or what satisfaction does it yield, for you to celebrate the Eucharist alone in the chapel?

It would be very frivolous to think that a priest celebrates Mass for his satisfaction. The Eucharist is a mystery of the faith, and the greatness of its celebration derives from the faith of the person celebrating it, not from the number of people who gather for it. A Mass before a congregation of a hundred thousand people isn't worth more than a Mass before a congregation of only one. In any case, my joy, not my satisfaction, would be to think that Christ is present among these people who don't know him.

Those who don't know or believe in the sacramentality of the priesthood or the Eucharist, which are visible signs of God's presence among men, placed by him in the Church, could say that a person who thinks Christ makes himself present through him is committing the sin of pride.

God knows very well that my hands are full of wounds, sins, and afflictions, but it was Christ who decided to make himself present only through the sacramentality of the Church. As I said earlier, I didn't invent the gospel, just as I didn't invent my vocation.

Why would a missionary, you in this case, go to Ethiopia, where there are no Christians?

Because I love the people there. Because I want to proclaim to them that God exists and that he became man in the person of Christ. Think how great God is, and how small I am, that God has linked his presence in a place on earth to whether I—as a priest, not as Christopher—am in that place or not.

There are people who say that instead of sending a sinful man, God should have sent angels. But the Lord has become man, and not an angel, associating his nature with ours in a way that's very different from how he has associated his nature with that of the angels. God is not an angel, and he is man. Do you realize the greatness of that?

Are you enjoying this experience as a missionary, which is so different from what you experienced in the Dominican Republic?

Yes, very much. But it's also true that it's because of the life I lived in the sugarcane plantations that my life is wonderful in the desert. I wouldn't be the person I am today, nor would I be experiencing what I am in the Horn of Africa, if I hadn't experienced what I did in the bateyes and the canefields. The Dominican Republic changed my life, and I give thanks to them, the poor, the catechists, my friends and collaborators who sacrificed so much to work beside me. I will never be able to thank them enough. I can't improvise what I am in Ethiopia. I didn't get it from my doctoral thesis or the faculty of theology. What I am is what the people of Los Llanos made of me.

Think about the fact that, if Christ had had no lost sheep, he wouldn't have had the capacity to love on the cross. If none of his sheep had been lost, he wouldn't have been a Shepherd walking through the mountains and hills. If the poor of the bateyes and the little campos hadn't lived in such dreadful conditions, I would never have had, as a priest, the opportunity to give the best of myself. On that account I see myself as a very privileged priest. It was a privilege and an honor to share those ten years. Only in heaven will they know what they did for me. So much of what I am I owe to them!

CONCLUSION

On September 25, 2009, a delegation of the Dominican government, headed by its ambassador to Spain César Medina, representing its minister of foreign affairs Carlos Morales Troncoso, hand-delivered to the primate archbishop of Spain Don Braulio Rodríguez a formal complaint asking the prelate—Father Christopher's immediate superior—to intervene "so as to procure Father Christopher Hartley Sartorius' definitive cessation of his campaign against our country and our national sugar industry", which was a diplomatic way of asking the archbishop to silence his priest once and for all. Don Braulio, after discussing it with his priest, did nothing more than calm him down and encourage him in the development of his mission in Africa.

On April 23, 2012, the Spanish news agency Efe reported that the United States Department of Labor had opened on that date in the Dominican Republic an investigation of the accusations of Father Christopher Hartley against the practices of the sugar industry in San José de los Llanos.

On the same day, the American embassy in the Dominican Republic reported the arrival there of a delegation from the Bureau of International Labor Affairs, part of the United States Department of Labor. Such visits are provided for in the Free Trade Agreement among Central America, the Dominican Republic, and the United States (CAFTA-DR, its acronym in English), in response to a petition made in December 2011 by Father Hartley, which cited "violations with respect to employment of manual labor in the sugar plantations of the Dominican Republic". The stated aim of the investigation was to determine "whether the acts of the Dominican Republic are incompatible with the obligations provided for in the chapter of the Free Trade Agreement relating to labor", according to the embassy's statement.

Commenting on Hartley's accusations, the Dominican foreign minister Carlos Morales Troncoso stated that the priest's purpose was to denigrate and belittle the Dominican Republic and added that "the advances in the improvement of working conditions in the sugar industry are evident to all, except to the Spanish priest", according to the newspaper *Listín Diario*'s April 23, 2012, edition. That statement is one with which I do not at all agree after having been a witness to the living and working conditions of the employees of the sugar industry, at least in San José de los Llanos, in January 2012.

These episodes show that a thousand books could have been written about this story, a thousand feature articles and documentaries. There are so many things that could be added without distorting the picture at all, that obviously some of the hues of the watercolor have been left on the palette. We have said nothing in these pages about other documentaries and articles, which are important even today, about the state of the cane workers and the efforts Father Christopher invested in protecting human rights and liberties. The reason so many things have been left out of this book is simple: when all is said and done, the heart of this story lies in the content of Father Hartley's letters and the testimony of people who know their author. It was my intention to write a book not about social conditions but rather about spiritual matters, based on those letters written by a missionary who had no purpose other than to describe to people close to him how his life at the mission in the Dominican Republic was unfolding. Having fulfilled my intention, I believe that digging into other subjects would perhaps distract attention from what was really important: that a lover of Christ, however much of a sinner he might be, is capable of doing anything for the sake of truth, freedom, and love.

I find it odd to think, as I am finishing the book, that there should be a tremendous uproar right now, in the U.S. State and Labor Departments, regarding some sugar plantations in the Dominican Republic. It moves me deeply that thousands of men should have woken up with machete in hand this morning, and with nothing to eat, to cut tons of sugarcane for which they will receive just pennies while we in the West keep consuming that sugar, in practically every product we buy, unaware that in other parts of the world that sugar is bitter and red, not sweet and white.

It surprises me that somewhere in the Ethiopian desert, near the border with Somalia, a hurricane dressed as a missionary stays calm, having made peace with himself and with those who, at times, succeeded in upsetting him. It is unmistakable proof that God calms everything, as he did the storm in the Gospel, and it is an echo of the gospel of Jesus Christ that this book aspires to be, in the people and circumstances that shape it.

To conclude, it is a blessing and a consolation to think that, all in all, those who have faith in God remain undisturbed in the face of the storm, firmly planted on the rock and looking to the future, having experienced so much, but as if nothing had happened. In short, I end this book with a vision of Cocola stirring her coffee, diluting the bitter taste of life with that of sugar, managing to summon a smile of hope from the face of her daughter Noemí, the lawyer for the Haitians in the bateyes of the Dominican Republic.

Jesús García, 2012

BETWEEN MUD
AND LONELINESS

An Epilogue of Sorts

It was about noon on a cool day in October 2006. I was walking anxiously along the Calle Ancha of my beloved Toledo, tossed this way and that by confused thoughts, a mixture of dreams and sorrows. It was this same street that had seen me set off, many years ago, for distant lands, with the eagerness of a sower of seeds and impatience in my soul. I then returned, with the patina of the passing years, the scrapes and gray hair of the weather-beaten missionary, worn with working the land. I left behind the canefields where I had roamed; I walked with the fresh taste of the cane juice still suffusing my soul.

Don Antonio, archbishop of Toledo, primate of Spain, was waiting for me. He opened the door himself. How well I remember that anteroom of the archbishop's palace, cradle of my priestly youth! He came toward me, with his arms and his heart wide open.

We talked for a good while, during which I was lost in the fog of my thoughts about the days and years gone by, among overflowing joys and unexpected disillusionments. There I was, on this cool Toledo morning, absorbed in memories of undeserved friendships that by their faces and scattered lives among those canefields had carved the face of the Beloved in my inner being. But I was alone.

Although I remember almost nothing about what Cardinal Cañizares and I discussed, I will say without offense or disrespect that, actually, it hardly mattered. What did ultimately matter for me was the sweetness of his gaze, the goodness of his smile, and the warm memory of his voice. I would not know how to recount what he said to me, but I do remember, before I left him, still enfolded in his brotherly embrace and the comforting certainty of his blessing, the following among his farewell words: "Welcome home again." And I knew at that moment, as I had never before experienced it, that the Church was Mother and that I now could also lean upon, and at last find support in, the crozier of this good shepherd.

I left in a daze of rediscovered fatherliness, almost instinctively, following the narrow streets and winding ways to the church of the Seminary of Santa Leocadia, and it was there that I understood everything. I knelt in the empty chapel on the marble of the tomb of Don José, Servant of God, father of my soul and the "Christ of the gypsies" of Toledo. His eyes—as blue as the Caribbean—seemed to be following me. They seemed to be looking at me like one of those winter twilights, when I sat next to him, in the warmth of the brazier of his *mesa camilla* (a small round table, often with a heater underneath). And it dawned on me that his eyes, looking down from heaven, actually had never stopped gazing at me. When my prayers ended, I slid down to sit on the ground next to the choir stalls and stayed there at his side, as on any other of those evenings of spiritual instruction.

The adventures and other incidents of a missionary life, spent between heavenly aspirations and the mud of the canefield, began slowly, one by one, to come back to me. Dear faces, sculpted by love and tears in this poor priestly heart; the recollection of those blessed Masses, with the taste of bitter bagasse, of faces blackened by sorrows and vinegar and especially those songs in their native Creole . . . Surprised and moved, I seemed to hear Yela, Francisco, and the others, singing, "Sa pov genyen" (What the poor man has), as, in their faith, they dream of a better tomorrow when all the privations and harsh shouts of an exploitative boss are effaced.

Blessed Eucharists on the endless green canvas of the canefields; immaculate banners of flowering cane between laughter and song; life cut to pieces in the press of an unspeakable life, fit more for animals than for people. In those years pregnant with priestly passion, how often would I raise my eyes to heaven, when dusk fell like a death-dealing diagonal across the cane, and cry out with infinite joy my unearned privilege, that of this extraordinary brotherhood!

You, O God of infinite kindness, were the only one who came with me into the canefields with a bundle on my shoulder swollen with fears and hopes, on the mud of the road, in the tracks of the workers, the oxen, the tractors, the carts, and the chainmen.

Yes, brothers, winding through the endless lanes, between the mire, the dust, and the mud of the canefields, to embrace them all, during the harvest, in the washbowl, in the foul cot, and in the barracks that were their prison . . . to celebrate one more Eucharist, so that the love and goodness of God would never be erased from their memory. Forgotten and despised by everyone . . . blessed in the heart of God!

It was only you, Christ of the plainsmen, who walked at my side among the interminable savannas to be taken farther, where no one had ever taken you before. These blessed people of Los Llanos, Dominicans of my soul, what good fortune and privilege were mine, that of shared faith in the light and the shadow of dusk and the glow of dawn.

Plainsmen of my soul, brave *Quisqueyanos*[1] who, with me and alone, for love of Christ, gave your all in exchange for nothing. Beloved plainsmen who walked with me along paths and through canefields, may you all be blessed in a shared faith like the friend who never fails you. You who reap the crop with me in the divine farming of the land, sowers of dreams, of ideals and hopes; sow while you sing, sow what will sprout in your tears, sowers of life, of joy, and of hope.

I look back and think of my fears, of the path I have just trod, with my doubts and pitfalls . . . So many fears hidden in the first fruits of my own harvest! Now I understand that fears are not conquered with bravado, with boasts, or with yearnings for revenge, and that in the face of the greedy sybarites or mercenary shepherds, love—love alone —can have the last word. Now I understand that the brave do not conquer fear, but rather only those who love, because all the courage in the world can do nothing if it is not rooted in love.

To you, good Lord Jesus, be all thanks, and to your blessed Mother be all praise, for these years of fishing, of nets, of hopes; for the years of struggling to navigate in the tossing waves of those oceans of cane. I know that there, on that distant shore, at the dawn of that infinite morning when your infinitude and my nothingness embrace—you will have prepared a banquet . . . of the Lamb and the Word, on a bed of coals . . . the fresh-caught fish.

. . . And there will I be, curled up with my soul's Don José, in the shadow of his smile . . . among prayers and thoughts, for it is enough for me that his eyes should have spoken to me and should have said to me—despite everything—that he, at least, is proud of me . . . the rest mattered not at all. . . .

---

[1] *Quisqueyano* is a demonym for a Dominican.—TRANS.

Thank you, Jesus, my soul's friend, thank you for these years of roaming and rowing in your boat, between the north wind and the gale, you the comrade of my lonelinesses. You . . . the God of the canefields!

Father Christopher Hartley Sartorius
Ethiopia, September 2012

AUTHOR'S EPILOGUE
TO THE ENGLISH EDITION

Winds and Whirlwinds

There is an old saying, an echo of the prophet Hosea, that "he who sows the wind shall reap the whirlwind", referring to acts that, with the passage of time, will spawn adverse consequences.

Father Christopher Hartley's turbulent passage through the Dominican Republic turned the saying around, and it is certainly true that after the storm of his transit, after the hurricane of his activity that uprooted some of the worst social realities planted deep in the canefields, the winds today breathe more gently, with an evidently beneficial effect.

Little by little, the rights of the workers in the canefields are very slowly being recognized, and this development is improving the lot of a great many families, while the father's condemnation of the sugar industry before international public opinion promotes the cause of human dignity and the rights of workers, whatever the color of their skin and place of birth.

The sower of that storm lived out its aftermath at a distance of almost ten thousand miles, in another country, on another continent, in another mission far from the eyes of the West. After leaving the Dominican Republic in 2006 and spending a year of rest and reflection, the father found on a map of Ethiopia the name of a city where the Church had never been established. Perhaps it had had an occasional presence there but never a stable one, with the continuous presence of a priest. "You mean there has never been a priest there?" Father Christopher asked the Missionary of Charity he spoke to in that long-ago year of 2006. "Then that's the place for me."

Gode is the name of a city in Ethiopia, on the border with Somalia in the apostolic vicarship of Harar, an area half the size of Spain with, at a guess, a population of eight million, though it is difficult to know precisely because most of them are pastoral nomads.

The people in this part of Ethiopia see themselves not as Ethiopians but as Somalis. Their skin color is different from that of other Ethiopians, they speak a different language, and, like most Somalis, they believe in Allah and his prophet Muhammad. (Ethiopians are mostly Christian, though Catholics are in the minority.) It is therefore one more arena of historical and cultural conflict, in which the average person has no choice but to make his way in life as best he can.

Every morning, under the gaze of Father Christopher Hartley, myriad members of the human race—endlessly varied in their beliefs, occupations, and education—pass by on the banks of the Shebelle River, alongside the crocodiles that infest its waters. "I'm living in an enclave where the main activity is commerce," he says, "whether it's herding livestock or arms trafficking." And here, in the middle of a nowhere filled with people, the father is a testament to and evidence of the fact that God has not forgotten any of mankind: the living presence of the Catholic Church who, in his ministry, gives Christ the Eucharist a presence every day, there where it has never been present before. And at the sign of peace in every Mass, which he often celebrates alone, he leans out the window and offers peace to all of Ethiopia, and also to all of Somalia.

Meanwhile, many, many miles away, in the green and torrid canefields of the Dominican Republic, the workers there are breathing the air of a certain good fortune, and the elders tell those to whom they have passed on their machetes that there was once a missionary who had the courage to bring change to their huts, thatched with palm fronds and straw, by preaching the freedom of the gospel.

ACKNOWLEDGMENTS

This book belongs to the workers in the canefields of the Dominican Republic, especially to all those in the plantations in the parish of San José de los Llanos. I thank all of them for opening their hearts so wide to me, without fear or reservation. If God is the meaning of this book, you are his hands, his eyes, and his lips.

Thank you, Father Christopher, for entrusting your life and works to me when you could have chosen many others before me, and for your unconditional yes, though beset by weaknesses, to the call of God in your life. The book was sown. All that was needed was to reap and arrange it.

My thanks to the publisher Libros Libres for daring again to join me in a controversial and risky literary expedition of immersing oneself in the heart of a missionary and in that of people who literally risked their lives for a shred of dignity and freedom.

My thanks to all who have accompanied me during my visit to the campos and bateyes of San Pedro de Macorís and San José de los Llanos, especially to Noemí Méndez and Álex Castro. Thanks to you, these pages of paper and ink have been given voice in my memory.

I recall, too, the people who, in the midst of absolute misery, smiled at my arrival: Fefa, Pedro, Francis, María, Tony, Quisia, Toña, Julio, Oliva, Lidia, Sonia, Yela, Roberta, Santiago, Rafelina, Yolanda, Joseph, José Francisco, and all the others who made it possible for me to see heaven in the midst of hell.

Thank you, my "brother" Jesús Pascual, for not hesitating for a moment to pack up and embark on this journey with me, and to María Carrera, for accompanying me in this and many other similar stories that will never emerge in a book.

To conclude, thanks be to God for showing himself so clearly through the events that have surrounded the story in this book since its inception in 1997 until its end in 2012.

APPENDIX

Report for the Meeting with the Vicini Family

I wanted to include this report in the book as a descriptive example of the circumstances that Father Christopher Hartley found when he arrived in San José de los Llanos, and of the legal work that was done by him and his collaborators, including Noemí Méndez.

~

From: The Diocese of San Pedro de Macorís
To: The Vicini Consortium
Date: March 16, 2000
Subject: The Situation of the Bateyes and Their Inhabitants

INTRODUCTION

Our reason for attending this meeting has its origin in the providential opportunity granted by the Lord to the Catholic Church on January 28, 1999, when the Honorable President of the Republic visited the Gautier batey. On that occasion the Church, fulfilling a sacred evangelistic obligation, prophetically called attention to the unspeakable penury and poverty in which so many men and women in our diocese live. This situation of penury and misery also affects the inhabitants of the bateyes belonging to the Vicini Consortium. For that reason they were mentioned by name before the President.

The Catholic Church was contacted immediately and with alarm by representatives of the Vicini Consortium, in the person of the public relations officer of the Cristóbal Colón sugar mill and, independently, its manager. A meeting with the Church was requested verbally, and

the Church gladly agreed. Before the written request of the Vicini
Consortium (dated February 9, 1990) arrived, however, the Consortium published a press release via many media outlets disputing what
the Church had said.

In the subsequent meeting at the offices of the diocese of San Pedro de Macorís, we believe it was made completely clear that, far from
being false, the revelations were the least possible expression of the
truth regarding the situation of misery, injustice, and poverty that is
being lived out in the Consortium's bateyes.

For that reason, it is the opinion of the Church that the statements
made in the Consortium's "public clarification" are false, because none
of what is stated there is confirmed by the raw reality in which these
poor people live. None of the children have access to an education.
None of the bateyes have latrines. None of the inhabitants have access to the most minimal medical services. None of the residents of
the bateyes have idyllic "family vegetable plots". None of the Haitian
workers are "recruited in different areas of the country"; everyone
knows that they are brought in herds directly from Haiti. Nor are
they properly documented.

In a subsequent meeting with His Excellency the Bishop we understood that the Vicini Consortium acknowledged the truth of the data
presented by his teams of consultants. In that regard, we find the explanation that "we did not know what was happening" to be inadequate.
Ladies and gentlemen, in our respective professional spheres, all of us
are responsible for the acts of our subordinates, and it is our duty to
supervise those acts on the ground, and not only through reports.

Let us remember that practically all the bateyes belonging to the
Cristóbal Colón sugar mill are located within the boundaries of the
Diocese of San Pedro de Macorís.

The Catholic Church has been working for several years in these
bateyes in pastoral and social matters: the pastoral being understood
as specifically related to the evangelizing and sacramental work of the
Church, and the social as referring to the overall well-being and advancement of individuals.

CONDITIONS IN THE BATEYES OF THE ICC
(THE CRISTÓBAL COLÓN SUGAR MILL)
—VICINI CONSORTIUM

Education

There are only five schools in the twelve bateyes that make up my parish of San José de los Llanos.

Most of the schools in the bateyes that have them are in deplorable condition. An example is the school in Contador, where the teacher, affectionately called Chea, must teach eighty-four children in just one group, teaching two different courses in just one classroom.

Until a few months ago they did not receive breakfast in any of the schools. There is not a single school in the bateyes between the Nuevo batey and Laura—San José, Brujuela Norte, San Felipe, Yabacao—an expanse of almost ten miles. We have counted 163 children in that area who are not receiving an education. We know of only three children in San Felipe who sometimes go to the school in Laura (on horseback, a distance of almost four miles).

Therefore more than 80 percent of the children who live in the bateyes that have no schools do not go to class, because they cannot cover the great distances they would have to travel.

In addition, because most of the Company's employees who cut and haul the cane are undocumented Haitian workers, the children of those workers are also undocumented, which keeps them from going to school.

We recommend, in the area of education:

—The construction of new schools.

—The repair, expansion, and modernization of existing schools.

—An application to the Secretary of Education for the appointment of more teachers.

—A limit to the number of students to forty per teacher; a higher number is, pedagogically, completely unsound.

—The delivery of an adequate breakfast at school to each student on
time.

—A request to the Secretary of Education to provide schools that
attain at least the level of basic education (sixth grade), which would
prevent so many children from having to walk so far or from putting
their lives at constant risk by riding in tractors and carts to continue
their education.

Health

Nominally, there are five medical dispensaries in these bateyes. The
ones that are operating limit themselves to offering first aid services.
Actually, the only one we have seen in somewhat regular operation is
the dispensary in Batey Nuevo. In view of the fact that the services
provided in those dispensaries are so minimal, by the admission of
those responsible for them, the vast majority of the patients are sent
to Los Llanos, at their own expense. A motorcycle taxi charges a hundred pesos to go from Yabacao to Los Llanos. This is one and a half
day's wages and does not include the usual cost of medications.

As the managers of the dispensary in Batey Nuevo have themselves
admitted, their work basically consists of distributing condoms, contraceptives, and abortifacients (the IUD is an abortifacient device because it acts by preventing the implantation of the fertilized egg in
the mother's uterus). All of this is gravely contrary to the teaching of
the Catholic Church regarding sexual morality. In the case of abortifacient devices, the Church explicitly excommunicates those who use,
produce, or promote them, or collaborate in doing so.

Only the pickup truck of the Catholic Church is available twenty-
four hours per day to transport the sick. The sugar mill's ambulance
is a figment because it is either broken down in Copeyito or is not
available when needed, and when it is available, it can gain access to
only three bateyes when it is raining.

Medical care is provided only to the employee, not to his family.
That means that 70 percent of a batey's population are left totally un-
protected by any kind of public health care.

The number of cases of AIDS and tuberculosis we have detected is
alarming, and these sick people are left to their fate; we know of no
program that attends specifically to them.

We recommend, in the area of health care:

—Improve the existing dispensaries: put in place public health staff and the means to provide adequate medical service.

—Guarantee medical care to the employee's family, with particular attention to children and the elderly.

—Implement a program that offers special care to those who are suffering from contagious diseases, such as AIDS and tuberculosis.

—Terminate immediately anti-birth and anti-life programs (sterilizations, contraceptives, abortions) in the bateyes.

—Improve ambulance service in all the bateyes.

—Introduce government-sponsored pharmacies in the bigger bateyes (there is no point in giving the patient a prescription at the medical station in the batey if he has to go to Los Llanos to obtain the medication).

Housing

While most of the houses of long-term employees are in acceptable condition, the misery, neglect, and overcrowding in which the workers, seasonal laborers, cutters of cane, and so on have to live are deplorable.

The barracks are made up of small hundred-square-foot cubicles into which up to five people squeeze themselves. They do not have latrines, adequate ventilation, or a place where they can cook under the most minimally hygienic and healthful conditions.

We are surprised that, although it is true that new barracks have been built—for example, in the bateyes of Sabana Tosa and Dos Hermanas—the new barracks are just as inhuman as the old ones, because they are identical to each other in their construction and dimensions. This is a fact that indicates the total lack of progress in your Company's interest in social welfare and in a policy that furthers a gradual improvement in the living conditions, health, and hygiene of the workers.

The lack of interest in the living conditions of your employees was glaring at the time of Hurricane Georges, when the roofs that were ripped off the houses were badly repaired with zinc taken from the old zinc that had been scattered among the canefields.

Speaking of Hurricane Georges, we are extremely surprised that the Vicini Company did not distribute from the sugar mill a single grain of rice, or food of any kind, and did not distribute clothing and other basic human needs. The people already had a hard and miserable life before, and in the immediate aftermath of the hurricane the hunger of the workers and their families became unbearable. It is not insignificant that September is dead time, there is no harvest, and the people therefore were not earning a penny. The sugar mill did not lift a finger to distribute food or clothing among the population. Hunger, malnutrition, and illness all went up. Would it truly have cost you so much to have had a little compassion for these your employees? The fathers of families cried out to us in their hunger and impotence because they were not earning their pitiful wages and therefore could do nothing to meet the most pressing needs of their families, especially of their small children.

At another level, only recently have any bateyes installed latrines, none of which are sufficient for the number of inhabitants. (Some bateyes that lack latrines are San José, Yabacao, and Brujuela, among others.)

We have determined, in addition, that many workers either sleep on the floor (for example, in the batey of Medina) or on the "springs" of their cots.

We recommend in the area of housing:

—In view of the size of the units in the barracks, they should be occupied by no more than two persons (to avoid overcrowding).

—Provide at least two toilets for every six cubicles for the inhabitants of the barracks.

—Provide every house and barracks with an enclosed space (a kitchen) for the preparation of food.

—Adopt a policy of constructing more decent housing (where a project is undertaken for the construction of more than one dwelling, it should include a toilet and a kitchen).

—Cots should have minimally adequate mattresses.

Basic Services

Of the dozen bateyes, only two have electric light (Cayacoa and Copey-ito), and they have it because they draw it illegally from the electric company.

After Hurricane Georges we had the opportunity to analyze the water that is consumed in some of the bateyes, with alarming laboratory results that showed it to be inappropriate for consumption because it contained even human feces.

We recommend in the area of basic services:

—Electrification of the bateyes; practically all the bateyes and campos of the Municipality have been electrified, and only your bateyes (practically all of them) lack electricity.

—Installation of manual pumps or other devices that will pipe water to the barracks.

—We request that you contact the tourist and hospitality sector to ask that they immediately terminate the daily visits to the bateyes in tours organized by the hotels. It is grotesque to convert human misery into a spectacle or attraction for foreigners. The misery of the poor is not a spectacle; it is a drama.

Labor Conditions

We have been unable to confirm any effort to legalize the situation of your workers there, the great majority of whom are illegal. Why is not a single worker, whether Haitian or Dominican, given a copy of the labor contract that he supposedly signs after he arrives at the sugar mill and before he is transferred to the batey to which he is assigned? The only workers who sign a contract are those who are transferred to the batey by the sugar mill; those who appear at the batey on their own have no contract at all.

The inhabitants of the bateyes say that the last time the immigration agency entered the bateyes was in 1991. For what mysterious reason does the Secretary of State for Immigration never conduct raids on undocumented workers in the Vicini bateyes, whereas it conducts them in those of the CEA and other plantation owners? What laws and state privileges protect the Vicini plantations when their workers and cane cutters are as undocumented as those of other private owners or the CEA? Why are the Vicini bateyes "untouchable" when they have as many (or more) undocumented immigrants living there illegally as the other bateyes?

The daily wage for cutting cane is 28 pesos ($1.75) if the machine loads the cane, and 41 pesos if it is hand-loaded by the cane cutters themselves. At the current rate of exchange, this amounts to exactly $2.50 (there is a compulsory withholding of two pesos per ton: a cruel and unjust way to retain the worker against his will).

Our recommendations regarding working conditions:

— Regularization of the immigrants' legal status: request that the General Directorate of Migration issue identity cards for all the workers.

— Employment contracts should specify the identity of the worker, the work to be done, the wages due, the working conditions, and the rights of the worker. The requirement that copies be filed in the local employment office, and that a copy be given to the worker, should be complied with.

— Regularize payment, so that the worker may go to an office in the sugar mill that is able to make immediate payment of the vouchers in cash, or develop a formula that will prevent the owners of the grocery stores from charging interest on the use or exchange of the vouchers.

— Abolish incentive withholding, which actually is a discount on the wage that the worker is entitled to be paid.

ACTIONS OF THE CATHOLIC CHURCH THROUGH THE PARISH OF SAN JOSÉ DE LOS LLANOS

Only the Catholic Church has attempted to work for the registration of the workers' children. We have helped in that regard with respect to a considerable number of children, obtaining for them legal status as persons and also guaranteeing them access to schools.

When, on September 7, 1997, I was named parish administrator by our bishop Monsignor Ozoria, I was informed by Sister Idalina Bordignon, the head of Pastoral Immigration of the diocese, that Don Juan Tejada, the manager of the sugar mill, had prohibited her and other members of the Catholic Church (of whom I am one) from entering the bateyes of the Vicini Consortium to carry out their work. I waited three months before violating the prohibition. I discussed this personally with Monsignor Ozoria, and we decided together to ignore this iniquitous prohibition.

At that time the parish, through the mobile pastorate led by Sister Idalina, taught reading and writing, assisted in the registration of children, assisted in the preparation and presentation of paperwork before the Haitian Consulate, taught sewing classes, assisted in the preparation and presentation of paperwork relating to pensions at the Dominican Social Security Institute, and so forth. But they were expelled and expressly prohibited from taking humanitarian aid of any kind to the bateyes. The wife of the manager of the sugar mill required that all aid be delivered to her because, she said, only she was authorized by the Company to take it to the bateyes.

Many of these bateyes have yet to receive their first visit from an official government agency or representative of the Vicini Consortium since Hurricane Georges. They themselves can attest to the fact that only—and I repeat, only—the Catholic Church has come to their aid. It was the Catholic Church that pursued and obtained from the Secretary of Education the distribution of breakfast in the public schools of the bateyes, although not uninterruptedly. I myself have distributed it or asked the teachers to do so. The managers of the sugar mill or of the bateyes have never assumed responsibility for doing so.

The situation is still not satisfactory because, as can be seen from the attached image, almost sixty children must share twenty buns, which means that each child receives a ridiculously small amount of food.

The Vicinis have given evangelical and Adventist sects land and the means to build three Protestant churches (in Copeyito, Contado, and San José). There is not a single Catholic church in a single one of their bateyes. The arbors that were used in some of them to celebrate Mass disappeared in Hurricane Georges and have not been restored. It has now been almost two years since the hurricane.

The Catholic Church has transported several ill men and women, and also several elderly persons, who were living in conditions of complete abandonment, to the home in Santo Domingo managed by the Sisters of the Congregation of Mother Teresa of Calcutta.

Every week, the Church similarly transports (at its own cost, and it also covers the cost of medications) patients suffering from AIDS, tuberculosis, and other illnesses to the Military Hospital of San Isidro, where they receive special care. Regarding the time of Hurricane Georges, with the collaboration of the Missionary Sisters of Charity of Mother Teresa of Calcutta, the parish of San José de los Llanos has carried out numberless distributions of food and clothing. The parish has conducted a census in every batey, prepared for each family a card recording the personal data of its members, and distributed as much in material resources as we could, at a cost of some five hundred thousand pesos. The sugar mill did not distribute anything. It may seem as though the Church has not distributed a significant amount, but it was an expression of our love for these suffering people and a reflection of the charity of Christ. The unanimous cry of that time, which today can still be heard during every visit to the bateyes, was and is, "Oh, Father, only the Church has remembered us!"

CONCLUSION

As the Church declared through its representative, on January 28 of this year in the batey of Gautier, before the Honorable President of the Republic, the highest officials of the government, the main elements of the media, and a large audience of others assembled there: *Señores*, life in the bateyes is a hell, fit more for animals than for human beings.